*More*
Contemporary Cinematographers
on Their *Art*

*More*
# Contemporary Cinematographers
on Their *Art*

Pauline B. Rogers

**Focal Press**

Boston   Oxford   Auckland   Johannesburg
Melbourne   New Delhi

**Library of Congress Cataloging-in-Publication Data**
Rogers, Pauline B. (Pauline Bonnie)
    More contemporary cinematographers on their art / Pauline B. Rogers.
        p. cm.
    ISBN 0-240-80368-X (pbk. : alk. paper)
        1. Cinematography.  2. Cinematographers—Interviews.  I. Title.

    TR850 .R64  2000
    778.5'3—dc21

                                                            00-032115


**British Library Cataloguing-in-Publication Data**
A catalogue record for this book is available from the British Library.

The publisher offers special discounts on bulk orders of this book.
For information, please contact:

Manager of Special Sales
Butterworth–Heinemann
225 Wildwood Avenue
Woburn, MA 01801-2041
Tel: 781-904-2500
Fax: 781-904-2620

For information on all Focal Press publications available, contact our World Wide Web home page at: http://www.focalpress.com

10 9 8 7 6 5 4 3 2 1

Printed in the United States of America

# Contents

## Nancy Schreiber, A.S.C.

*Amnesty International World Tour*
*Blair Witch-Hunt*
*Buying the Cow* (Destination Films)
*Chain of Desire* Distant Horizons)
*Lush Life* (Chanticleer)
*Middletown*
*Nevada* (Storm Entertainment)
*The Other Half of the Sky*
*Possum Living*
*Reaching Normal*
*Scorpion Springs*
*Shadow Magic*
*Trapped*
*Your Friends and Neighbors* (Gramercy/Propoganda)

## John Schwartzman, A.S.C.

*Airheads* (20th Century Fox)
*Armageddon* (Touchstone)
*Benny and Joon* (MGM)
*The Conspiracy Theory* (Warner Bros.)
*EDTv* (Universal)
*Mr. Wrong* (Touchstone)
*Pearl Harbor* (Touchstone)
*The Rock* (Hollywood/Buena Vista)
*You Can't Hurry Love* (Lightning Pictures)

## Dean Semler, A.S.C.

*The Bone Collector* (Universal/Columbia TriStar)
*City Slickers* (Columbia)
*The Cowboy Way* (Universal/Imagine)
*D-Tox* (Universal/Imagine)
*Dances With Wolves* (Orion/Tig)
*Dead Calm* (Warner Bros.)
*Farewell to the King* (Orion)
*K-9* (Universal)
*Kitty and the Bagman* (Forest Home)
*Let the Balloon Go* (Film Australia)
*Lonesome Dove* (2nd unit/mini-series)
*Mad Max 2: The Road Warrior* (Kennedy/Miller)
*Mad Max: Beyond Thunderdome* (Kennedy/Miller)
*Nutty 2: The Klumps* (Universal/Imagine)

*The Crossing Guard* (Miramax)
*The Deer Hunter* (Universal)
*Deliverance* (Warner Bros.)
*Fat Man and Little Boy* (Paramount)
*The Ghost and the Darkness* (Paramount)
*Hired Hand* (Universal)
*Heaven's Gate* (United Artists)
*Intersection* (Paramount)
*The Long Goodbye* (United Artists)
*Maverick* (Warner Bros.)
*McCabe and Mrs. Miller* (Warner Bros.)
*Obsession* (Columbia)
*Playing by Heart* (Miramax)
*The River* (Universal)
*The Rose* (Fox)
*Sliver* (Paramount)
*Stalin* (HBO Television)
*Two Jakes* (Paramount)
*The Witches of Eastwick* (Warner Bros.)

# Preface

As a staff writer for *International Cinematographer* (formerly *International Photographer*) magazine, published by the Cinematographer's Guild, I spend my days haunting sets. I am always trying to find interesting camera and lighting setups for my monthly "On the Set" column. Or, I am doing research for in-depth feature articles on television productions, documentaries, or motion picture films to run as they are released.

Over the past ten years (and some 700 articles), I've gotten to know a lot of these talented cinematographers. Some have become good friends. How they got to where they are and the choices they made has always fascinated me.

This is one of the main reasons I began a series of books for Focal Press. Telling cinematographers' stories in long form has allowed me talk about the whole person — not just the details of his or her work.

To me, Nancy Schreiber's struggle as a woman entering a man's world; Daryn Okada's comeback after a crippling accident and Mike Benson's near-death experience on *Sliver*; the working relationships between Peter James and Bruce Beresford (some nine features) and Neil Roach and Peter Werner (some 21 projects); and, of course, Vilmos Zsigmond's courage in starting over in America after becoming a top cinematographer in Hungary are just as interesting as how they did what they did on a particular project.

As with *Contemporary Cinematographers on Their Art* (part one), choosing the subjects was quite difficult. I consciously included a wide range of "big picture" people, that is, cinematographers who do movie-length productions (or high-ticket commercials). Whether they are typed (unfortunately) or do a broad range of genres, they have interesting stories to tell.

It is my hope that those who read this second book will get to know these talented cinematographers as people — as well as the artists — who have brought us tears (as Peter James did with *Driving Miss Daisy*) and laughter (as Ueli Steiger did with *Austin Powers: The Spy Who Shagged Me* and *Godzilla*), gasps and thrills (as John Schwartzman did with *The Rock* and *Armageddon* and Ward Russell in *Blackwood: The X-Files Movie*), the will to rage at injustice in this world (as Dean Semler did with *Dances With Wolves* and Dante Spinotti did with *The Insider*), and memories that will last forever (as Vilmos Zsigmond did with *McCabe and Mrs. Miller, Deliverance, The Deer Hunter, The Ghost and the Darkness*, and *Close Encounters of the Third Kind*).

They are one of the main reasons we fork over our hard-earned money to be entertained. Because, if not for the cinematographers' talent and knowledge, there would be no way to make a writer's words into pictures for everyone to see.

*The operator is the one who knows if a shot is in focus, not the video assist. The most important thing today is focus. Nowadays, if there is a screw up, there is technology to correct most of it. But, if the shot is out of focus, there is no technology to change the focus.*

# Michael Benson

It is early on a beautiful California day, and Mike Benson is trying to reacquaint himself with his spacious Woodland Hills home. It's his escape, a place to reenergize, a place he hasn't seen much of lately.

In the past year or two, he's been on location more than home — doing his first main unit Director of Photography (DP) job (*Universal Soldier: The Return*) and traveling to Canada to DP the second units for films like *The Bone Collector* and *X-men*.

Benson is acknowledged to be one of the top, if not the prime second unit DP in the industry. Aside from talent, he has the most important quality for this line of work — the ability to put his ego aside and amalgamate himself into the tone of the first unit cinematographer's style.

"That's what you have to do, whether you agree with the look or even the kind of equipment used, when you are hired to shoot extensions of first unit shots — or the huge action sequences that can't be completed because of a tight schedule," says Benson.

Literally raised on the 20th Century Fox lot, Mike Benson would travel from set to set with his construction coordinator father. He would watch the various departments at work, and from a very early age knew he wanted to be a Director of Photography. "I thought what they did was artistic and elegant," he comments.

It was a typical start — the mailroom at Fox, while he was in high school. He would visit various television sets, as well as watch the progress of Fox's highly touted western, *The Commanchero's*. "It was still a family," he remembers. "It was the tail end of the old studio system."

"There were freelance cameramen (DPs), but the crews were on staff. The operators and assistants were all employed by Fox and you would be employed 52 weeks of the year."

Knowing that he wanted to get into camera after school (USC), Benson made friends with the camera department at the studio. Every chance he got, Benson would try to learn on his own — loading film magazines for a start. "One day, I was coming out of the dark room and someone asked me what I was doing there. It was Sol Halprin. I told him the truth — I was learning.

His one comment — 'Don't blow it kid' (regarding white light on a roll of film), always stuck with me."

That was how Benson got his foot in the door.

Eventually, he worked his way over to the equipment room. One day Halprin came walking through. "Without stopping, he told me there would be an opening for a film loader on Monday. Did I want it? Of course I did!"

Benson officially began working "in the industry." Three years of shuffling between the loading room and equipment room, and no sign of breaking into the camera department. "In those days, when you did a good job, it was hard to get out," he comments. "I finally took the step and went to my department head. 'I want to get on production.'

"I knew it would be iffy, but I was ready.

"Fortunately, Billy Croniager, A.S.C., on *Peyton Place* really liked me and got me a job as second assistant."

It was a start. From *Peyton Place*, he moved to *Patton*, which was being shot in 65mm. Fortunately, he'd learned the tools while in the equipment room, and as cinematographer Fred Koenekamp's, assistant. At the time, operator Chuck Arnold was looking for a second assistant. Even though there were ten other people in line for the job, Benson got the chance because he'd gone out of his way to learn 65mm Todd-A-O equipment.

Six months in Spain was not hard to accept, for your first feature. "We ended up forming a second unit," Benson recalls. "Mickey Moore was the director and there were only three other Americans. The rest were Spanish technicians.

"Second unit was different then," he recalls. "You didn't use the principals. Today, that is almost a given. Back then, it was back up — battle sequences and so forth. On this picture, we were averaging 30 set ups a day on 65mm. In the Battle of the Bulge sequences, they moved 500 to 1,000 men and tanks over night, from one end of Spain to the other. It was a logistical nightmare but well organized."

For some reason, a lot of production was being done in Spain at the time. With all the A-list crews booked on other productions, the producers for *Patton* had to "make do" with what was available. When Chuck Arnold realized he had a technical problem with the first assistant on the main unit, he asked for Benson's transfer from second unit. "It was the beginning of my career in features," Benson recalls.

Benson and Arnold had now formed a solid partnership that lasted 11 years, with Benson as assistant for the minimum union requirement of five years. In 1973, the two began working on the television series, *Kung Fu*. They were told if they stuck with the show for one season, they would both get promoted at the same time.

"It was unheard of," Benson recalls. "But in 1975, we got it. Chuck was moved up to lighting and then I became an operator. We literally learned on the job.

"In those days, we were shooting with        Panavision reflex cameras (PSRs). We had mobility but the cameras were still very big.

"The producer, Jerry Thorpe, was extremely supportive," he recalls. "Director Dick Lang told me he was going to ask me ten questions after every take and they weren't going to be about the mechanics. They were going to be about what the actor was doing and saying. I was forced to look beyond the mechanics of the job. Learning about the actors and what they were doing brought me to another level of operating."

Often, the questions were obtuse. Which handheld what in the shot? Little things. This taught Benson to look beyond the camera frame. He began to look at everything that was going on, to study it.

"At the end of the take, I was required to say only two words — 'good' or 'no good,'" he recalls. At that time, with no video assist available, the camera operator was the definitive memory on the set. "A camera operator played (and still plays) one of the most important roles in making a film with the director. A premiere operator instills confidence in that director.

"Frankly, I hate video assist," says Benson. "I feel that it has encroached on an operator's or a cinematographer's job. The director is now watching the scene on video and doesn't have to rely so heavily on the operator. Sometimes, directors use the video assist too much as a crutch and don't go with their guts.

"There is a triangle of director, camera (and operator) and actor," Benson explains. "When that triangle is broken, the communication line is broken. It can go in any form but the triangle is an important part of the film and the storytelling can be affected by it.

"I have found, lately, that the director can often become much too mechanical. They have become so aware of the camera that they lose what the actor is trying to say. The most important thing has been and always will be the script. What the actors are saying about the script and the mechanics of it — this all helps tell the story.

"When I was working with directors like Franco Zeffirelli, Robert Wise, Franklin Schaffner, and Richard Brooks, I worked with the masters. They were involved. Totally involved. Robert Wise, for example, would place his chair in certain positions by the camera and watch what the actors would do, based on the scenes he had them doing.

"Now, I know, we're moving into a new century. Making films is entirely different from 20 years ago. But, at the same time, those directors were smart. They set down some pretty good rules for us to follow. Yes, sometimes we break those foundations, and often it becomes ordinary storytelling.

"Crutches like video weaken those foundations. The operator is the one who knows if a shot is in focus, not the video assist. The most important thing today is focus. Nowadays, if there is a screw up, there is technology to correct most of it. But, if the shot is out of focus, there is no technology to change the focus. Maybe, to a small degree, if we manipulate the pixels, it costs thousands of dollars; we are still in the baby stages of dealing with this technology."

The Mike Benson of today is as passionate about what he and others are doing as the Mike Benson on his first major project. His vision hasn't changed all that much. He is still a camera operator at heart, with the instinct that makes a shot work. He knows his tools. And knows how to use them.

"Today, there are a lot of new tools. The problem is that people aren't always knowledgeable about what these tools really do," he says. "Or, how to use them to the best of their ability. Take a remote camera, for example. It has one function — to get a shot that is too dangerous or not accessible by a manned camera.

"Using a remote camera is not the same as putting a man behind the camera. Do you really have what you want, or will you be surprised in dailies because you didn't get what you really wanted?

"Take the Steadicam. I've used it. It works. It's a great tool for certain shots. However, directors have to be aware that there is a focus problem, just like when using the video assist on other cameras. It's a mechanical thing and it isn't foolproof. Whenever possible, I will choose a man behind the lens over a mechanical and electronic device. There is no substitute for putting your eye in the eye piece."

These are things that he learned early. On *Kung Fu*, for example, he was often using long lenses, or zooms (25 to 460). He would be shooting from 150 feet away from the set. "*Kung Fu* was a trendsetter," Benson recalls. "The show was stylistic and set big standards for other shows. We would do things like use infrared film, try new things that weren't done on television. For example: Flashing the negative, force development.

"Director Dick Lang loved all the gimmicks — black lights, flashing, even scratching the negative. With 36 episodes per season, Chuck Arnold and I were allowed total freedom. It was a great way to start."

Already, Mike Benson had the itch to move up to Director of Photography. He made the rounds, but nothing happened. Still, he kept working. *Rocky* was one of his favorite projects. "I was one of five operators," he recalls. "I remember going to the script supervisor and asking what the director liked in the shots. He liked to see banners and hands. So, that's what I went for.

"Suddenly, I went from fifth bimbo behind the camera, to first. Doing what my instincts told me irritated a few people, but got me noticed and got the shots that the director wanted."

It is at this time in his career when Mike Benson did some of his favorite projects in 1979 and 1980 — *Rocky, The Champ, The Formula*, and *Vision Quest*. "The director and camera operator were really one on these projects," he says. "No video assist to get between them. They had to really work together to make the picture what the team envisioned.

"Filming *The Champ* with Franco Zeffirelli was a prime example of how great it can be when the camera operator and the director are working on the same page. For instance, we were shooting a scene with Jon Voight and Rick Schroeder at Hialeah Race Track, and, at the end of a take, Franco looked to me and asked: 'How was it Mike?' My reply was 'mechanically, everything's OK.' Zeffirelli said, 'Forget about the mechanics, what did you feel, what did the lens see?' I told him that I felt Rick Schroeder was out of character. I could see it in his eyes, he was just saying the words, just going through the motions. Franco said, 'That's what I want to hear Michael — you have to be my eyes.'

"A camera operator cannot rely solely on composition, he must have creative instincts, like that of a director." Mike Benson was paying his dues and learning as he worked. "I can see why there is a system in the Union," he says. "Being forced to do a job for a certain amount of time gives one a basis to work from. Today, everyone wants to get to the top — fast. Not everyone is willing to spend the time to master the craft.

"As a cinematographer, today, I look for operators who have come up the hard way. That tells me they have learned their lessons properly. Unfortunately, there aren't that many of them around.

"I often sit in screening rooms and hear remarks about what this one or that one doesn't like on the screen. How he or she would have done it differently. It's easy to criticize, when you are sitting in a projection room. You don't really know what is going on during the filming of a movie. There are a lot of factors that come into play, the least of which is the talent of the operator."

Benson has worked with most of the top-named directors and cinematographers in the industry. He spent four years as cinematographer Adam Greenberg's A-camera operator. "Of course, at times, it was a little difficult to understand what he was saying," Benson jokes. "After several pictures, I was finally able to interpret for the rest of the crew. And, I didn't have to learn a lot of Polish or Hebrew! 'Choka,' for example, meant 'show card.' It was worth the struggle.

"Greenberg will always be, in my mind, one of the top directors of photography in the business, second only to John Alcott. I have learned an incredible amount from both of them."

He has learned things like just how involved a good operator should be. "As involved as the director and cinematographer will allow — and then more," he says. "You listen, and keep your eyes open. John Alcott was the best teacher. He made me look and listen.

"What he could do with one light, was more than what most cameramen can do with four. He was into total creativity, taking suggestions from wherever they came, as long as they worked.

"Kubrick trained, Alcott would light 360 degrees of the set. It came from knowing that directors, especially those like Kubrick, would like to be able to go anywhere in a given shot."

Alcott and Greenberg gave Benson other invaluable lessons that helped him when he became the second unit Phnom. "John Alcott's 'reckies,' as they were called, were so educational. We would survey the locations. But more, he would have me organize the crew. By doing this, I knew everything he wanted almost before he told me what he wanted. This made us all work faster as a team."

This is where he learned how invaluable preproduction planning really was. "I remember on *No Way Out*, he had a model of Gene Hackman's office created," Benson recalls. "By looking at it, he could see the problems. He would talk about them, even had an art director change a wall. By the time we got to the actual set, he knew exactly where the Lowell package lights with the umbrellas would go. He knew he would have an overall basic overhead, with space lights that he brought in from Arriflex in Europe. They were like a coup, with silks that could be teasered down.

"Anyone can come in the day of the shoot and say, 'I want this and this' and wait for it. Masters like John and Adam have everything in their head and on paper. This allows them to light fast and save production money."

Benson was fortunate, when working with Alcott. His projects were run on the English system. While Alcott dealt with the lighting, Benson was thrown into the pot with the director. Having to step away from the lens and discuss different possibilities in staging and lighting gave him an invaluable grounding. "Still, I was always aware that my first responsibility was to the cameraman," he adds. "That never changes, no matter what system you work in."

Benson admits that he sometimes would take the "allowance" and "freedom" a little too far. "There was one time when I really caught it from mild-mannered John Alcott," he admits. "On one show the director wanted a 360. He had a great idea but he was a little lost. We brought the first team in for a rehearsal, and I had suggested a 180 handheld instead. But, he was adamant. Before I knew it, 'where is John going to put his lights,' slipped out!

"John overheard and led me to a corner. 'Never say we can't do that shot because John doesn't have a place to put his lights,' he literally hissed at me. 'If a director wants to do five 360s, I will find a place to put the lights.' That's the job, I learned quickly. He lights. I shoot. No matter what. It was amazing. We got the shot the director wanted."

Benson learned different lessons, but just as valuable ones, with Adam Greenberg. Eight pictures really refined his interpretive techniques and his ability to move with the flow.

*Terminator 2: Judgment Day* was probably the most crucial pairing of the two. "One of the most important things to find out is just where loyalties are placed," he says. "A cinematographer must stand with the director. There are too many cinematographers who forget that it is the director who hires him — not production. That is the team to work with."

The team, however, will always vary. Sometimes there is a lot of unacknowledged pressure and personalities. Benson is very up front about what he has seen and how he gets around the "challenges."

Take the teaming of director James Cameron, cinematographer Adam Greenberg, and Mike Benson on second unit for *Terminator 2: Judgment Day*. "Going in, I knew there would be a problem," Benson admits. "First, Cameron hates second unit. But, at the time we were working on the project, it was the most expensive picture ever made.

"Originally, Cameron had decided to tag the 40 days of second unit onto the first unit schedule. This way, he could keep control of the picture and make the action sequences as seamless as possible.

"The idea didn't last long. To finish it on time, he had to have a second unit and he knew it. So, a unit comprised of more than 125 people was set up (with more than 200 on first unit). Adam moved me from A-camera first unit, to second unit.

"I often say, you can measure how big a picture is by how many walkie-talkies there are," he laughs. "On *Terminator 2: Judgment Day* (1991), second unit alone had more than 75. We also had ten generators, and five and a half miles of cable in Long Beach.

"On this picture, our job was to extend Cameron's work. To make it seamless. Adam would come over to the set I was working on and discuss his lighting. 'You fill it in, Bensoni,' he would say. 'I trust you. You have a good eye. Just remember — don't worry about exposure. Exposure will take care of itself. You create contrast.'

"Adam taught me so many things on this film. He taught me to think of the picture as a whole, of what the effect was that I was creating.

"At times, we couldn't tell what unit was creating what work, it meshed so well.

"Take the freeway sequence, where the big tanker is chasing the pickup truck. We had both units working at the same time. Adam was at the north end of the freeway, by the 101, and I was at the south end at the bridge. We were doing completely different sequences, but they had to MATCH!"

Short conversations between Greenberg and Benson were crucial. "Not always easy, because we were not always on the same location. But, I always knew what Adam was using and what Jim wanted. Although," he laughs, "at times things got a little confusing.

"Take the shots at Cyberdyne, for example. I was inside and upstairs, shooting secondary action. Adam was outside, shooting the helicopter stuff. Sometimes, I would hear him yell that our lights were interfering with his. At other times, we would have a shot set and suddenly his lights would swing around and change the lighting we were using. That's when you have to be innovative.

"We ended up moving our sets around, to take advantage of their lights.
After all, we were the second unit."

To help both teams to keep things seamless, Greenberg brought in a Moviola. He would send footage to Benson, so he would know the direct cut. "It was a lesson I carry with me today," Benson says. "I look at everything I can, and ask all the questions, right or wrong, before we get to the shooting part. It saves a lot of time and energy."

Ask Mike Benson about working with a legend like James Cameron, and he will hesitate, for a moment. "He can be a difficult man to work with," he admits. "Not everyone would take the challenge. When it says a 'James Cameron film' that is true. His hand is on everything, whether you like it or not.

"Dailies were always an adventure," he laughs. "There were times when Adam just wouldn't go — the communication break down had become that difficult. So, I'd be sitting there and Jim wouldn't like something, so he would blame me. Sometimes, I would shut up. Sometimes, I would try to tell him I hadn't shot the sequence. He could care — he had to vent!

"Part of a cinematographer's job description, I guess, is to know when to let the director rage, and not take it personally. Right. We are all creative people. We want to be accepted as that — not as whipping posts!"

One of the things that Benson learned from Cameron was how to work under pressure and maximize creativity. "He is a perfectionist, so you strive for perfection."

So, Mike Benson had been inducted into the hall of fame by fire. He survived second unit with James Cameron, and it made his reputation.

Now he was "in demand." *Patriot Games, Clear and Present Danger,* and *Sliver* added to his reputation.

"So did an accident I had, while shooting in a volcano," he says, dryly. "I am the first one to advocate safety, yet I got caught. On *Sliver*, we were sent to Hawaii to do some background and beauty shots of the volcano, Kilaeua, on the big island of Hawaii. On the morning of November 21, 1992, we had just filmed our beauty shots with the Westcam. We then decided to change the helicopter mount to a Tyler Scorpion front mount for plate work.

"After completing one pass and reviewing our videotape, I realized the shot was too short in screen time. I asked pilot Craig Hoskins if he could fly slower and I would overcrank the camera. This would increase our screen time.

"We did another take. As we dipped over the lip of the volcano and descended, we lost engine power and we started to autorotate 290 feet (a controlled crash) to the bottom of the volcano. Unfortunately, our main rotor hit the side of the volcano at eight feet above the ground causing us to drop like a rock.

"By the grace of God, all three of us escaped the crash with only minor scrapes and bruises. I spent more than 60 hours in the world's most active volcano with no food or water. I hold two world records: first one is the most number of hours a human being has spent in an active volcano, and second, the most number of meal penalties accrued by a single film crewmember!

"Our rescue was one of the largest and most expensive rescues ever undertaken in Hawaii's history!"

*Sliver* (1993) was an interesting mix according to Benson. "The film didn't test all that well," he admits. "So, they wanted to go back and shoot more footage. By that time, first unit DP Vilmos Zsigmond, A.S.C., was on another picture. I had to make my shots work as his.

"The object was to give the editor material that could cut with his shots and not know the difference," he says adamantly. "Not only did I have to follow his trend, I had to follow his style of shooting, no matter what I wanted to do."

One of Benson's tricks is to run the shot footage backwards and forwards, continually checking the continuity. This allows him to know if he is keying from the same side, using the same props and wardrobe, and that every other detail is correct. "It is usually a piece of film that has already been cut," he explains. "That way, I know what the next piece is going to be.

"If I can't get that, then it is the dailies. I will watch the film and see how the light is, how high things are, and where the light comes from. I have to know a little bit of everything — not just camera — and how it all fits together. I'm there to enhance and duplicate what the main unit cameraman has done. I am the extension of the first unit, not a standalone piece."

Of course, there are times when he can take liberties. It all depends on the cameraman, the director, and the shot. "That happened on *The Saint* and on *Virus*."

*The Saint* was Benson's fourth time doing second unit for director Phillip Noyce. "Okay, I'll admit it, *The Saint* was another logistical nightmare," Benson says. "It was shot in Moscow. We had to do things like turn out all the lights in Red Square then relight with movie lights. That had never been done before. We literally had to light the whole area in two different directions.

"Of course, not only did we have to light it, we had to deal with the political pressure — we didn't have 'total' approval from the Russian government.

"And, we didn't get all the equipment we needed (from the UK) in time. So, it was 'What do you need?' to first unit, and I would get back 'What do you need?' from DP Phil Meheux. We literally pooled our equipment and kept our fingers crossed."

Sometimes, one unit would interfere with the other, so Benson had to be creative. "It's amazing, how fast you can put blacks up when you are watching for the soldiers to come to close you down," he jokes. "We had five nights to get everything, and not a minute more."

When Meheux's first unit finished certain sequences, Benson would do clean up. Then he would tackle one of the most difficult jobs of the picture — crowd multiplication. "We literally made a grid pattern of Red Square and figured out how many people could stand in one square of that grid," he explains. "The crew then placed the grid on a map of Red Square and put people in different sections at all times of the night.

"For each movement, lighting had to change accordingly. And, when the night hours ran out, the crew had to adjust for interfering sunlight by adding shadow areas with postproduction computer generation. The point was to make it look as if one crew filmed the shot straight through."

Benson admits that working second unit for Philip Noyce is different than working second unit for most other directors. Unlike James Cameron, Noyce really welcomes the abilities of a second unit crew, even plans for them and lays a lot of material off on them.

"On *Clear and Present Danger*, he had a new idea. After Don McAlpine, A.S.C., had shot a certain sequence and moved to light another set, he would send the principal actors back to us for additional material.

"I'd studied Don's lighting and knew where things would leave off and pick up, so my 'second unit' really became sequences of first unit, but by a different team."

One of the most crucial things in any production, according to Benson, is preproduction planning. "You don't realize how important that is, until you are on a picture far away from all the toys," he says. "With *The Saint*, we tried hard to map everything out before we left.

"However, we learned something valuable. The equipment we have in America can't always be found overseas. And, if you don't pay attention, it can hurt you when you start shooting. Some of the lights and cabling available overseas are very old. They are harder to control, for one thing. It's important to know what limitations you are going to have to work within, and how to do just that!"

That same year, Benson did second unit on a rather difficult film called *Volcano*. Again, Benson found a challenge in that the first unit director wasn't a fan of second unit. "Mick Jackson, the first unit director, respected what I did but had a problem with letting go of some of the shots," he explains.

"Finally, Mick realized we could pick up certain shots — shots where he simply didn't have the time to troubleshoot the problems. What really happened is that we became the guinea pig.

"When Mick had a shot where he wasn't sure where to put the equipment or what lights to use, he would give it to us. We would then work out the kinks, shoot what we were assigned to shoot, then he would avoid the problems on the first unit.

"Take the time we duplicated Wilshire Boulevard's Miracle Mile in seven-eighths scale in the parking lot of McDonald Douglas in Torrance, California. The set was three city blocks long and the second unit was to start filming at this location before first unit. The first night we had only two 'BFL lights' (Musco lights) with only eight hours of night shooting.

"We could only shoot in one direction without moving the lights. The schedule required us to shoot in two directions. We told production that in order to shoot in two directions we needed to goal post the set, which means using four huge lights, two at one end of the set and two at the other end of the set. At first, production would not pay for the four lights. They gave us three.

"The next night, production saw how we moved faster with the third light, but not as fast as the work was scheduled, so they reluctantly gave us the fourth light. When the first unit Director of Photography and Director realized we could move fast and shoot the schedule with our lighting technique, they encompassed our lighting scheme into their shooting mode.

"That's a key element to our work on second unit," Benson admits. "We can become the testing ground to make a film go faster. We can also help when the first unit is bogged down. We can pick up the slack.

"It's a budget thing," he admits. "Second unit's daily cost is often half that of first unit. We can usually do two days for the cost of one, so to speak. Ever since *T2*, producers have realized that. This is why we've become so crucial. Budgets are getting bigger and bigger.

"Production can't add days for first unit, but often can slide in a few extra second unit days without the financial cut. That is, if they have faith in the second unit."

That happens on many films. "*Broken Arrow* (1996) was a good example," he recalls. "First unit had only so many days with John Travolta. They used up their days with him, quickly. So, I had to come in, look at the footage, and pick up the slack — like adding the additional train sequences. It was a logistical nightmare, but we were able to get the material."

*Virus* ran 22 weeks. More than 35 percent of the picture was done by second unit — and these were major units. "Sometimes, the first unit had to leave for another location, and we didn't have a choice. We did the job. Whether we had the principal actors or photo doubles, we still had to make it look like one seamless series of shots."

This was probably one of the trickiest second unit jobs Mike Benson has ever done, because he needed to make several major shots look real, even though he was using doubles. "Take the fuel tank sequence, where we had to reshoot without Jamie Lee Curtis," he says. "The first unit team had used a lot of close-ups, but not the medium shots as often in the second unit.

"The tank was lit high and we shot down through the girders using a lot of cross light. Hard light for a night sequence. We had to make it look dark (no light source) but be bright enough for the audience to see the action. To do this, we used Kinoflos, lighting the back walls (an old trick from years gone by) then added a lot of smoke," he explains.

That meant constant conversations between first and second unit. He would tell them what he was doing and first unit under Director of Photography David Eggby, would tell him what they were doing.

"You know, probably the worst part of doing second unit is the 'credit,'" he laughs. "When you do things right, the first unit gets the credit. When something is wrong on the screen, often it is your second unit that gets blamed, whether you did it or not!"

Just what is it that Mike Benson has done to make his second unit work so special? He says it's that he doesn't treat his work as second at anything. "I try to take all the years as an A-camera operator and apply them to the second unit," he says. "I try to make it look and feel like a first unit.

"You don't just pan. You can track with the shot, do a dolly move, crane up and down, try to do a different kind of transition. The first unit may have the toys, but we have the fun!"

In 1998, Benson got to have all the toys and have the fun as well. He finally made it to first unit Director of Photography on *Universal Soldier: The Return*. "And I didn't have to match anyone but myself!" he laughs.

Ironically, it was director Mic Rodgers, who had worked with Benson on *Volcano's* second unit, who gave him the break to "move up" to the first unit DP. "I guess we really clicked on that film, because we had the same constraints — to match the first unit director (Mic for Mick Jackson) and first unit cinematographer (Theo van de Sande)," says Benson. "Now, Mic had moved up, and he wanted me to move as well."

The picture was a great challenge, in that no scene was longer than two pages, giving them about 1,500 setups in the 56-day schedule. Benson had only seven days of daylight exteriors and the rest were night exteriors, and day and night interiors. "More lighting equipment and setup time," he says.

Since the two were shooting pure action (something they had been doing together over the past seven years), they didn't go for the big toys. We had one philosophy in mind," he laughs. "K.I.S.S. — keep it simple stupid!"

Ask Benson about the shot he is particularly proud of on *Universal Soldier*, and he will immediately go past the jet ski opening or one of the dozen other fastcut scenes, right to the Steadicam shots down the hall into the biochemical room. "See, I told you, there is a time and a place for all the tools," he laughs. "I said earlier that I wasn't a fan of Steadicam — but that is only when it isn't used properly.

"I met with the production designer and told him something cinematographers rarely do — that I wasn't afraid of putting lights in the floor, lighting from the top or bottom. I just didn't want to light flat. And, I didn't care if there was all glass.

"Right — I got glass — in the floors and the walls — and everywhere. That gave me sleepless nights, trying to figure out how to get rid of the reflections of lights and cameras!

"I knew I could use smoke and specific lights. But I still had to get rid of the reflections.  Could I gimbal the glass? The best way was horizontal and vertical. But, the show cost $25 million, with not quite $9 million for below the line. There was no way I could convince the powers—that—be to gimbal. The next trick was a 50/50 mirror. But, that meant we couldn't keep the camera moving. Back to gimbals.

"To convince production, I had a small set designed with gimbaled glass. That did it. We got the gimbals, or at least some of them. Then we added fluorescent tubes in the floor and down the center of the hall. We left the ceilings open and put in the grid work for the lights, so they could shoot in any direction. Those meant just a little more fill light. It worked! And, on a budget!

"This past June I joined Phillip Noyce in Montreal, Quebec, on his film, *The Bone Collector*. I shot added coverage on the finale with Denzel Washington.  It's always great working with Phillip especially when he is satisfied with my work; he and first unit Director of Photography, Dean Semler, were pleased that the additional photography was seamless with the footage already shot.

"At this point, I am working in Toronto on 20th Century Fox's feature, *X-men*. This second unit is as large as any second unit I've done. *X-men* is a photographic challenge for me in that we are using *The Matrix*'s concept of 'bullet time' — a slow-motion visual effect.  We are taking 'bullet time' to the next plateau.  In the click of a finger, the action will start at normal and go to high speed and vice versa. To accomplish this, we over-cranked our camera at 96 frames-per-second, and then, through the use of the computer, in postproduction, we'll create the 'bullet time' effect."

*I do a chronological script breakdown of a script. Then I color code it, rule it all out, then punch it on the left side of the page. I have four columns — camera, grip, electric, and special effects. I then rule across, when I would have the look changed. In this picture* (Driving Miss Daisy), *you can feel the time going by with the seasons. I couldn't give a different look for every time change. There were too many. So, I selected the big emotional changes in the script. After all, the cinematography should reflect the emotion of the film.*

*Peter James*

The directions to Peter James', A.S.C., house in Los Angeles are rather ambiguous. They take you from the busy Sunset Strip up and up and up into the hills, where you end up on a one-way road looking for a set of mail boxes. Parking is by luck. Hiking is in demand. The walk is short, around another house. Finally, tucked away is a hilltop marvel — with the most incredible view of the city. When James is in town, working, it's a great place to relax. When he's out of town, working, or home in Australia, people like Milos Foreman or Richard Dreyfuss gets to stand on the deck and watch the lights of Hollywood.

It's a little different view from James's home in Australia. There he craves the beaches and water that nurtured him growing up. "My house is very simple," says James, as he gets comfortable on that Los Angeles hills deck. "It is Australia's version of a Frank Lloyd Wright house, which I built myself.

"I'm on the beach of a small fishing village on the East Coast, halfway between Sydney and Brisbane. It is 20 acres overlooking the ocean. The view, well, it's as if Walt Disney's brush went down the screen. Perfect. I literally grew up on the beach, swimming and surfing. It was my first passion."

James documented that passion for the water in a 1983 book (called *Lifesaver — Still Photographs* in Australia and *Down Under* in the States). It is about the lifeguards on Australian beaches, and the competitions between different beach groups held each Saturday afternoon. "It's also a history of lifesaving," he adds. "And, about the group called the 'Nippers,' who are junior lifeguards."

These men and women are important to Peter James, for when he was a child, he was washed out in a riptide and rescued by one of these "lifesavers."

Peter James has always been lucky — able to combine his love for the waves and for documenting life in the same place. He began his career in the movie industry at 15, working in the camera department of a Sydney film studio. For five years, he trained in all aspects of moviemaking, from work in the metal shop to laboratory, animation, and construction. He even had a chance to do sound, editing, shoot animation, and titles.

"My parents really didn't know what to do with me," he laughs. "It was either be a photographer or a butcher! Photography won out. I had a box Brownie when I was young. I would shoot everything. I remember stacking all the chairs in the house on top of each other so that I could get a high angle."

At the time, the small company James was working for shot television commercials and trade documentaries — mostly 35mm projects. Occasionally, there would be a drama or a television show.

"The first real job I photographed was a film about a packaging plant. The company sent me off to an area not far from where I live now. I was supposed to photograph a man boxing up bananas.

"In those days, we didn't have color correction," he explains. "I went to a news agency and bought blue wrapping cellophane and hung it on coat hangers in front of the light to correct the color.

"Another time, I had to do a big display shot in the Woolworth Supermarket," he continues. "We were shooting on Ektachrome (25 ASA), and the store wasn't very bright. I shot the film without a correction, then corrected it when we printed.

"While they were cutting the film, they showed the original at a test screening. I remember the client running out of the theater, screaming 'I'm not going to pay for this! The bananas are still green!' The fluorescent lights had turned the bananas green.

"That was a valuable lesson on how to deal with clients. Don't show them anything that is not color corrected!"

Peter James's first real camera job on a television project was as a focus puller for the Australian television series *Riptide* (not to be confused with the American series starring Perry King and Joe Penny). While the commercials and product films were mostly in black and white, television was shot in color. The cameramen of the time were lighting with 5ks and backlight from 2ks.

"This series was all hard light, and shot almost like multi-camera," James explains. "It was very much like the way theatrical productions were done.

"Years later (1977) I remember doing a film called *The Irishman*. I photographed it in black-and-white style lighting. When we had light outside, we still had to bring all our lights out for the bright exterior. We didn't have acrylics to put on the windows, so I shot the whole thing at T12.5, often polarizing it to cut down some of the glare of the exterior.

"I photographed it at a high stop, to keep the background in the shot," he explains. "This was very effective, because you never felt that you (or the characters) were alone. There was always the land to keep you company.

"When people saw the film, they said it was like a John Ford film," he adds, smiling shyly. "I was a little upset. I had no idea who John Ford was, and didn't know, until years later, that this was a compliment!"

The commercial and trade world were great training grounds for James, but enough was enough. James realized he needed to learn about other areas of production, and became one of the first freelance focus pullers in Australia, working mainly in television commercials.

An interest in the idea of "editing in the camera" led him into documentary film work with the BBC. "I started on the Time-Life *History of the British Empire* series with a very experienced documentary cameraman by the name of Ron Lowe," he says. "We went off to the jungles of Malaya, where we reenacted the battle that won the first Victoria Cross under gorilla conditions.

"We dressed the people in red coats, pillbox hats, and old rifles. We then marched them through the jungle and shot before we ran out of light.

"At one point, I had the camera low and was running along a log that was across a river, following these men as they attacked a fort. I then ran into these bamboo spikes that were a massive wall. I raised the camera up and passed it over to Ron, then ran around to take more shots, shooting until the 'soldiers' had literally mowed the bamboo down — so there was no longer a place to hide. It was a pretty scary sequence.

"I think the shot took 15 minutes — and was one take!"

The experience he garnered on these productions and his second television series, *Barrier Reef*, led to his first short feature, *Willy Willy*. "It was done on a budget. We did the film on short ends, maybe 50 feet. If the scene didn't work, we wouldn't even bother to process the film.

"We made up a curved track out of water pipe. It was a 360, around a carousel set up in the Australian countryside. We had an Elemac dolly and an Arri 2C, allowing us to do continuous dollying with the actors. Every foot of film we shot ended up in the film," he laughs.

The ability to experiment and push the envelope learned on documentaries and other run-and-gun type projects really helped James make this 1973 film work. At the tender age of 25, he received the Australian Cinematographer of the Year award for the project.

Peter James was now a "recognized" Australian cinematographer. Careful about the direction of his career, he chose the hard—hitting *Who Killed Jenny Langby* docudrama for his next big project. It was the story of a woman whose life had become too much to handle. She commits suicide, leaving several children behind.

"At this time, Australian television was switching from black and white to color," he recalls. "So, shooting in 16mm, we chose to use both techniques. The black and white was for the previous period, the color for the television magazine coverage.

"We were so effective with the two techniques that people believed that this was really a true story, and not a 'docudrama,' made up for entertainment."

This set the tone for James's future. Suddenly "hot," whatever he touched got attention. His 1975 film *Caddie* was the first "really big film" on his résumé. It ran in theaters for some 16 months.

"In those days, films ran in the theaters for a long time," he explains. "*The Sound of Music*, for example, was there for two years. So, 16 months was a nice run for us," he smiles.

*Caddie* won him another Australian Cinematographer of the Year award as well as the Golden Triangle and Sammy in 1975. It was the story of a woman from a rich background who was a barmaid. Battered by her husband, she took her two children and went to a rooming house.

"It was set between WWI and WWII," he explains. "While she was working as a barmaid, there were always men around demanding drinks, drunk, getting sick, and creating chaos. She meets a Greek man who is absolutely charming, and takes care of her and her kids."

James believes his ability to create different moods and a look with three distinctive film styles is what caught the various awards committees' attention. "The film takes place in spring, summer, and fall," he explains. "I photographed it in those three seasons and changed filtration and lighting, working very closely with the production designer.

"I remember him coming into the office one day with a packet of sprinkles you would put on a cake. He showed them to me, and we decided to use those pastel colors for a party.

"We might be shooting in Australia, but the style we used was very 'English' on this film. We went with the 'English look,' which was soft light and natural sources coming from outside. The idea was to make the light soft and invisible.

"It was important not to see where the lighting was coming from. It was just there, and you weren't aware of harsh shadows.

"I don't think the American cameramen had started to light like that yet, so we were doing something different.

"True, they had access to more lighting equipment, but I had come through the documentary era. When we ran out of natural light, the set ups got smaller or we went home. It was very difficult to create a mood that wasn't there, due to the limited lighting resources."

No, there weren't studios in Australia at the time. Film production was growing, but in the world of the independent. "It's still like that today," James comments.

One of Peter James's favorite earlier productions in Australia was called *The Wild Duck.* "We shot it in six weeks, on 85,000 feet of film. We rehearsed, did a take, and that was it. It was a nightmare to light, but worth it.

"We shot it with the 'light flex,'" he explains. "We preexposed the film as we shot it. We then shot through a glass, with a colored gel in the top. The reflection from the colored gel changed the look of the film stock. In candlelight scenes, for example, I used a yellow gel for the glow.

"You really have to watch it when you are shooting with something in front of the lens like that," he comments. "You can't have anything on the glass, or you will photograph it.

"By preexposing the film, however, you don't have to put in as much fill light. The color affects the black shadows, but doesn't change the highlights.

"You can't put too much in, because you will fog it completely," he adds. "The tests were a nightmare. In prelight, we had to switch from night to day and back, to make sure we had the right level."

Determined to keep his career on the move, James made the conscious decision to nurture his work and his résumé in Canada. Over a ten-year period, he made television commercials and short films in Toronto. "The Canadians thought an Australian would be good at lighting out-of-doors scenes," he laughs. "So, I did big-budget projects for Ontario's tourist board, for Beer clients and airline commercials.

"The use of filtration on the camera was becoming popular at this time, so I was stacking up to eight filters on the camera to create a painterly look for directors like Jeremiah Chechik and Bruce Dowad (Director of *The Avengers*).

"I remember one commercial with Bruce, where we shot a minute—and—a—half spot – using about 85,000 feet of film. That was more stock than I used on *The Wild Duck* starring Liv Ullman and Jeremy Irons!"

James's first American project came through his relationship with Bruce Beresford. The young director had asked him to shoot *Tender Mercies*. However, James had agreed to do another film at the same time. "Those were the days of handshakes and a person's word," says James. "There were no contracts.

"This film was called *The De Niro Boys*," he recalls. "It was a huge WWII saga, following a Jewish man from Chrystal Night, as he goes across Europe on a train to London. From London, he goes by ship to the Australian desert, and ends up in an internment camp."

Unfortunately, as often happens, this film fell out. By the time James was free, it was too late to do the Beresford film.

"Fortunately, Bruce didn't forget about me," he says. "So, when he got the script for *Driving Miss Daisy*, he called. I adored the script, the moment I read it. To me, the Morgan Freeman character, 'Hoke,' was the most wonderfully written part I'd ever read." James knew it was going to be good — but "just a little film."

The look was a challenge for James. "I wanted to give the film a very different look," he says. "The difficulty was that we were tracking Miss Daisy over many years. She isn't young when Hoke begins to drive her. By the end, they are both really old."

To capture the feeling of the transitions, James and Beresford broke the film down into time frames. "I do a chronological script breakdown," James explains. "Then I color code it, rule it all out, then punch it on the left side of the page.

"I have four columns — camera, grip, electric, and special effects. I then rule across, when I would have the look changed.

"In this picture, you can feel the time going by with the seasons," he explains. "I couldn't give a different look for every time change. There were too many. So, I selected the big emotional changes in the script.

"After all," he adds, "the cinematography should reflect the emotion of the film."

James would change little things, when certain elements came into play. "For example, the first part of the film is very soft," he explains. "So, I had smoke and a pink chiffon net on the camera to make the cast look younger.

"When the maid dies, there is no more smoke in the house. A certain spirit has gone out of the house. The sun never shines in the kitchen. It's an emotional shift.

"After Martin Luther King's speech, we went from white diffusion to black diffusion.

"At the end of the film, when they are very old, and in the nursing home, there was absolutely no diffusion. We made it very harsh, harder lighting from outside.

"When we did the scenes where the house is being cleaned out, the light is also harsh. It's the harsh reality of dying.

"We had four different looks, but each fit the moments in the story. The combination of story, production design, and lighting made for a seamless transition."

Ask Peter James what his favorite shot in this 1990 Academy Award winning film is and he'll immediately jump on the car shots. "There were so many of them," he recalls. "The triumph was not one particular shot but that we were able to create so many different looks in a car.

"That, in a good part, goes to Bruce's credit," he adds. "He really blocks and storyboards the shots.

"The drama is inside the car. So, the triumph is to give it a feeling that they are actually going somewhere and often to reflect the relationship of the people in the film as to how they are getting along and how they are getting there as characters.

"Bruce would either put the camera where Jessica looked, that she is right behind Morgan. He would be in front of the camera on the driver's side. So, we could see that she is being driven. Morgan is in front, driving, and she is very much behind, being the passenger.

"Or, Bruce would move the camera to the side more. It would be, say, in the side front window. This way there would be a big gap between them across the frame. Morgan in front and she behind.

"When Bruce wanted them to have a conversation, he wanted them more equal," he adds. "We would also do singles in close ups. They would be almost side by side. Sometimes, he'd have her sit forward a bit. That would soften the relationship.

"In the scene where they are going for Christmas, as an example, he wanted to have Christmas lights in the side window of Miss Daisy's side.

"We put lights on a C-stand and ran them along the curb. So, when we went by and shot the scene, the lights photographed into the window. You would see the lights reflected over Jessica's face when she was looking out."

In 1989, Peter James did two more pictures with Bruce Beresford. *The Black Robe* garnered him four distinct awards, including The Australian and Canadian Academy Awards. *Mister Johnson*, shot in Nigeria, also brought him major attention.

"*Mister Johnson* was a challenge in that it was started and finished in Nigeria," says James. Set in 1923 British Colonial Nigeria, *Mister Johnson* was considered an oddity — and educated black man who doesn't fit with the natives, or the British. The film starred Maynard Eziashi (as *Mister Johnson*) and Pierce Brosnan (as Harry Rudbeck)," says James.

"We brought all our equipment from England. Just getting it in was a challenge. There were palms to be greased, and . . . Not to mention the blood tests we had to take so that we could give other crew members direct transfusions, if needed. Then, there were those shots we had to get for immunizations!

"I think, of all the shots we did, the day-for-night work really stands out in my mind. I had to design a filter for the work. It's a green/blue color," he explains. "I put together a combination of blue and yellow with neutral-density filters to make that green/blue color.

"This was as close to the light gels we used for moonlight," he explains. "When we were doing day for night, it would cut in for night for night sequences quite well. It was an experiment that I hadn't done before and I have been using it ever since.

"At that time," James continues, "I didn't have a filter tray large enough to carry the three filters to make up the colors. Plus, we were adding other neutral density to reduce the depth-of-field.

"While moving the camera one day, the crude pack we'd made fell off and broke. We had to stop doing day for night for a few weeks, while we sent the filters back to America to be remade into one filter pack. "

The challenges were fine, for James. It was his chance to solidify his relationship with Director Bruce Beresford. "We were beginning to develop a sold working relationship," James comments. "I was beginning to understand what he wanted and how he wanted to work.

"With *Mister Johnson*, it was all about capturing the relationship between these two men who were trying to build a road across Africa," he explains. "It was a difficult shoot because the art department didn't have access to earth—moving equipment, so the roads had to be built by hand.

"That really worked for the story, since that was how it was done in those days anyway. We had hundreds of laborers doing the work and, Herbert Pinter, in our art department, did a great job of putting the golden African background in the shots when we were observing the two men."

*The Black Robe*, on the other hand, was a story that takes place during the 17th century. "It's about a Jesuit priest who goes to Quebec to convert the 'Indian' tribes."

Traveling along the same lines as *Dances with Wolves*, Beresford and James painted a truer, more graphic picture of the era. "There is a lot of violence," James agrees. "However, Bruce felt it necessary to bring out the story. We tried to make it strong, but not over—the—top.

"It was a beautiful film to shoot," he continues. "It had a range of weather, starting in autumn and going through winter.

"Since it was an early period, we were dealing with fire and lamp light. That's always a tricky thing to do," he adds. "When you are lighting to make it look like fire and lamp, the challenge is to get the light source in the right place. We would dig holes in the ground or hide the lights behind rocks. Or, use the old cinematographer's trick of putting an actor in the way to block the equipment.

"The other challenge was to get the correct amount of flicker so that it doesn't look mechanical," he adds. "We used gas bars on the fill side of the face to soften the effect and give it a more realistic look."

The biggest challenge, however, was the weather. It was a six-week shoot, with no cover sets for unshootable exteriors. All we had was this teepee that we carried around with us," James recalls. "I didn't want to shoot in the dull sun. When we couldn't get the dull light outside, we'd go into the Teepee. Fortunately, the teepee was only employed once," he laughs.

"My most vivid memory is the end shot," he says, a little smile coming to his face. "It is where the main characters are outside a church. We wanted to start inside the church and frame to see the whole village. Some of the Indians would come in and some would go away. We wanted to see the village, the snow coming down, and the sun setting in the background.

"However, the weather was so bad that you could reach up and touch the clouds! I turned to Billy Two Rivers, our Indian advisor, and said 'I'm praying to the Holy Spirit, you have a word to someone.' I had had a dream that the sun would come out, but needed a little 'insurance,'" James laughs.

"Billy was calm. 'The sun will come out,' he said — even though we hadn't seen it in six weeks!

"By 4:30 in the afternoon, it was freezing cold – but we could see the clouds opening up, like in my dream. We turned the snow machines and fans on, and opened the lens from a 4.5 to a 16. We got 15 minutes of sun, and Bruce got a great scene of the Indians being baptized!

"It was one of those magical moments in film that you walk away from, knowing you can never reproduce it again!"

James's relationship with Beresford was now firmly in place. It was time for the two of them to do an "American" film in the present time. "*Rich in Love* was wonderful, not just for the cast but also for the location," says James. "To capture the beauty of the location and the story, I decided to shoot the film with Fuji film. It would give it a completely different feeling."

Ask him to pick one shot, and he will hesitate. It was all about feeling. "The inspiration for the story was the American painter, Hopper. Beresford and James used him as a reference, even having postcards of his work stuck to the side of the camera. "This would remind us to use Hopper-like compositions — his canvases were always broken into thirds.

"We used negative space a lot — especially in the last shot, where Jill Clayburg's character leaves Albert Finney alone in the house waiting for her to come back."

Although Peter James had now become Director Bruce Beresford's cinematographer of choice, James was always free to do other projects. Frank Marshall's depiction of young Rugby players stranded in the Andes was on the other end of the cinematic spectrum. It involved snow and extreme Alpine locations. James's experience on *The Black Robe* was a good preparation for filming *Alive*.

"The biggest problem was the location," James admits. "Each day we had to fly from 4,000 feet, where we were staying, to 10,000 or even 14,000 feet to shoot. It was a big deal and took a lot of production coordination."

For Peter James, the most impressive shot in *Alive* was the daydream and the end sequence. "The end sequence was a night camp out at the top of the summit," he explains. "We had Dave Crone on the Steadicam shooting the boys as they get to the top of the mountain.

"We wanted to see the sun in the west," he adds. "But, because of the location and logistics, we had to shoot the scene at sunrise. If we'd done time for time, we could have had nothing.

"Dave had to hold the Steadicam at 14,000 feet, and climb with the actors to get the dialog and a huge confrontation. Without any lights to help the shot! We did it all with the sun!"

James's effort was worth it. It helped him win the 1993 Australian Cinematographer of the Year award.

That same year, James began working on a film that could have been extremely claustrophobic and boring, but that was the challenge of *My Life*. "Most of the story is filmed through Michael Keaton's eyes," says James. "We used the Handicam, but we didn't want to have grain or texture or any of that normal stuff in the way.

"We needed to make things as natural as possible. So, we shot it handheld on the Panaflex." James agrees that, today, many of the shots would have been done digitally and with CGI, but at that time, reality was the most important factor.

"Director Bruce Joel Rubin was always challenging the crew," says James. "There is a scene where we are swapping between a baby and the camera.We used a Panavision handheld to look like the Handicam.

"We choreographed the shots, filming the baby and then we would pass the camera over and the baby to Michael Keaton, still filming the baby with the other person having the camera. It was tricky, but it was great and exactly what the director wanted."

"Of course, we wanted to make that body of water a character in the story," he adds. "One of the reason's that Richard Dreyfuss closes up his practice is that an autistic student had drowned in that lake. So, I wanted to use the beauty as a juxtaposition to his feelings.

"That meant bringing light from the lake and bouncing light off the lake's surface, which is right at the front doorstep. I was always trying to fill the rooms and the house, to get the feeling of light. It's a great contrast to the ending of the film, where the lake becomes a menace. When it freezes over, Richard's character almost drowns too."

To bring the light into the house, James used simple cinematic tools. "We had mirror trays, HMIs, and mirror reflectors," he recalls. "This created the bounce that worked so well."

He also wanted to make the house less important than Dreyfuss's character. To do that, he had the walls changed to darker tones. "When we get to the young boy's environment, we wanted to make his house more important, so we left the walls white and let them consume the character."

In 1996, James did two Sharon Stone films. *Diabolique* was directed by Jeremiah Chechik (with whom James had shot many commercials in Canada years before). It was a challenge because "we were shooting two Divas from two continents," James explains. "Every day was like going to shoot a *Vanity Fair* cover — only the characters were moving. A lot of work!"

James was lighting two stars, constantly mindful of what the sun does to beautiful women. Everything was done to keep the sun off their faces, give them flattering shadows, and create individual looks for each actress. "Sharon Stone has a classic look," he explains. "She has wonderful cheekbones, fabulous features.

"Isabella Adjani, on the other hand, required lighting that made her look like she swallowed a light bulb. She needed to glow from the inside.

"We, basically, needed four sources of light to cover these two women. When they were looking at each other, it was more difficult than when they were looking in different directions. However, I encouraged two-shots because this showed the differences in the characters.

"When they were in the same frame, face to face, I would do something like try to light Sharon with a harder light than Isabella. I would keep the light off Sharon.

"On the other hand, I had to light Isabella with a rather soft light from above and below, trying to keep this light off Sharon.

"If we could keep them apart, I was able to give each their own special look. That usually consisted of George Hurell-type lighting for Isabella. For Sharon, I would use four sheets of polystyrene, two above and two below, to give the beauty look."

That same year, James reteamed with Beresford for the hard driving story of one of the first women to be executed, *The Last Dance*. Here, James wanted Sharon Stone to look sympathetic. A challenge for an actress who wears virtually no makeup throughout the whole film.

"There are two distinct worlds in this picture," says James. "The prison world — which was lit with florescent and sodium vapor lights to exploit the harshness. And, the real world, for which we tried to make use of natural light."

James used the walls of the prison as effectively in this film as he did in *Silent Fall*. He did not want to create another *Shawshank Redemption* type prison, so harshness and Dickensian visions were out. He chose to create an image that was closer to a hospital look. "We changed the walls to a greenish/gray," he explains.

"That allowed us to use color and fluorescent lighting in combination. This enhanced the characters, rather than swallowed them."

Sounds easy but it took time and concentration. "One of the first things that you have to do when working with green and blue is to test the color of the paint on the walls," he says. "We thought we had what we wanted, then we brought in the fluorescent lights and everything turned very green. Production design had to go back to the paint department and get another mix.

"John Stoddard, the designer, was a great help to us on this film," he continues. "With so much in prison cells, the sets had to be flexible. He did things like putting rubber on the ceilings. They made this sound padding look like cement. Often, the cells were so cold it even hurt to talk in them. The echo was really hard to break. These added extras helped a lot.

"They also blacked out the overhead lights and gave me places to insert special lamps," he continues. "This way, we could get rid of a flat look.

"The windows were small, and very little outside light could get in. At times, it was hard to tell day from night. We added sodium vapor lights like the ones used outside government offices. By controlling them with ballasts, we were able to switch out main lights and bring in these lights upstage — getting a distinctive day and night look. We kept the night just bright enough so that you could see the video surveillance cameras."

During preproduction scout, James found something else interesting. "Prison bars don't throw shadows," he says. "Bruce, of course, wanted to use shadows as a metaphor in the film. He wanted a slight film noir-style —not black-and-white shadows on the wall, but still, a sense of the drama of the moment when we were in the cells.

"We used open eye 1ks, placed in the holding areas, where the officer sits in a cage. They gave us the wall pattern we needed, and added a more dramatic feeling, something the audience might be familiar with, for a 'prison' effect."

In 1996, James and Beresford took on another challenge featuring women. This time an anamorphic saga with a huge ensemble cast of 12 stars and 300 extras, in the water and the jungle, under appalling conditions in Australia, Malasia, and Singapore. "Glenn Close was barefoot for the entire shoot of *Paradise Road*," he says. "There were a lot of digital effects, where we turned a small shoot with airplanes into a squadron.

"The most challenging shots on this film were probably the ones in the camp kitchen," he says thoughtfully. "It was very hard to photograph this set because we had to have it quite dark, but still not underexposed. If we didn't have the people bright enough to see, you were not able to expose the background properly. The background was important, a character if you will.

"The added challenge was the harsh prisoner-of-war conditions," he continues. "We had little or no electrical lights in the shots, so we had to make it look like the only lighting came from a single bulb or oil lamps. We used two light bulbs in the long hut, just enough to see the actresses.

"The exteriors were technically difficult," he explains. "We shot a lot of scenes in the prison kitchen, which was an open thatched-roofed building. This was difficult because we had the tropical sunlit exteriors. That gave us a deep shade under the thatched hut.

"We needed to pour a lot of light in to see, but not so much that we had a different exposure, so we could get the action inside and outside. We didn't want it too dark, or the background to burn out too much."

Another challenge James faced on *Paradise Road* was the sinking of the ship and the characters jumping into the ocean. "We had 300 actresses and a large support crew. The women had to jump in the ocean where there were sharks!

"We had to keep the camera steady, while we were making the boat look like it was listing over," he recalls. This is not the ocean that he loves! "That meant weighting the side with water tanks to make it look like it was going over on an angle.

"Add to that, we had only one plane to 'simulate' the attack of the Japanese Zeros. Second unit cinematographer Andre Fleluren, A.S.C., made it look like a squadron, thanks to the digital enhancement done later.

"And, we had to have depth charges and bombs hitting the ship —again, thanks to the digital world! When you see this on the screen, you can't tell what is real and what is digital. The shot really works!"

And, the challenges were worth the effort. The film won James the Australian Golden Tripod — his second, after winning for *Diabolique* the previous year.

By 1997, Peter James was ready for the challenge of a movie icon —the Western. Pairing, this time, with Richard Linklater, he photographed the real-life story of *The Newton Boys*, the nation's most successful bank robbers, who never killed a single person. "Who can resist a Western?" James laughs. "Even if it is a 'road' picture that starts in the Wild West and ends in Chicago's most notorious era."

Again, James assigned lighting, filtration, and lensing for the different periods. The film begins with the traditional Western look of wide angles and strong shadows. "As they became more adept at robbing banks, we began changing the angle and moved into a film noir-style. The final look was of the speakeasy era — subdued colors and lighting."

When James was shooting the old Western-style images, the challenge was to be able to keep everything in focus, whether he was inside or outside. "Richard would want to do things like carry the focus from outside the bank, with the gang waiting to a gun, and then into the actor's faces behind the bank bars," he explains.

"At one point, we had to pull focus from a medium close-up of Matthew McCohaughey to an extreme close-up on a gun barrel."

To do this, James had to be careful of the film stock — but more important, concentrate on keeping everything in focus. "We used a diopter on the 75mm lens," he explains. "Yes, it was hard on our focus puller, but necessary.

"The trick was to get enough light above the windows and doors but still see details on the images in the guns and the bullets."

One of Peter James's favorite sequences, of course, was the most difficult shot to capture. This was a complicated train robbery that involved a steam engine, five carriages (20-feet high), a tender, and a caboose. "Two of the cars were historical mail cars, which meant we had to be very very careful with out lighting and cameras — and, of course, we had to shoot inside them!" he says.

To capture the remote "Western" look, James had to light about a quarter mile of track. "It took about a week to do this sequence," he recalls. "All nights."

One of the things that saved James was his ability to get light into specific areas or in a general ambiance via the Musco light. "It was the main back and side light for the train, fields, trees, and tracks," he explains.

"The opposite angle was lit with three 18ks and one 115-foot Condor as a backlight source. We used another 18k for side light on the trees and the background.

"There were small units in the woods and fields. For close-up work, we added two 12-by-12 muslin pieces to bounce 6k PARs into for ambient and light on the actors."

One of the difficulties in shooting a sequence such as this was giving the audience an identification point. "In vastness, there are often few landmarks," he explains. "Do these shots at night, and it is more difficult.

"You can easily lose the geography of the location, but more important, you can forget who is the 'good guy' and who is the 'bad guy,' especially when you are doing over-the-shoulder shots and covering fights and confrontations from all sides.

"To give the audience (and ourselves) reference points, we lit the two sides of the train differently. We had the lighter side in 'moonlight,' and used carriage lamps as sources. Of course, we used 2ks with half CTO to help the car lights out.

"The other side, the shadow side, had to be dark. We used a lot of reflection, with bounce light. The train reflected the bounce to silhouette the action against it. Steam helped with the separation and atmosphere. We also lit the trees, for an added contrast.

"My gaffer, Brian Gunter, used the train to the best effect. Packing two Honda 6500 watt generators inside allowed them to light the practicals as well as our lights when the train was moving and move at the same time. "When the train wasn't moving, we hooked into the main generators," he adds.

"There is a wonderful shot, where Matthew and Ethan Hawke are running along the top of the car, across a bridge, and then jump into the cabin of the train engine," he comments. "This was a combination of shots. Some done at dusk for night and Poor Man's Process. All we had to do is add a few sparks and smoke to the handheld camera.

"To do this, we used a wire cylinder filled with cedar chips. We lit one end like a torch, then blew the sparks into the action. This gave us the 'moving train' look."

In 1998, James returned to his film roots — in a way. He paired for his ninth project with Bruce Beresford, and traveled back to Canada for the newest version of the classic film, *Double Jeopardy*. "It was a great action film," says James. "One of my favorite sequences is on a car ferry when Ashley Judd sees Tommy Lee Jones coming after her, and she tries to knock the handle of a car door off to free herself from handcuffs.

"She accelerates the car too fast and the car drives off the back of the ferry. He smashes the window in, and jumps in, just as she is going off. They both go into the water and sink — and she's still handcuffed to the car. He has to undo the handcuffs and get her out while under water then swim to the surface away from the sinking car.

"The shot was done on several locations, including a huge water tank at NASA in Mississippi, where scenes of the car going away into the abyss were done. The actors coming up past the camera were shot in Vancouver, in a pool with a blue screen. These two images were then put together.

"We also did a low angle in the tank in Mississippi, as the car came toward the camera. Two doubles swam out of the car.

"The actors had to do a lot of their own underwater work for the close-ups — like Tommy pushing Ashley out the window, as the bubbles are coming up. She had to go back to get the gun and then swim to the surface. They did this extremely well."

It is no secret, Peter James loves working with Bruce Beresford. The two have a great working relationship, and can often get each other "into trouble" with their creative ideas.

"I remember a time when I was just finishing a series of commercials and got a call from Bruce in New York," James smiles, as he looks over the rail of the house at the city below, his mind on a different map of buildings some 3,000 miles away. "'An ice storm is coming!' he said, without delay. 'I need it for *Daisy!*'

"Of course, the film was still in 'negotiations,'" James adds. "But, I knew it would happen. So, I grabbed a camera and we met in Stow, Vermont. It was just an assistant and us! We went out and got the wonderful ice storm sequence that we put in *Driving Miss Daisy.*

"It is often those little scenes, when you get on the second camera and pick off a close-up or do some inserts that really make a sequence," he smiles. "This is where you can come up with ideas that really contribute to the story.

"After so many films together, Bruce knows how I think and I know how he thinks. It is that rapport that really works for us.

"True, he doesn't always take my suggestions, but he always listens! And, sometimes he does use them. That's part of the relationship — we can comment and criticize, and we still know where each other is coming from. It's a respect — the benchmark of a relationship to work from.

"Bruce leaves a lot of the look of the film to me," he adds. "This allows me to work closely with the production designer, makeup, and wardrobe. It helps in the testing and in the creation of the film's look. It's an area I really enjoy.

"It's also a help when you are stuck on a frozen location, or up a river, or in the bush and you don't want to be there. That's one of the difficult things about being on location – you don't want to be there – conditions are not the greatest, to say the least. But, it makes it a lot nicer when you are among friends and with a crew you get along with."

Peter James takes a deep breath and a long glance at the city below. It's going to be a while before he sees LA's smog and traffic again. He's getting the house ready for another guest — probably Milos Foreman, again. James is off to New York to shoot a comedy called *Meet the Parents* starring Robert DeNiro.

Then, if all goes well, back to his homeland to team with his friend and cohort in filmmaking Bruce Beresford, on a "small" project that is very close to the director's heart.

*Comedy is as challenging as trying to scare someone. You are rhythmically trying to lead someone down one path, then surprise them instead of frightening them. Making the material come alive by leading them one way, then popping them with a joke takes a whole lot more than timing and bright lighting.*

*Daryn Okada*

It might be a holiday to the rest of the world, but for Daryn Okada a day when the banks are closed, mail isn't delivered, and most businesspeople are almost psychotically trying to enjoy their "day off" means he can wear shorts instead of jeans and drive close to the speed limit as he goes from meeting to meeting. This is a man who doesn't know the meaning of the words "down time" or rest. When he isn't prepping or posting a project, he's spending time with his family. Sure, he'd like to take a vacation, but this is Hollywood and you have to strike while the iron (or the cinematographer) is hot. So, when the calls come, he goes for it.

"It's great to be doing something you like, in a time when less movies are being made," he says as he takes a breath and tries to relax. As he sets his Powerbook on the table, he gives it a look. You know he longs to turn it on, check his e-mail, and feed some thoughts into the program designed for his latest project.

"I thought I was just lucky," he smiles, as he pushes his long black hair way from his shoulders and tries to concentrate on the cup of tea before him, the computer still drawing his attention.

"Don't look at it like that!" he says, glancing at the small monster. "That thing has saved my ass on more than one occasion. I don't know how other cinematographers prep their jobs, but that little Powerbook does more than keep me organized!

"If we didn't have the computer, GPS, and Digital Camera on *Anna Karenina*, we would never have been able to pull off that film in Russia.

"And when I'm photographing live concerts, like the last Celine Dion one in Memphis, that four-pound 'briefcase' helped me keep track of the 15 film cameras, digital pictures of their various angles, and floor plans of locations in the arena for two concerts and I don't know what else!"

In an industry where time is money, Okada has found a way to get the most out of every moment he spends on a project. "I'm not the only one who plans my projects with the aid of a computer," he says, stubbornly. "Every one of us does extensive preparation for a feature film. I've just found a way to get rid of a lot of the paper!

"How did I get hooked on this method? I got into using a Powerbook because I hated having to write my notes again and again. As each script revision and schedule came in, I had to find a better way to manage and keep track of photographic details with visual references and the means to accomplish them.

"At first, I made lots of lists. Lists of visual ideas relating to the story, of camera movement, lighting, equipment, etc. I'm always writing some idea on some piece of paper. Soon, I began copying them into a notebook but thought it would be great to be able to always refer to the script and schedule, except as we all know, those elements keep changing during the preproduction process. So, I began to try programs and compartmentalize everything.

"Now," he laughs, "I don't think I could do a project if I didn't have a Macintosh with me!"

That's a typical Daryn Okada pattern. If one method doesn't work, noodle around until you find another.

A second-generation Los Angelian, Okada's parents are both from Hawaii. The oldest of three children, he grew up in the San Gabriel Valley. "It seemed far from the entertainment industry, not knowing anyone who actually worked in it," he says.

"I guess I sort of became interested in motion pictures at nine, but wasn't sure how to get into the business," he admits. "So, I studied still photography. I eventually got a job projecting films for a foreign film series at East Los Angeles Junior College at 16. I knew nothing about the job, by the way! I'd do things like start an anamorphic movie with a nonanamorphic lens!

"What was great was that we had films from Mexico and Japan that were incredible. I'd watch these classics not knowing anything about them prior to screening them. Because the projectors were so loud in the booth, I couldn't hear the sound, so I just watched through the window and got hooked by how the photographic style told the story and set the mood of the films. I think it was at that time that I was determined to find a way to get into 'cinematography.'"

Okada thought about going to film school at UCLA or USC, but the entrance qualifications and finances were a little daunting. Still, he checked the boards at UCLA and found ways to get practical experience in the business by working on student and ultra-low budget projects.

"Every movie title had the word 'blood,' 'kill' or, 'demon' in it," he recalls. "My first experience in the business was working weekends on a horror film. I choose this one over the others because a friend told me the director was 21 and had directed two other features. I would put up lights, moved Styrofoam grave markers, and watch.

"The other thing that made this worth doing was that they didn't cut corners in camera and film. We had Kodak film. It was processed at Technicolor. And the camera was a Panaflex with, I think, four lenses."

This was great experience for a would-be filmmaker. "Proves you can do with very little, if you know what to do with what you have," says Okada. "I learned little tricks like not showing the parts of a set that we couldn't afford to light, and hiding things in darkness.

"Usually, the issues my friends and I discussed all had to do with lighting. We would go to foreign films during the week, then on weekends do these low-budget movies, trying to make very little mean and look like something.'"

Even on the earliest projects, Okada had a feel for the camera. He went to Panavision and said he was a new assistant on this film and for the next two days he wanted to learn everything about their equipment.

He practiced loading, pulling the movement, and changing circuit boards. Back at the set, however, he could only watch the loading and operation of the camera between setting up the lighting and other equipment.

But spending time in Panavision's Tarzana office came in very handy. "One night, we were working and the camera stopped running. Of course, the shoot came to a halt. This was the most expensive piece of equipment we had. It was a Sunday night and the camera was on a one-day rental for Saturday so they didn't want to call the 24-hour help line. They debated what to do for about 40 minutes.

"I offered to open the camera and change the circuit boards.    At first, I got a firm 'No!' But, as the night wore on and nothing happened, they relented. In no time the camera was working.

"My payoff? They let me look in the eyepiece once in a while and watch how they were shooting this very strange feature called *Phantasm*. The film, by the way, grossed a lot of money for its time," he adds.

Looking back, Daryn Okada admits that, if he had had a choice, he would have liked to go through the studio system during his learning process. "Observing others work before getting tossed into the fire would have been helpful," he says. "But, that was the breaks. My fires came early, and there were times when I had no idea what to do but to make the shot work on the spot."

Okada's first real film was additional photography on a picture called *Falling in Love Again*. It was a time when many European cinematographers were shooting independent films in the United States. "At various times on this film, I worked as the dolly grip, key grip, gaffer, additional camera assistant and, when the DP had to return to Europe because we were over schedule he recommended that I continue the last few weeks because I knew the lighting style.

In the independent world, the DP's operated their own camera, so Daryn Okada decided to concentrate on other aspects of filmmaking that would benefit him when his time came. Molding soft light through grip equipment, choosing the few lighting units for the desired effect, also spending time in editing rooms to see what pieces were needed to tell the story was the training ground he created for himself.

Also learning and operating the Tyler Major mount led to an entry into commercials. This led to shooting some very small action movies that were released in Europe and a feature in Sri Lanka with virtually no lighting equipment.

Back in the states, after six months, he began photographing and directing commercials, and music videos, still seeking a feature film where he could use all his skills.

In 1984 Frank LaLoggia, who had directed a film that Okada worked on as a key grip and postproduction supervisor in 1980, was preparing a feature, *Lady in White*. Okada and LaLoggia planned the shots needed for a trailer to raise funds for production of the film. The week before the two-weekend shoot, Okada was photographing and directing a commercial in Arizona. It was scheduled to end on Thursday with Friday as a contingency, which left time to get back for the Saturday shoot on *Lady in White*.

Unfortunately, the helicopter that Okada was shooting from crashed after getting the last shot on Friday morning. As he was figuring out what was happening to his body, he was telling the producer of the commercial that he had to call Frank LaLoggia and tell him that he wouldn't be there.

Of course, they thought it was shock setting in, but Okada knew everything was set to go for the trailer shoot and did not want LaLoggia to be unable to shoot. The Producer got ahold of LaLoggia, and they were lucky to get Russell Carpenter to photograph it.

For the next two months, Okada was in the hospital in Arizona. The crash left him with a burst fracture in his lower back paralyzing his legs, and his right shoulder was fractured. He made a deal with himself that he would leave that hospital on his own feet, and did, barely walking with the help of a cane.

After a year and a half Daryn Okada had done only a few commercials for people he knew. He would go on interviews for features but got the feeling they felt, since walking in with a cane, he would not be able to keep up with the schedule or operate the camera. He worked at physical therapy to strengthen his legs, and kept a positive attitude.

He finally did end up shooting the features *Survival Quest* and *Phantasm II* for Director Don Coscarelli, in addition to *Boris and Natasha* for Charlie Martin Smith during this period of fighting to get back.

His first taste of having his work noticed as Director of Photography was ironically a television series shot in Memphis called *Elvis — The Early Years*. It was 1989.

"I remember getting a call from a writer/producer friend who was about to meet the Executive Producers on a new series — about Elvis," he says. "All I could do was laugh. There was no way, I thought, anyone would care to watch a television show about a dead rock-and-roll icon. I was shocked, shall we say, when my friend called and said they were going to do it — the story of Elvis's early years. And, he had recommended me to shoot the series."

Once Okada looked at the pilot, he became interested in shooting the series. Done in Memphis, with a non-union local crew, the edict was to make the audience feel the location and the world Elvis grew up in. "We did a lot of long lens work," he recalls. "That way we could stack up the set dressing in a linear fashion elongating the view. This gave us the impact of the surroundings.

"Since I worked on features prior to this, I could only visualize each episode as a short movie. Keeping the lighting dramatic but simple, making an effort to set a visual mood for each scene.

"To stay on schedule, the deal I had with the ADs was, if we could photograph the exteriors for the best light, I could shoot efficiently and get a better look using less equipment off the truck, making moves faster. Also, we dollied instead of using the zooms.

"On this show, we used various camera speeds," he continues. "It was an idea Steve Miner, the director of the pilot and first four episodes, had. It would convey the atmosphere of Elvis in the late fifties."

Somehow, Daryn Okada was lucky not to be typecast as he began shooting. He moved freely between features, commercials, and television pilots.

"Is *Wild Hearts Can't Be Broken* a feature?" he asks, lightly. "I thought it was a television movie when I saw the schedule was 33 days.

"This was a 1930s period film with a lot of exteriors and horses," says Okada. "Honesty of the image was important. So, one of the first decisions we made was not to diffuse the picture, but to keep as much realism of the locations as possible. By not putting any diffusion in front of the lens, we were able to use the warm look of the environment and diffuse the look by color and lighting.

"For most of the picture, we used Rosco soft frost and Lee chocolate gels on the interior lighting. Kodak 5245 just came out and we used a lot of it. Also, the Canon 150 to 600mm lens had been just modified by Century and after testing it, I shot about 50 percent of the film on this. The lens enabled me to go into a field and find many compositions without having to reposition the camera every time.

"People who have seen the film think we only shot at magic hour but that would have been impossible with 33 days," he continues. "It was, again, a matter of looking at the story and the schedule and figuring out how to be in the right place for the right light and keep shooting scenes you can control when the light's not right.

"My favorite scene is when Gabrialle Anwar is blind and a doctor is testing her eyes. I wanted to convey this atmosphere that the film is going to take a different turn. Darkness and the last bits of light seemed to have the right mood for the scene.

"So, I lit this upstairs bedroom with one 2,500 watt HMI PAR light through the window and used bounce cards to catch little details. I still wanted to see Gabrialle's face which was backlit, so I kept pinning white handkerchiefs on the doctors suit so that, when he leaned toward her, the light that bounced off him would light her face.

"I thought this was pretty clever until I saw his ear backs glowing red. We tried to cut the light off his ears, but we lost the outline of his head in darkness, so as a last resort, I stuck on black tape cut to the size of his ears to block the light."

Now established as being able to handle a television shooting schedule, in addition to features, Daryn Okada was called by New World Television, which produced the *Elvis — The Early Years*, to consider a mini-series. "My breakthrough, if that's what you could call it, was a mini-series called *In A Child's Name*," he recalls.

"Not only did the story fascinate me, but the opportunity to interweave different parts of the country and give each an individual look that would support the story was important. We wanted to show the variety of cultures visually so that the audience would feel like they were progressing from one place to another."

Warmer colors and backlight for the New Jersey home where family was important. The camera moves always complement the characters by moving with them. Overcast, and stark lighting for the murderer's home. "The camera moves are independent of the characters, opposing and-or creeping when there is no other movement," he explains. "White walls for the small Indiana town. Very little camera movement showing that beliefs and way of life don't change very easily."

It is probably the separation of visuals that garnered Okada an A.S.C. nomination for the project. "I remember one sequence we simply had no idea how to approach," he recalls. "We wanted it to be frightening, but not like the horror films I'd worked on years before. After all, this was television.

(For cards outside the US, please affix a postage stamp)

# BUSINESS REPLY MAIL

FIRST-CLASS MAIL   PERMIT NO. 78   WOBURN MA

POSTAGE WILL BE PAID BY ADDRESSEE

DIRECT MAIL DEPARTMENT
BUTTERWORTH-HEINEMANN
225 WILDWOOD AVE
PO BOX 4500
WOBURN  MA  01888-9930

NO POSTAGE
NECESSARY
IF MAILED
IN THE
UNITED STATES

**B**UTTERWORTH
**H**EINEMANN

**www.bh.com**

## Keep up-to-date with the latest books in your field!

Complete this postage-paid reply card and return it to us now! We will notify you of upcoming titles and special offers. Visit our website and check out information on our newest releases.

**www.bh.com**

What title have you purchased?

_____

Where was the purchase made?

_____

Name _____

Job Title _____

Institution _____

Address _____

City/Town _____

State/County _____

Zip/Postcode _____

Country _____

Telephone _____

email _____

(FOR OFFICE USE ONLY)

"In the story, a murder takes place in the bedroom of a house. The visiting parents of the killer have no idea that their son participated in this horrible deed. How could we show that the murder took place in the bedroom, show the horrors, without showing the blood?

"In the script, it said the entire room had been scrubbed clean by the murderer. The police can't find anything. However, just before they give up, they use a chemical which, after applied, glows if there has been blood in the area.

"The idea was to have the parents of the killer go to sleep in this room, and when they turn the lights out, they realize the horror of the murder by us showing the green glow of hand prints and spatters all over the room, the  walls, everything. A struggle for life is shown by the glowing marks left behind.

"Wildfire had just come out with their blacklights," he recalls. "So, we brought them in to expose the fluorescent paint that was used to make it look like blood from a fight. The color spectrum of the light was real narrow, so there was no violet cast in the room, giving away that this chemical is self-illuminating.

"By doing that, we could show the room, and even do cut-aways to pools of green to show where the body was dragged across the room. It is, probably, one of the things that caught the A.S.C. Awards committee's attention and got me the nomination," he adds.

Since there were no "period" projects available, after *Elvis* and *Wild Hearts*, Okada signed on for his first of several big "comedy" projects. Admittedly, he is somewhat of an authority on the genre and can speak from first-hand knowledge that the light-hearted venue is not as easy to capture as it might appear to be.

"Discount the fact that *Captain Ron* was done on a boat and on water, and you still have a whole lot of challenges," he says. "Comedy is as challenging as trying to scare someone. You are rhythmically trying to lead people down one path, then surprise them instead of frightening them. Making the material come alive by leading them one way, then popping them with a joke takes a whole lot more than timing and bright lighting.

"When I began prepping this picture, the first thing I thought of was the Marx Brothers. Everything was simple and hilarious. That's what I wanted. I needed to find a way to make shots that would sustain them and be funny. Too often, comedy is done with the cut, cut, cut, cut mentality. That doesn't allow for the audience's intelligence or interest. There has to be a balance between how much you lead them and how much you entertain them.

"Of course, we wanted postcard images, after all we were shooting in the waters off Puerto Rico so that had to be incorporated into the visual scheme. There's a scene that I think incorporates all these elements. It has only two shots. Martin Short is walking down a beautiful sunset beach with Mary Kay Place, only he's been temporally blinded by a flare gun and can't appreciate the great place.

"The first is a wide shot of the two of them and the setting sun followed by a second shot tracking them as they walk and talk on the beach. At the end of the shot, he's bummed that he can't experience this wonderful place and bumps into a tree that enters frame just before the camera is cut."

Okada's next film was called *Airborne*. A fish-out-of-water, hero's journey type story, it takes a young California surfer to his relative's house in the Midwest during winter. Here, instead of king of the waves, he becomes the object of jealousy and scorn by 'the powerful kids.' It is only when he shows himself to be a championship rollerblader that he wins respect, from others, and from him.

"Again, my idea was to find ways to support the story, taking the audience along for the ride. A major element was the classic 'Western showdown' climax," he continues. "Instead of horses and guns, we had kids on rollerblades. We scouted lots of hills in Cincinnati, and could not find one, so we put several together to create one big hilly road on film that would lead into the city.

"I knew that, to get the best footage of this, I would not be able to do it all myself. So, I spent most of the prep period working with Second Unit DP Candy Gonzales and operators Guy Bee and Bruce Bennedict in setting up how each segment should be photographed and how each progression of the race should build to."

With two successful projects on his résumé, Okada thought he would take a break and do a "little relationship comedy." "Yes, there is a difference between the *Captain Ron* type comedies and a film like *My Father, The Hero*," he says, adamantly. "Most important, we wanted to show the sense of tenderness that came out between the father and daughter.

"This being the third project with director Steve Miner, we knew how each other worked. We would discuss things like the number of times we would see father and daughter together in the same shot, and how many times we would have them separated in their own shots.

"When they were in the same frame, how close would they be? As she begins to separate from him, emotionally, we would move her farther away in the frame and finally move her out and have him looking at her and then after her."

For *Big Bully*, a Tom Arnold and Rick Moranis comedy, Okada tackled another style of shooting. This was a tough one," he admits. "What we prepped and shot really has little relation to what ended up on the screen."

He sighs, then re-focuses on the present. "Sometimes, you simply have no control over what you have done. Originally, *Big Bully* was supposed be a black comedy. That's the way we shot it. However, when the production company got into the editing, they wanted to make it more of a broad comedy.

"The two aren't really compatible, visually. If you are doing a black comedy you do things like create a more stylized mood, a darker tone, but still be natural. In a broad comedy, you might open it up a little more.

"There were several scenes that are not in the film that have a real dark dramatic quality to them. This balances the rest of the film. In trying to make it a broader comedy, the elimination of these scenes leaves the film with a visual indecisiveness. The viewer is not clued in as to what they should feel while watching.

"Scenes are always dropped out of movies, but in this case, it was all the scenes that would have told the audience this film is funny, with tension and suspense. But, then, that's what the studio decided they did not want after it was shot."

Fortunately, Okada didn't let the uncontrollable circumstances consume him. He went on to do another comedy project, with a highly successful director, Penelope Spheeris. "*Black Sheep* was probably done in the broad style they wanted on *Big Bully*," he laughs.

"This was a comedy where the star's physicality really was a big part of the story. In planning this film, one of the most important things we had to do was give actor Chris Farley room to do what he did best, use his body."

*Black Sheep* gave Okada a chance to capture Marx Brothers's type movements, with his style of camerawork. "There is a scene where Mike (Chris Farley) is determined to give out every last campaign brochure he has. This, he thinks, will help get his brother elected to a state office.

"At one point, we had this slapstick sequence where he tries to give two elderly people a brochure. He scares them, and they slam the trunk of their car and race to get in. They don't realize Mike's tie is caught in the trunk. As they speed off, they see him running after them. Panicking, they hit the gas, go over a speed bump, and drag him on the ground.

"As he is dragged, the various campaign buttons he is wearing set off sparks against the road."

Okada and Spheeris discarded the idea of using a massive series of cuts with stunt doubles, and decided to use Farley, in a way that they could show off his comedic work and protect him at the same time.

"We just put him on a skid plate with metal that would spark against the road. One handheld camera in the trunk looking down at Chris and another dollying parallel to him. Simple and low tech."

Comedy, especially physical comedy, might look relatively easy on the screen, but it takes just as much or even more planning than any other type of project. "Well, not as much as *Anna*," Okada laughs, his eyes sparkling with excitement.

After Daryn Okada finished *Black Sheep*, he got a call from the producers at Icon Productions whom he had met while doing *Airborne* and additional photography for Mel Gibson's *Man without a Face*. They wanted to know if he was available for a little picture to be shot totally in Russia, called *Anna Karenina*.

Was Okada available? "Was I available?" Okada laughs. "The moment I read the script I knew I would do anything to shoot this picture. This was where I wanted to be, cinematically since photographing *Wildhearts Can't Be Broken*."

Daryn Okada's face nearly glows. He pulls his Powerbook close, nearly rips the cover off, and flips it open. "Doing our version of this classic story was a challenge, and I knew I was up to it. All it took was a lot of planning and planning, and praying."

It takes a moment for the computer to power up, but that doesn't stop Okada from getting impatient. "Everything that I had done up until that moment, for me, was preparation for doing this film."

The computer screen comes alive and he moves his finger across the touch pad gently. "When I started planning my projects on the Macintosh, I knew the graphical logic of the system would come in handy. It was more than a life-saver on *Anna*."

Soon the computer's "table of contents" appears. It reads like a book, chronicling the history of Okada's career. Prominent among the list is a large block of entries with *Anna* written in them.

"When I start a project, I read the script three times," Okada explains, as he moves the cursor through the list. "Once, to get a sense of the movie as a viewer. A second time, to stop and think about things. Then, a third time, to input detailed notes," he adds as he opens a file.

"My notes have the same scene headings as the script, so I can refer back to either, easily. Take this one, for example, it details one of the most difficult shots in the picture."

The computer came in handy on *Anna* for many other unexpected things. One of the biggest challenges on this picture was the isolation of the crew. "This was the first time an American production company was allowed to do a whole film on Russian soil," he explains. "We even got to shoot inside the Kremlin. Although these people are no longer our 'enemies,' there were certain inherent problems we still had to deal with.

"One of the challenges was simply getting current information on time and accurately. When you are doing so many exteriors as we did, knowing exactly what the weather was going to be is vital. In Russia, the weather is not something they follow with great accuracy or interest. They know it is going to be cold. How cold, and where the wind would be coming from wasn't important to them. It was to me."

Fortunately, he was able to tap into the Internet. He would then download data from weather sites or contacts outside the country. Okada used this "underground" system of information gathering to a great advantage.

"It was even more vital while we were prepping," he explains. "Back at 'home base' outside the country, my crew would be checking out equipment. We would send digital photos and requests back and forth over the Internet. By the time we were ready to join up, everything had been taken care of."

To Okada, it is all about logic and elements, and taking things one step at a time. Easy to say, when the job is confined to planning the lighting and camerawork. However, it is a lot harder, when the cinematographer has to split his attention and operate the camera as well.

"There is something to be said about having someone else do the operating," he admits. "However, on *Anna,* our time schedule, the complications of the shots, and the crew restrictions made it more logical that I wear several hats.

"Actually, half the fun was getting behind the camera!" he adds. "Of course, there were times when I wished I was a safe distance away – like when we used two 'wolves' in one of the opening sequences with just us and the camera in the snowcovered forest.

"And then, there was the time I had to make this long move through a series of historical rooms, roll onto a crane and execute an extremely complicated move through a huge ballroom in one take."

It has been a while since Daryn Okada finished *Anna Karenina.* The film has garnered him quite a lot of attention. Everyone who sees it, says it is magnificent. He is always asked, "How did you do that?" about many shots. "I'm also asked what it was like working in Russia," he adds.

"That was as fascinating as the project itself," he says, seriously. You'd think that this film would get Daryn Okada some more very serious jobs. In the long run, it might. However, right after finishing *Anna*, he went on to another Penelope Spheeris project called *Senseless*. "The strange part of this project was shooting in Los Angeles, something I was not used to now," he laughs.

"In the fall of 1997 Steve Miner gave me a script written by David Kelly. It had wonderful characters involved in a situation that is bigger than they ever expected. It takes place in a small lake town in Maine. It would involve plenty of water work in the day and night, animatronics, and computer graphic effects.

"When we were done scouting, the ideal choice for lakes close to a crew base with technical support would be Vancouver, British Columbia. The only problem was El Nino was coming and with it the chance for record rains. That would be very bad for a film that has only ten interior scenes. Also, we decided to accomplish this film, we would need to build a very large tank that could support a set that looked like the lake where this takes place.

"So, in pushing that film to a summer 1998 start, Jamie Lee Curtis asked Steve Miner to direct the 20th anniversary *Halloween* film that spring."

Daryn Okada made a major departure from comedy. "The 1998 horror picture *Halloween: $H_2O$* took lighting and camera back to the roots of where I got into this business," he says. "It was fun, striving to set up the look and mood, creating a scary but accessible atmosphere while keeping the film fun.

"The thought was to be as close an homage to John Carpenter's *Halloween*. We wanted to show minimum gore in creating the suspense. Since this project came up very quickly not enough anamorphic lenses were available at Panavision because of demand, so we shot in Super 35mm composed for 1:2.40. There are differences but, after testing the process through dupe negative prints, we were able to compensate with exposure, lighting, and choice of colors in the frame."

As soon as *Halloween: $H_2O$* was completed, a site to construct a tank for exterior night filming was chosen for *Lake Placid*. John Willett and Daryn Okada designed a 180-by-200-foot tank from scratch. It was angled to match the light at the lake location for day work and gain maximum depth and lighting accessibility for night work. In addition, it had to accommodate an anamatronic 30-foot crocodile.

*Lake Placid* is about a small lake in Maine where no one lives, but it is discovered that something in or around the lake had attacked and killed a Fish and Game officer. A tooth is found and a museum curator is sent from New York to identify it. These characters get caught up trying to unravel the mystery before word gets out and panic sets in.

"Steve Miner wanted it to have a warm, dark look and to always include the lake as a character," Okada explains. "Photographing this film in anamorphic was a must and the lenses had been reserved six months in advance.

"We tested various combinations of filters and flashing for the look, but settled on a more simplistic approach since I needed to blend production footage with digital effects. I wanted the day exteriors to be affected by natural changes in light.

"To get a sense that nature is a power to reckon with. My collaborators in this were First Assistant Director Mark Cotone who scheduled the best he could for being in the right place for the light and Production Designer John Willett who choose locations and colors. Even with this kind of help you still face unexpected changes that you wish could be better."

This film had everything. Large natural lakes as sets, air to air, underwater, animatronics in the water, digital effects, and an ending that takes place at night on the water.

"On the large exterior lake tank set we used two Musco 80 lighting trucks that moved at least four times a night around the tank. The Muscos were the only way we could shoot in continuity and, if we had to change plans in the middle of the night, we could quickly reconfigure the lighting.

"Three days before getting to the tank, I would stop there after wrap at the lake and do some prelighting at night. We painted positions on the ground for the Musco 80s for the different angles we would shoot. We also built a 12-by-20-foot 'moonbox.' It had two 12K HMI's on a 120-foot articulated arm that could provide soft fill for a large area. This had to be approved by an engineer before being use because of the wind factor.

"We came up with the idea to attach the Rosco grid cloth and the surrounding black panels with Velcro so that it could blow apart. We did have heavy winds and after lowering the arm it did exactly that. From there, we just put it back together."

The real test of the prelight plan was the first two nights of shooting on the tank. In the story, they have lured the crocodile by dangling a cow from a helicopter as bait in the water. "We were approved to do this right after sunset, and had to complete the shot in ten minutes due to regulations.

"Condors and Muscos could not be left up from the previous night as a pre-light because of the winds in the day and getting men out of the condors. Also, we had to turn around from our day schedule to a night one.

"So, an hour before sunset we moved our lighting in our predetermined marks around the tank and hoped that when it got dark it was right, and I hoped we had lit enough air for the helicopter to be seen.

"As it turned out, the sky still had a slight glow in it, the lights were all on, and the helicopter with cow attached descended on our set dipping the cow in the water with three cameras rolling. Wind, noise, and water were everywhere and when it left and the camera was cut, I was relieved that the plan had worked because there could be no Take Two that night.

"During postproduction, Digital Domain sent effects shot in progress to my Macintosh, where I made comments and e-mailed them back to the digital artist. Of course, there were many trips to Digital Domain to see the work in progress but this cut down on the time there, while also giving us a way to get instant feedback.

"During the postproduction of *Lake Placid*, director Steve Miner and I began an accelerated preproduction on a Western called *Texas Rangers*. Shot in the badlands around Alberta and Durango, it was a chance to photograph a period film and have it appeal to a contemporary audience. Steve's visual references were paintings by Remmington. They were vivid in color and captured a moment of action.

"Steve Miner would have liked to shoot in 65mm, but with the short prep and the use of multiple cameras with different units, we decided to shoot 35mm anamorphic," he continues.

"The Panavision-Kodak Preview System was used to aid us technically, in choosing a color scheme, since we would not have time to shoot extensive exterior tests at the beginning of prep," he adds. "There was still snow on the ground, and the picture takes place in the fall.

"While shooting, we also e-mailed images to Delux in Toronto, to use as a guide in timing dailies," he adds. "Most of the film was shot with Harrison and Harrison Sepia A filters. We didn't choose it because it said Sepia. I tested a lot of filters with the Preview System. We wanted to bias the color, and this particular filter affected the image just right. It also crushed the contrast a little.

"It was a challenge, capturing up to 60 riders on horseback during the battle scenes," he admits. "We also had awful weather! The coldest, rainiest summer that had hit that area in a long time. It was apparent that we could not shoot everything before we lost our lead actors to prior commitments, so we shot the beginning and several other scenes in Durango, Mexico, four months after wrapping in Alberta."

It has been a long way from trying to shoot anamorphic films without anamorphic lenses in the student days to planning the logistics of *Anna Karenina* and *Lake Placid*, and Daryn Okada has enjoyed every moment of the ride. At the moment, he may be slightly "typed" in comedy, but that's okay. As he says, "it is harder to do than it looks." And, that's okay, too. There aren't many cinematographers out there who can make something "look funny" on the screen, and still give a project soul. Daryn Okada is one of them. So, until another *Anna* comes along, he'll keep digging into his "bag of tricks," and his Powerbook, for all the tools needed — to bring to the screen what he's read (three times) on the page.

*The cinematographer is one of the key set dressers on a picture. The most important things are the script, the performance of that script, and the director's vision. I see it as my role to create a certain kind of reality that supports the director's vision of that script. Hopefully, the cast senses the reality in the lighting, which adds to their comfort and security and, just like good props and set dressing, may present them with opportunities to interact with the environment that I have helped create.*

*Neil Roach*

It takes more than a little negotiating to get to Neil Roach's home in the hills above Santa Fe, New Mexico. Using the obligatory four-wheel drive, you climb up and up, following a rutted one-lane road for miles until you finally get to a beautiful and open Southwestern style house with the most incredible views imaginable.

For a while, parking was out of doors, the garage space taken up with a small single-engine plane — one that Roach literally put together with his own hands between pictures. It took some time, but not too long ago the little single-engine plane was towed to the local airport.

It is another tool that will allow Neil Roach to do what he loves to do — make moving pictures. And, to keep his unofficial title of "the king of the short shoot" — television movies, mini-series, television pilots, and video released features.

Over the years, Neil Roach has shot more than 100 projects, ranging from horror to drama. Several of his projects, including the Glenn Jordan directed Hallmark Hall of Fame film *To Dance with the White Dog* have been nominated for various awards, including the 1994 A.S.C. Award. He counts among his favorite projects *House of Frankenstein* and *The Substitute Wife*.

A native of Kansas City, Missouri, he is doing what he set out to do at seven years old — making movies. He admits, when he started, he really didn't have any idea what that was all about. While in high school, Roach and a friend began shooting their "movies" on 8mm.

During his years at the University of Kansas there was no film school, so the only classes that really interested him were photography. And, those were really only in press photography. Since he already had some knowledge of the camera, Roach ended up tutoring other students in the dark room.

"School bored me," he admits. "In my senior year, I had had enough. It really angered my father, but I couldn't waste my time anymore. I quit. I went home, determined to be a movie cameraman."

With the Vietnam War looming in the background, Neil Roach literally let his fingers do the walking. He opened the phone book and called every company in the book relating to camerawork, asking if there were any job openings — for any amount of money. By the second day, he had gotten to the "C" section — Calvin Productions.

Roach had lucked out. The company was huge, with their own laboratory. They even manufactured their own processing equipment. He was offered a job, with one stipulation. He had to like traveling.

He started in the camera department, where everyone did all the jobs — from gaffing to electrician to grip. "Of course, I started out sweeping the floors," he interjects. "But, after a few days, the guys started showing me the lights and how they worked.

"Soon, I was troubleshooting with broken lights and learning how things worked," he adds. "I was constantly being taught to do things in the department. But, the best lesson I learned was to 'volunteer' for anything. You never know what you can pick up along the way."

Roach was soon out on shoots, working on the stage, and moving around the Production Company. In the machine shop, he learned design and even built a modification of the TelePrompTer.

"Unfortunately, it was a time when all these big companies were coming to an end," he says sadly. "Just as I began working at Calvin, things were winding down. As much as I enjoyed every day, I knew we were coming to the end of an era."

Fortunately, a Hollywood production company came to town and, although he wasn't a member of the union, he got a job lifting equipment. Not only did this job teach him what the Hollywood system was all about, he formed friendships with several of the veteran crew, who showed him some of the ropes.

Looking for warmer weather and more opportunities to work, Roach went to Dallas and got a job at a company called Jameson Films, a smaller version of Calvin. After a year and a half of commercial and industrial work, Roach embarked on a freelance career.

At that time in Dallas, people working on film crews would do any job available, from assistant camera to grip, electrician or whatever else was needed. It was a great learning tool for all involved and a way to build a group that worked well together.

When a local production company geared up to shoot a filmed called *Benji*, Roach applied for the job as camera operator. Unfortunately for him, there were others with more experience. However, he was offered DGA scale for the job as Production Manager, "with half my salary deferred," he recalls. "As Production Manager, I learned a lot about how to manage people. I learned how to plan and how important a team is. I learned to handle locations, work as an AD, drive the mobile home, and for a portion of the show, even served as key grip. All positions were invaluable lessons."

Roach knew that he didn't want to work on the production management side of films for a living. At 25, he was ready to establish himself as a cameraman, even though most men his age in the industry were barely loaders.

That didn't stop him. Roach made the rounds, landing at a studio in Dallas. "The guy that owned the studio knew I needed him as much as he needed me. So, we struck a deal. I got time behind the camera. For the first year, however, I was traveling at least 330 days."

One of the most important lessons Neil Roach learned in these days was that making movies is all about collaboration. "When you are working with the right director, you can turn out some beautiful work," he says. "But, no matter what director, you have to do the best-crafted work you can.

"Because of the nature of a cameraman's job, you are always being told 'No'. No, you want too many lights. Or, 'No,' you can't do this or that. In self-defense, I was always figuring out a way to satisfy myself, and get what I wanted out of the job at the same time, giving my employers everything they needed.

"It makes me a manager, really. But, being a clever manager allows you to buy yourself the time and resources necessary to inject your notions of craft to get the product you are happy with. Yes, sometimes that means being demanding and tough. But, always reasonable. I've learned to expect people to do their jobs well."

Several years after working on *Benji*, the film took off. Since part of Roach's salary was a percentage of the film, he started receiving substantial checks. This gave him a comfortable cushion, allowing him to pursue work as a cinematographer exclusively.

Roach's next step was to join the Chicago camera local. He admits paying his dues was terrifying. He was now a union cameraman. But, would he work? He didn't have to wait long. B-camera operator on second unit then a variety of productions in Dallas that required almost a full local crew. Through this experience, he was able to move around in the camera department, learning more of what he needed to know to do his job well.

"B-camera on *Semi Tough* led to a call for second unit on a film called *The Island,* which was a huge Universal Picture," he recalls. "Then, $20 million was something. It was an interesting five-and-a-half months.

"Director Michael Ritchie told me what he wanted but not how to get it," he admits. "Being rather new at the game, I had to improvise – and call people for advice, like how to handle special effects!"

The most difficult assignment on this second unit involved a scene where 40 pirates in three small boats attack, disable, and board a large (250-ton) sailboat. "Since the scene would be filmed over a number of weeks, out at sea, there had to be a plan for matching the look of the scene," Roach explains. "It wasn't just the light but also the angle of the sails, the tilt of the ship, and its speed, as well as dozens of other factors."

With matching and logistics as well as dramatic and photographic considerations in mind, Roach worked with the ship director, stunt coordinator, and an assistant director to lay out a shooting plan that would accomplish all these goals, keeping safety in mind at all times.

Film director Michael Ritchie gave Roach a simple assignment, create an action scene where the pirates attack and stop the ship, then get them on board. The first unit would take over from there.

With a very small camera team and huge support crew of up to 120 people, Roach methodically photographed the scene over a period of six weeks. At times, after finishing a day on the water, he would join the first unit and operate a camera for a few hours. The planning and work resulted in a great scene that satisfied the director, producers, and most of all Roach himself.

"The lesson," he says, "is plan, execute the plan, and be ready for targets of opportunity when they come along. Breaking a job into its component pieces reduces a big job to a manageable task. This is the key to success when you are faced with large photographic challenges."

After returning from the Caribbean, Roach continued working as an operator and second unit cameraman. He finally secured an agent, which ultimately helped him get a DP job on a CBS television movie. *The Wild and the Free* was filmed in Florida. "It included 14 chimps in the cast," he recalls. With 22 principle first unit days and 14 days of second unit, Roach knew he had to surround himself with a good crew, listen to the director, and make the days.

This project could have launched Roach into the ranks of full-time DP, but a writers' strike came along about that time. It had a major effect on the industry for several years.

"One of the nice things about working out of the Chicago camera local, was the operator/DP classification," says Roach. "This allowed us the freedom to move back and forth between categories, while making the transition to full-time DP."

Roach returned to Dallas from Florida, and started working as a camera operator for DP Robert Jessup, A.S.C., on a picture called *Skyward*. The film was helmed by a new young director by the name of Ron Howard. "It was wonderful to work with such a great, young talent, and to see him get started," says Roach. "*Skyward* was a pleasure because Ron was so prepared and collaborative."

Aside from the normal challenges presented in making a picture with a short schedule, airplanes, the hottest summer on record in Dallas, and a big cast (including Bette Davis), Roach was asked to solve a tough problem. He had to get the 12-year-old female lead into the rear cockpit of an old Stearman biplane. "How do you get numerous shots of her which pan and tilt from various places both to and from her face?" he says.

"There was no time for elaborate camera mounts, which could be remotely panned and tilted," he continues. With the pilot's help, Roach worked with his key grip to build a lightweight harness that allowed him to be strapped almost anywhere on the outside of the plane. When Roach had an open period of time during the production, he would shoot aerial footage. He got more than expected — and kudos from the crew. Of course, when they realized the danger he had put himself in, there was a consensus of opinion. Roach was a crazy man!

For a while, he continued to operate on features like *Breaking Away*, *Southern Comfort,* and *Barbarosa*, as well as various television movies — waiting for another DP job.

When director Reza Badiyi wanted to bring the classic book *Of Mice and Men* to the screen, the project was going to be shot in Dallas. "I admit it, they gave me a chance because they had no money and wanted to do the project as cheaply as possible. It didn't matter. This was another chance. The shoot was 17 days and it turned out great." Even Siskel and Ebert called attention to the project, saying it was one of the best versions of this classic story.

"What did we do? It was all about natural light and how to use it. And, finding just the right place to put the camera. Reza trusted me to do my job, and that helped a lot."

Roach believes the cinematographer is one of the key set dressers on a picture. "The most important things are the script, the performance of that script, and the Director's vision," he says. "I see it as my role to create a certain kind of reality that supports the director's vision of that script.

"Hopefully, the cast senses the reality in the lighting, which adds to their comfort and security and, just like good props and set dressing, may present them with opportunities to interact with the environment that I have helped create.

"I remember, while shooting an episode of a series called *Early Edition*. We had a scene where the star is waking up in a darkened bedroom early in the morning. I placed a little shaft of sunlight across the pillows, which did a couple of things. It gave a beautiful highlight to an otherwise darkened room.

"I told the actor what the room would look like on the screen. He realized he could react to that little shaft of bright light as anyone might when they roll over and their eyes are assaulted with that intense early morning sun after a deep sleep.

"That little shaft of light added beauty and depth but, it also blended the reality of the performance with the photography.

"The notion of reality in any given project, however, may range from a factual recreation of a documented historical event to a completely made up world or universe," he continues. "The point I am making is that I see it as a part of my responsibility to work with production design and set dressing to help create a stage on which the cast and director are free and comfortable to satisfy the dramatic needs of the script.

"My best efforts as a cameraman are not going to save a bad script. My job is to try to get inside the head of the director, to figure out what he wants and help the performance where I can. I must also stay out of the way while I figure out how to satisfy my own creative needs as a cameraman."

Neil Roach has been encouraged to direct, but he prefers to focus all his attention on the image that goes on the screen. He knows how to handle a crew. He inspires the confidence that is needed to get the best out of a cohesive camera department.

"You have to treat each and every member of the crew with respect," he says adamantly. "On many projects, I've seen how badly some of the crew was being treated. They made fairly good money but they were working their rears off! I've seen crew-members get fired, sometimes for no reason. However, how many times have we seen a producer who doesn't do his or her job replaced?

"You have to recognize that everyone makes a contribution to a project. You have to allow them to accomplish their jobs in the most efficient way. I don't believe in work for work's sake. I will never ask someone to do something just to keep that person busy.

"I always try to come to the set prepared," Roach says. "That does not mean every decision has been made in advance. What it does mean is that I arrive with an appropriate plan to translate a rehearsal into blocking, blocking into a visual plan, that plan into shots and lighting design, and all of that into explicit instructions to the crew.

"Finally, as things develop, you have to be ready to listen to, recognize and implement ideas that may come from the director, producer, cast, or any of your trusted crew members."

This is what has helped build Neil Roach's reputation for getting the job done. Ironically, that doesn't always make him friends among the producers or other cinematographers. Although he doesn't like to "take over" for other DPs, he has been called in to finish something that has gotten out of another artist's hands.

"When that happens, I try to make this transition as easy as possible," he says. "I try to talk to that cinematographer, making sure things stay comfortable between us. We all do the same job, we just approach it in a different way. It is important that we all understand this and get along."

For a while, Roach was a fixer. He would come in and finish what was bogged down – usually small features and television movies. "I wanted to do features on my own," he admits. "So, I turned down operating on projects like *Terms of Endearment*, hoping that little television projects for DP jobs would come along."

What did come along was a Jessica Lange feature called *Country* (1984). "Several DPs turned the project down. I was relatively new, but they allowed me to shoot some tests with writer/director Bill Wittliff. Jessica and the people at Disney liked what I'd done.

"We had three weeks to prep the project," he recalls. "I'd never shot anything of this magnitude, so it was a challenge. Fortunately, we had some wonderful people on the project; however, a conflict developed on the production side."

Roach got caught in the middle and became the scapegoat. The problem — he was told — was "the cameraman." He was asked to leave. "They wanted me to continue working until David Walsh (the new cinematographer) arrived, and even asked me to introduce him to the crew the next day. And, I said I would.

"It was the hardest thing that I've ever done," he admits. "But, this is all part of the deal when making movies. You have to roll with the punches.

"To this day, I really don't know what happened. Was it creative conflicts with the producers or the stars? I knew Bill had confidence in me. So, was it other things? I don't know. I do know that, once in a while, you get involved in a project that goes sour. It's your call, just how much you take before you get out. The trick is to keep going and not let what happened get to you. I know, it is easier said than done sometimes."

Roach then took over on the series *The Mississippi* for a cinematographer who was going on to other projects. Then, he got a call to go to Toronto for *Alex, The Life of a Child*. Next, a television movie with Larry Elikann called *Dallas, The Early Years*. "What a great opportunity," he says. "The show was completely the opposite of the original series (which was very glossy and high key). We had fabulous production value. They built huge sets for big bucks (for 1985), all to explain how the series got started. It was a 40-day shoot, often with up to nine cameras."

Later that year, cinematographer Jack Priestley fell off a ladder and broke three ribs. Director Gary Nelson needed someone in Texas to take his place on a show called *Houston Nights*. "It was a wonderful one-hour pilot, a 12-day shoot — with terrific actors.

"Seymour Freedman (in charge of production at Columbia Television) wanted me to do the series, but there was a hitch. I wasn't a West Coast union member. (This was before the Cinematographers Guild became national.)

"While I was in Los Angeles making the rounds with my agent, we were walking across the Paramount lot and into Bob Marta, whom I'd known from other projects. 'You shooting here?' he asked me. 'I can't, I don't have an LA card,' I replied. 'Maybe we can help you with that,' Bob replied.

"Bob was connected to the LA local. Technically, I wasn't supposed to shoot in Los Angeles, so he decided to change that. The union people were amazingly cooperative — a corporation and a contract, and I was legit."

Things weren't all that smooth sailing when production on the series started, however. The producers wanted the look to be hot and contrasty. The darks were jet black. They didn't like the direction of the first episode. Out went the director, and Roach was afraid he would soon follow. However, there was something about his lighting style that caught production's eye. "They came to me and asked what we could do to make the look better," he recalls.

"I came up with an interesting visual style that really hadn't been used in television before," he explains. "The use of extremely hot light in unexpected places, a higher key to fill, is common now. But, back in the mid-1980s, it wasn't done. I was one of the first cinematographer in television to push the visuals in this direction.

"It kind of became a learn-by-doing," he admits. "I put super hot spot lights in, teaching myself the limits of the equipment and film, as I went along."

For a year and a half, after this show, Neil Roach realized he was hopping back and forth between union and non-union projects. "I was and still am a firm supporter of the union issue," he says. "But, there was and still is a lot of work in the non-union world. I had no choice. I had to work.

"Even when I am working 'non-union,' I make sure my crew is treated fairly and safely. No 20-hour days. No danger or abuse."

Roach was now working steadily on a series of independent productions including Hallmark Hall of Fame projects. One of the most powerful was *My Name Is Bill W*, starring James Woods. "It was a typical 24-day shoot," he says. "But with a powerful story. I think Hollywood really paid tribute to the subject (alcoholism) as much as the acting and cinematography, when it was nominated for a series of awards, including the Emmy for best actor."

When Roach was nominated for the A.S.C. Award for cinematography on a movie-for-television or mini-series category, he was thrust into a new world in Hollywood. "Suddenly, I was up there on the stage with Haskell

Wexler and Steve Burum (in the feature category) and on the ballot with John Toll, Eric van Haren Noman, Shelley Johnson, and Gayne Reicher. I had been Gayne's operator earlier in my career, and thought of him as my mentor.

"At the dinner for nominees, the night before the awards, I even got to see Chuck Wheeler again. He was the cameraman on a show I did in Kansas City when I was moving equipment around."

Although Roach did not win, the nomination brought him into the limelight. "What image from *Bill W* sticks in my mind?" he asks, rhetorically. "It's a poster shot where Bill is leaving his apartment and his wife is looking out the window, watching him go away. He walks across the street, drunk."

Roach shot the sequence from the other side of the street then moved into an upper floor (6th) window, where his wife is watching. "We then got into a cherry picker and shot the reverse of her watching him running away," he recalls. "The way we lit it was interesting. We set lights so that his shadow was stretching all the way across the street, with him in the shot.

"Lighting on the shot was very simple," he smiles. "It took all of ten minutes to put a LTM 1200 watt HMI PAR on the ground. The time? Finding the right angle for the shadow! All we needed was a little light coming out of the building. We then simulated street lights for him to walk through," he recalls. "We mixed incandescent lights with HMIs coming back at him, which created the long shadows.

"It was feature style — something that I always do, even when I'm doing a short television shoot. I always strive to light shots in an interesting, yet natural, way."

Roach was now being sought after for projects. What he chose to do was always story driven. *The Image* for HBO was an important project for him. Not only did he get to work with one of his favorite directors, Peter Werner, but he also got to go to New York for a week. "Working with HBO is wonderful," he says. "They bring great actors into a project, allow time for rewrites if necessary, and allow us to do what we do, without screaming 'budget' all the time.

"Still, these projects are short (30 days)," he adds. "We tried to get the most out of each day. And, even though I had all the tools I needed, we were looking for ways to get things done simple and fast.

"I remember getting to the tenth hour of a long day, and realizing we had a three-page sequence between Albert Finney and John Mahoney to go. The moment was a philosophical conversation between the two, as they sat on the floor of the rural airport waiting room where they were stranded. We wanted to see their isolation and the rain outside the door.

"I had a notion of how to do this, without the need of coverage. I went to Peter. 'If we can get all this in one shot, what do you think?' I asked him. 'If you can, go for it,' he told me.

"I set the shot up so that we started on a dolly at 250mm on a zoom lens. This allowed us to see depth. We could see out the door with the rain in the shot and a person mopping the floor in the foreground. We also saw someone closing up the ticket counter in the background. We then moved diagonally in on the dolly, while zooming out to maintain the size — ending at 25mm. The actors remained the same size in the frame throughout. The massive change in perspective pulled the viewer into the scene.

"It was a great shot — no coverage — and we made it in a reasonable time, allowing us to get the much-needed rest we had to have to come back the next day."

The team of Roach and Werner was cemented on this picture. Doing the run-and-gun killer short shoots can often be difficult, so when a cinematographer and director form a partnership, it allows them to develop a shorthand and get more punch out of each project.

A few months later, Roach shot *Hiroshima*, an NBC-TV movie, with Werner. The story featured four or five parallel stories revolving around the days before the bomb was set off. "We really had two looks," he recalls. "The world before the bomb, and after, when everything was destroyed.

"It was a great project," he admits. "A huge cast, dedicated Japanese extras, and a lot of tricks to deal with. Like effects.

"For me, the other visual highlight was the scenes with the fire and smoke. I got the idea of how to handle these scenes from a cute little Disney project called *Goodbye Miss Fourth of July,* which I had done years before," he says.

"There was a sequence in this Disney film, featuring Chris Sarandon, where the factory was burned down. I needed smoke, but the wind was blowing our smoke the wrong way. We had smoke but we couldn't see it. Instead, what we saw were the shadows going across the set. This gave an unexpected energy to the scene, and helped tell the story when we couldn't see the fire.

"I remembered that look, so I used it on *Hiroshima*," he says. "For this picture, most of the shooting was done in the Los Angeles Basin. On sunny days, for the post bomb look, I had to make things look not so pretty. So, to sell the 'after-the-bomb' shots, when we couldn't always create fire, we used this technique. We had two huge foggers on condors, and created shadows and smoke. I knew, we would ruin the sound track with the noise, but the director liked the idea of the look.

"To do this, I had to break my long-standing rule of backlight. We had to frontlight the set and drift the shadows across the set through the light. It was effective, and created a lot of attention.

"The look, here, wasn't about the light and what we used, but how we placed the shadows and their movement across the set."

The toughest scene to accomplish on *Hiroshima* was the actual moment of the bomb's explosion. The script showed each main character at the moment of detonation. Roach had some experience in trying to create the effects of a nuclear blast, as the second unit cameraman on a movie called *The Day After* for ABC-TV. "On this one, we had quite a few resources and considerable budget for opticals," he recalls. "Still, we struggled to create images that in any way replicated historical footage of actual bomb blasts."

On *Hiroshima*, there was little or no budget for major effects. "So, it was obvious that another approach had to be found." Roach and Werner decided to stick their necks out and film the pieces of the scene in very short takes, concentrating all of their limited resources into a few frames of film, covering each of the principal characters.

"Each of these pieces replicated some different and accurate effect of a nuclear explosion," Roach explains. "The risk was that there would be no extra footage for editorial fixes. Cut the slate off, splice it together, and pray.

"Through the use of experience, planning, and a clear vision of what was needed dramatically, we had a scene we hoped for but, initially, had never dreamed we could accomplish on our budget."

Many months later, Neil Roach went to another award-nominated project called *To Dance with the White Dog*, directed by Glenn Jordan for Hallmark Hall of Fame. "We had incredible exterior locations," he recalls. "And, all I really had to do with most of them was find the right time of day to exploit them. The Nestor Almendros style of shooting," he laughs.

"It was summer and we were 200 miles south of Atlanta. It was miserably hot. We had two wonderful actors (Hume Cronin and Jessica Tandy). Jessica was sick and we knew we had to get the shot right the first time. We could never say, 'camera need another take.'"

Pressure — but not anything Neil Roach couldn't handle. He was behind the camera and he had a strong focus puller. "We lit the full set, so the actors could concentrate more on their performances than hitting their marks. This meant I had to require a lot of the assistants. Wherever the actors were, they had to be in focus.

"I wanted to be able to turn the camera on as soon as our actors walked into the room and not interrupt the action until we had to reload the film."

To do this, Neil Roach lit without a piece of equipment on the floor. He had lights hanging from above and coming through windows. "They could miss their marks a mile, and it still worked.

"What I had to do was work backwards," he continues. "I had to work, not from what I wanted the project to look like, but what I could get, with the guidelines that I had. I took the limitations and developed the style from there.

"Ironically," he adds, "they were letter-perfect, not only in performance but also in hitting those marks. Still, the extra care didn't matter. It was a joy to work with these two consummate actors — a few of the only 'true old Hollywood' performers."

As a cinematographer, Neil Roach finds that it is easier to start with the limitations, as opposed to coming up with a preconceived notion of how he is going to make a project look good. "That can make for disappointment, because you get all enthused about what you can achieve, only to find you don't have the tools to achieve it.

"I have to see the locations, find out what the director wants, and read the script, of course. Then, I create a template in my mind. That's pre-production for me. It helps me maximize what I have to work with, in a minimum amount of time. I can plan a 12-hour day, and still work the 12 hours and nothing more. The bottom line – don't get in the way of the performance or the word."

Whatever the formula, *To Dance with the White Dog* won Neil Roach an A.S.C. nomination – and more attention from the industry. He went on to bigger projects, including the mini-series *Texas*, and what he likes to think of as a "beautiful movie," *The Substitute Wife* directed by Peter Werner. "Peter gave me carte blanche," Roach says.

"We had one main set, which was their two-room sod hut," he explains. "The interior was built in a Texas warehouse, with walls that were not only wild, but on wheels so that they could be moved easily. This was a great help, considering we had nine days of shooting in that two-room hut.

"The exteriors of the sod hut and this prairie farm were an interesting challenge," he continues. With eight or nine days of filming on this location, Roach insisted that they take the time to find the perfect location to build this set.

Patience paid off, and after hours of trekking around hundreds of acres of pasture, they found a site that satisfied everyone's needs. "Though, it was only a half a mile from an interstate highway, signs of civilization were only evident in a 30-degree arc, as viewed from the main set. The company could park close to that arc," he says.

"It was no accident that the least desirable angle to shoot, from a lighting standpoint, was in that arc." By solving practical problems in the location selection, Roach found what was a production friendly location, one that could be crafted into a beautiful set.

There was another exterior set that was needed for *The Substitute Wife* that production could not afford to build and which could not be found as a practical location. It was a short scene involving a character driving a wagon up to a house in the middle of the prairie.

Roach asked director Werner if they could have the scene take place at dawn in the story and if the set could be filmed as a silhouette against a red sky, substituting sunset for sunrise.

With the permission in place, Roach had the art department create a large flat, cut out to represent what the profile of this house would look like. The cutout was painted flat black. "At the end of the day of production, when the clouds promised a beautiful sunset, the grips erected the flat on the top of a hill," he explains. "The prop master hung a little glass lantern at the appropriate place on the set. It caught the fading rays of the sun.

"Actress Lea Thompson drove the wagon past camera and up the hill toward the cut out set. As the camera paned around 180 degrees, it was stopped down five stops to make the end composition a stark silhouette against a red sky.

"The end mark for the wagon and actress was set in such a way that the perspective matched the half-size set. What started out as a problem of limited resources, turned into a solution that was better than it would have been with unlimited resources.

"When I saw the final cut, I was really proud of what we did. It's great, when you have an image in your head and you are given the time you need to accomplish that image for the screen. As I always say, it is all about cooperation and trust. That is one of the most important elements in bringing these kinds of projects to the screen."

Neil Roach and Peter Werner were a winning team. They went on to do a short Disney Channel program called *Four Diamonds*. This was the story of a boy dying of cancer who daydreams and then writes out his fantasies of a quest with knights in shining armor. "Again, Peter gave me total visual control," he says. "We worked fast, kept it at 11-hour days, and lit it with a 'Hallmark' look for the modern times, and a fantasy medieval look for knights in shining armor."

On another project with Werner, Roach made an exception to the "always shoot 35mm" rule (under duress), and did *Almost Golden* in 16mm. "This was a real challenge," he admits. "We had hundreds of television monitors in the frame at various times. It was impossible to convert all of them to 24 frames. So we did it in the 30 frame, avoiding the 24-frame playback," he says. "We shot everything at 500 ASA, overexposing everything half a stop. The 16mm format doesn't scare me," he adds. "It's all about making what you are shooting look good, no matter what the format.

"The project won our lead actress Sela Ward a Cable Ace, and a lot of attention to the look." Making Ward happy with how she looked was one of Roach's biggest challenges. "She is a beautiful woman. As a cinematographer, it was my job to bring that beauty to the screen. I had shot the pilot for *Sisters*. She was happy with that. I thought I knew how to handle her.

"Early in the shoot, we had a scene in an editing room, where Sela (as Jessica Savitch) is viewing footage. The room had to be dark, with just light from the doorway and the screen's monitor. She was a little nervous, and voiced her fears. 'Don't worry, I won't make it look like *Eight Is Enough*,' I teased her. That wasn't a smart move.

"I got a call from her at about 6:00 P.M. that evening. Would I meet her in the bar for a drink? I was sure that was it. I was gone. She told me she was nervous about the look. She was patient, so was I. 'Look, Sela, if you don't look good, I look terrible. You are the focal point of this film. I would be a fool to make you look bad. Trust me to create the look that is appropriate for the scene. I can make you look good, and keep a sense of realism for the story.' I guess what I said made sense, because we both left the meeting feeling comfortable. And, she got an award for her performance."

In 1997, Neil Roach had several different challenges – two of which really stick out in his mind. One was a creative challenge that many cinematographers enjoy – the ability to do something out of the ordinary. "*House of Frankenstein* had some wonderful photography," he says. "It was another Peter Werner project, and it allowed me do what we call 'vampire vision.'"

Roach had a minimal amount of prep — a week — to find a way to fly the vampire in the shots, or show him lurking on the edges. "There were times when we could use a helicopter, and other times when we couldn't get close enough to people," he recalls.

"Although Frank Holgate (second unit) did most of the 'vampire shots,' I did a few myself. At one point, I had the effects guy rig a 150-foot crane with a sling so that I could hang face down with the camera in my hand. They could then swing me as far as they could around and we could get the 'vampire point of view.'

"There is a video of these shots," he laughs. "The crew dubbed me 'pinnate man.' In the video, I'm hanging above the set, and the crew is following me around — with sticks in their hands. See, you do have to have a sense of childishness and humor to get you through some of these projects! You have to have fun, even when you are on a short and tight shoot."

This is what Neil Roach loves about filmmaking, it is the pure adrenaline rush of making something work. "You have to be clever," he says, "especially when you are up against bean counters who don't care about creativity, but just about the bottom line. You have to know what you are doing, and know what you can make work.

"Basically, I've developed my own kind of formula — the same camera and lighting package — and I will always work with 500 ASA stock for television projects. That helps, because it cuts down on the testing, and I know intimately what everything I have can do.

"Of course, there are jobs where you do have to bring in a few special tools. *Into Thin Air,* directed by Robert Markowitz, was just that kind of deal," he explains. It is a project he did right before the massive *House of Frankenstein.* In contrast to that project, which involved hundreds of extras and massive locations, this one took place almost entirely on an ice glacier.

"I had two weeks of prep, which included going to the top of the mountain," he says. "The producers had slated a lot of the snow shots up there for a second unit. That wouldn't do, for me. If I could crawl up there, I could do the shots. I was determined to make the shots work myself, regardless of the hardships and how hard or difficult it was to get to the locations. I convinced them that I could shoot in the remote areas."

Roach realized that he could make the picture work if he had two cameras running all the time. He brought in another operator and several assistants, warning that the conditions would be difficult, to say the least.

"We were a mixed bunch," he admits. "The gaffer was from Israel and the crew from Prague. It was like shooting a Western," he admits. "Instead of sand and boulders, we had snow and a glacier that was more than 400-feet thick.

"I was probably crazy, going down the side of a 4,000-foot cliff, roped in, with climbing guides who would help me bring the camera package and batteries into place. It was incredible, dealing with the elements and things like glare and cold air (great for cameras and film). But, it worked."

Roach really faced two different challenges on this project. The first was to shoot the actual locations, making sure the actors were safe and getting as much depth into the shots as possible. The second was to light many of the night shots – and not make them look lit.

"In testing, I found that I could put an old-fashioned cukaloris in front of a 12k, then back cross the snow and we could get shafts of light on the snow and darkness in other parts. This gave texture and depth to the shots. Mountain climbers at night wear little headlights on their hats. We used these to our advantage, as they talked to each other. That and a hint of fill light was enough to see them. On the screen it looked extremely real."

In the past two years, Neil Roach has done a dozen more projects. There was the story of Hugh Hefner (the unauthorized version), "not as much about the playboy side, but the man and the state of human emotions and morality at that time in history," he explains. "We shot some of the picture in 8mm as well as 35mm. It was to be another way to show the reality of the day. Unfortunately, due to budget considerations, we weren't able to print the 8mm to 35mm. So, most of the shots designated for 8mm transfer were scrapped and their 35mm counterparts were used."

Then there was *Mama Flores Family*, the chronicles of a black family through five generations. "I don't light black actors any different than other skin tones," he comments about this project. "It was just another interesting story, and we did what we needed to bring it to the screen."

He also shot *Ballad of Lucy Whipple* in Park City, Utah. "In the gorgeous summer!" he comments. And, *Songs in Ordinary Time* in Nova Scotia. "Also, a beautiful project," is all he will say.

In the first months of the new millennium, Roach paired for another project with his close friend Peter Werner. "Peter and I have done 21 projects together," Roach says. Roach believes working with one director many times allows a cinematographer to create a shorthand for problem solving. In the case of his long association with Peter Werner, he maintains that they have always approached each film in the same basic way.

"After a few careful readings of the script, we will try to visit each location with the production designer," he says. "These visits will define the basic uses for any given set, probable angles, and an assessment of any limitations. Later, in preproduction, we will spend many hours going through the script scene by scene. What we hope to accomplish is to come up with a shooting plan that works for every scene and a plan that also unifies the look of the picture.

"Before we start, we have made the movie in our heads," he continues. "This gives you a kind of security and hopefully takes a little pressure off of each day."

Roach admits that, though many times they complete a scene just as planned in pre-production, as a film evolves they frequently take scenes in directions they had not considered at the outset.

"Peter's challenge is always — 'That's good, can it be better?'" says Roach. The director's basic trust in Roach's visual solutions make this pair a great team and has, incidentally, resulted in a lasting friendship.

All this came into play for their first pairing of the new millennium. "It's called *The '70s*," says Roach. "I lived through it, I don't need to talk about it!" he laughs.

It isn't that Neil Roach does not want to talk about every project he does. They are all interesting and different. It is just that he does so many. "I know I'm known for the television movies," he says. "And, don't get any ideas that I don't like them. I do. The problem is, like so many other cinematographers, I've been typecast. When someone hears the name Neil Roach — they instantly think — short shoot — that is, television movies.

"These projects bring a different challenge every time," he says. "Each network has a different look that they like and each project demands its own visual style, which somehow must be reconciled with the needs of the network. Then, there is always the director!

"One of the newest challenges (and opportunities) is the dual format now needed for television production," he adds. "We have to compose standard television format, but now we must also compose the new 16/9 Hi-def format.

"There is a lot of resistance among directors and producers to make concessions to protecting this format, let alone composing for it. But, it is the wave of the future and definitely here to stay."

Roach believes that this format is going to open up opportunities for those who want to make the most of it. "When you color-correct a film in this format and on a Hi-def monitor, you see how much more of your hard work is going to show as this format is seen in more and more homes.

"The difference between the quality seen in a theater, and what is seen at home will become significantly smaller as more people purchase these sets."

Like most cinematographers, Roach feels he is trained and experienced in many types of productions. He, too, would like the big budget features to come his way once in a while. But, even if that never happens, he feels that whatever venue he shoots — television, features, commercials, industrials, even inserts — the challenges drive him, and success rewards him for the hard work.

"Mathematics teaches us that, no matter how large or small the frame, within its boundaries there are still an infinite number of discreet points. Limitations only tell us what we don't need to think about.

"No matter what boundaries are placed on us, we still have an infinite number of choices to contemplate and deal with. How well you use the resources you have will determine the success or failure of your endeavors. This is certainly true in life in general, but most particularly, in the endeavors of a cinematographer.

"No matter what venue I work in, however, I love what I do. I get to travel to a lot of places — challenge myself (climbing glaciers or hanging from a harness) — and learn about different people and different approaches to life. Now, who can tell me that that isn't a great way to make a living!?"

*You can learn more from looking at a shadow than you can by looking at the light. You can tell the direction, the softness, the intensity, and the fill-to-key ratio by looking into the shadows. Shadow is what gives you contrast and contrast is what gives you shape and drama.*

*Ward Russell*

A roaring fire in the corner fireplace of Ward Russell's Santa Fe, New Mexico, home provides an interesting soundtrack to a series of videotapes playing on his living room television. As he settles into an overstuffed chair near the huge picture window looking out onto the snow-filled front yard and clear sky, he sighs with contentment. This has been a very busy year, commercial-wise, and he hasn't really had that much of a chance to enjoy the home he and his wife built away from the bustle and hype of Hollywood just a few years ago.

"We just sold our properties in Los Angeles and bought a small condo in Marina del Rey for the days when we both have to be in California," Russell says with satisfaction. "One of the great things about working in the commercial world is that you don't have to be on the coast. Since the projects are done at a wide variety of locations, it only matters that the agencies and production companies can reach you."

Russell has not lost one assignment, film or commercial, because of this move. The contentment of the New Mexico lifestyle, in fact, has probably brought the calm necessary to handle the frenetic pace of prepping and shooting commercials done from Canada to Argentina and from Los Angeles to Yugoslavia. One of his most recent was shooting a dozen 250-pound flying "cupids" on Venice Beach for Tostitos.

In between the national and international spots, he's also found time to do several exciting features including *Days of Thunder, The Last Boy Scout,* and *Blackwood.* "I do love the camaraderie and familiarity you develop, when you are doing a feature," he admits. "However, there is also something really fascinating about the challenge of compressing an often big-budgeted and complicated 'mini-movie' into a few days, and selling the product at the same time."

How did Russell get involved in this particularly competitive and invigorating end of the world of make believe? "Just lucky, I guess," he laughs lightly.

Russell was born in Lawrence, Kansas, and stayed put until he graduated from the University of Kansas with a degree in scenic design and lighting. "My father's hobby was still photography," he explains. "So, he introduced me to the darkroom when I was very young. Although I was interested in pictures, theater was the real driving force in my life. My senior project at college was to design the sets and lights for *Macbeth*.

"For the three witches scene I hung camouflage net that I had dyed white from the grid in a big, sweeping, arc. Then, I borrowed a 16mm camera from the film department and shot footage of the apparitions, which I then projected onto the netting. That was the beginning of my involvement in film."

Russell seemed to find lighting the most fascinating of all areas, and began pursuing that avenue of work. "When you think about it, lighting is really 90 percent of what photography is all about," he says. "I just didn't realize it at the time. I wanted to be a theatrical lighting designer."

Even when he was in the Navy, Ward Russell pursued his interest. He always had a still camera with him. "In fact, I still have many of the shots I took from a bar in Hong Kong, where I'd concentrated on a line up of beer bottles. See, I was doing product shots, before I had even thought about shooting commercials!"

Although Russell was quite successful, working for several years as resident lighting designer for the American Conservatory Theatre and the San Francisco Opera in San Francisco and the Old Globe Theatre in San Diego, he soon found out he couldn't make a decent living in theatrical lighting outside of New York and Broadway. He left San Francisco, moved to Los Angeles and worked his way into movie lighting. He served his apprenticeship at Universal, working his way up from electrician to best boy and then to gaffer.

He quickly discovered the technical differences between theatrical and movie lighting when he was asked to light several commercials by a DP friend. "I met gaffer Art Kaufman through his daughter, and from the first moment, hit him with a lot of these technical questions.

"You want to work in the movie business," Kaufman asked Russell. The "yes" was immediate. Kaufman picked up the phone and called the I.A.T.S.E. electricians local. "Tell them Art Kaufman sent you as soon as you get in the door, and then tell them who you are," Russell was told. Two weeks later he was working on the rigging crew at Universal studios.

"Those were the days (early 1970s) when studios realized that the average age of their crews was 56. If they didn't wake up and get in some new blood, there wouldn't be enough crews left!" Russell says.

Early in his gaffing career, he met Tony Scott and did a series of commercials for him. "He was living in London at the time," Russell recalls. "So, whenever he came to the States he would always call me. Over the years, I gaffed for other cinematographers like Bob Steadman on MOWs, and several mini-series including one in Yugoslavia starring George C.

Scott in a story about Mussolini. I also worked with Tom Ackerman who gave me my first couple of gaffing jobs. I had gone to college with his partner Mike Robe, and their commercial production house was really popular at the time."

Being a gaffer, even in the tail end of the days of a somewhat studio system, prepared Ward Russell for the slide into camera. "When you are at a studio, you learn lighting but you also learn all other aspects of the work, if you have your eyes open and are aware.

"I remember working as a best boy or even an electrician with Jerry Finnerman on several Universal television shows. He was a brilliant hardlight cameraman and allowed me to come to dailies at lunch each day to see the effects lighting had on film. With my background in theatrical lighting, I was already prepared to see and understand the visual nuances of what film recorded and what it took to achieve them."

Russell would bounce from *Murder, She Wrote* to *Six Million Dollar Man* and other television shows. He would watch the lighting, and the camera, and begin to store the knowledge of different departments. He also began to see how theatrical lighting blended into film.

Russell's background in theatrical lighting taught him to design for a total production all-in-one set up. "Since you can't stop and relight every scene, you have to light each one and hang instruments, then add individual specials, so that you can use them when you want theatrical conventions. This allows you to play with the mood a lot more. You create the reality you want not the imitation of reality that is the basis of movie lighting.

"When you transfer over to film, you have to reign yourself in as to the mood you can create. You get more intimate with people. The theory of modeling the faces, however, is the same whether you are on stage or film," he adds. "You are just doing it differently. You do it from far away and in broad strokes on stage and close up and personal in film. In film, you are able to light each moment and make it the best you can. You aren't locked into one look through the whole scene."

While working at Universal, he met gaffer Joe Pender, who is now a cinematographer also. Pender brought him on as a best boy — "which is really a misnomer when you think about it," says Russell. "It sounds like a rinky-dink job, but it is extremely important.

"The best boy is a CEO of sorts," he explains. "He is the one in charge of all the manpower and equipment. He makes sure you have enough people and equipment where and when the gaffer needs it. That allows the gaffer to take the equipment and create the look the cameraperson desires. It is up to the best boy to be the behind-the-scenes guy. It is one of the most important positions on any job."

At this time, soft lighting was coming into play. However, since the film stock was still slow, that meant a lot of equipment. "I had the opportunity to learn about bounce lighting from Mario Tosi on *The Betsey* and other productions.

Soon, Russell was gaffing on his own. He did a series of Tony Scott pictures, gaffing *Top Gun, Revenge*, and *Beverly Hills Cop 2*. "Gaffing is all about interpreting what the cameraman wants," he explains.

"Lighting of a picture is ultimately the responsibility of the cameraperson," he says. "However, he has more on his mind than whether it is a 1k or 2k or what kind of cable to run. A DP conceptualizes what he wants the look of the picture to be. A good gaffer can implement that look.

"Every camera person is different, however. People like myself, who have come from the lighting end, have more input, sometimes to the chagrin of many gaffers.

"There are two types of gaffers," Russell explains. "There are the nuts-and-bolts ones who make sure the equipment is there and make sure it works. This kind of gaffer will do exactly what you tell him or her to do. Then there's the kind of gaffer who understands lighting concepts, so when you tell him the look you want him to achieve, he then can run with it. He or she makes it all happen and you don't have to get involved in the nuts and bolts."

During his years as a gaffer, Russell handled a variety of different projects. *Top Gun*, however, was probably one of the most difficult of the features. "Tony Scott is always a challenge for a gaffer because he is so visually oriented," Russell explains. "He knows what he wants, but he can't tell you what it is. So, you end up experimenting a lot. He is also a perfectionist. If it doesn't feel right to him, you will continually relight, until he is satisfied.

"Scott would never compromise on the lighting, and that's what I liked about him. Sometimes, we would light a set three different ways. You knew you were working with a director who knew what he wanted and would back you to get it."

By 1987, Ward Russell made the move into the position of Director of Photography — working in commercials at first. "By then, I'd spent enough time watching dailies that I knew film stocks as well as the cameraperson. I was working along side the cinematographer, so I also knew lens choices.

From the first moment that he "stepped up" to Director of Photography, he gave his gaffers sound advice. "I always tell them you can learn more from looking at a shadow than you can by looking at the light. You can tell the direction, the softness, the intensity, and the fill-to-key ratio by looking into the shadows. Shadow is what gives you contrast and contrast is what gives you shape and drama.

"My exposures are always based as much, if not more, on how much detail I want to see in the shadow as on how bright I want the highlights. To me, once you have found the right spot for a light, the really creative process is how much of that light you then take away."

The only thing that Russell felt weak about, when he started working as a cinematographer, was how the camera actually worked. It was still a mysterious black box.

At that time, Bill Russell at Arriflex was starting a camera systems program for assistant camera people, so Ward Russell took the course. He learned not to be intimidated by the box. "It was just a highly sophisticated piece of machinery that was not to be feared. You just had to know how to make it work. That's what he taught us.

"I also learned the value of a first-rate camera assistant. Not only did he follow focus if something went wrong with the camera, the assistant would take care of it."

Ward Russell was now ready to start shooting. He went to Crossroads Productions and talked to Cami Taylor, who he had worked with as a commercial gaffer. "They brought a 16mm art film director in from New York and wanted someone to introduce him to commercials and show him how to use a 35mm camera, so they hired me for very little money," he recalls.

"We did a Boy Scout promotional commercial. Actually," he laughs, "he taught me more about the 16mm format than I did him about 35mm. He taught me new tricks — like dutching a camera, not commonly accepted in those days."

The challenge to break into commercial cinematography then and now was to build a reel of work showing what you could do. "I had several small commercials, but I needed some beautiful day shots to round the reel out," says Russell. "I borrowed an Arri III, rented a motor home, talked my wife and a camera assistant friend into accompanying me, and we set off on a week-long odyssey of sunrises and sunsets all over California.

"We went to Morro Bay, Mount Shasta, various lakes and waterfalls. We shot sunrises, sunsets, tracking shots from the door of the motor home, that sort of thing. I had it edited into a 30-second montage and showed it to my agents. They added music, and I had a 'save the universe' commercial.

"It was edited at the same time and place where Tony Scott was editing *Revenge*. He walked in one day and saw the reel being built. It was the first time he took me seriously as a cameraman. Six months later, I got a call. Tony wanted me to shoot a race for *Days of Thunder*."

So, Ward Russell started a career in the major leagues of cinematography, shooting the infamous race for Tony Scott.

"At that time, there was only one night race in the NASCAR circuit, Bristal, Tennessee," he says. "And, Tony wanted it for the movie."

Russell had never shot cars (something he's become very proficient at since), and had never really commanded a large crew. For this race, he had four crews working at the same time.

"The first thing I had to think about was where we could best see the race," he explains. "We had to pick our spots. Fortunately, the track was well lit by four Musco lights, the type of job they were originally built for. Then, I had my grip build a rig in the fenderwell of a car so that we could get action shots from the track during the race."

Tony Scott loved what Russell was doing. When Jeffrey Kimball (who had shot *Revenge* for him) wasn't available to shoot the first unit, he called Russell. "There was a mad scramble to get me into the camera union," Russell recalls. "But we did it. Then, I had the challenge of this, my first, major motion picture."

Russell and Scott decided to shoot everything, including the close-ups, with a minimum of three cameras. It was a continual, "where do we put the cameras?" situation. "We couldn't put them on the track when there was a race," he recalls.

"We shot some footage from the actual race cars and a lot of what were actually drive-bys of the race cars during the Daytona 500. For all of our on-the-track racing and wrecks, we spent three months staging our own races with our cars and stunt drivers. We shot something like nine real races, just to get establishing shots of the various tracks and crowds of people.

"In all that, there wasn't one wreck!" he laughs. "We had to create one!"

The staged races were a big challenge for Russell and the team. "We had to find a way to run the cars at 100 miles an hour, and make them look like they are going 150 to 200 miles an hour.

"Yes, we had to speed up the cars by adjusting the speed of the camera, but that was something that had to be calculated extremely carefully," he explains. "If they go too fast, they get jumpy. So we could do 20 or 22 frames, and get down to about 18 frames, after that it looked artificial."

An interesting result of this groundbreaking race film was that the style Russell set began showing up on ESPN and on NASCAR commercials.

Russell's baptism by fire in features ran the gamut of filmmaking. One day he was shooting racing footage and the next a steamy love scene between Nicole Kidman and Tom Cruise.

After *Days of Thunder*, Russell started doing a lot of car commercials because people readily identified him with automobiles. "That's funny, considering there wasn't one beauty shot of a car in the whole movie," he laughs.

Back in 1990, car commercials were all about looking for beautiful locations and beautiful cars. One of his first was about miniature race cars that were run by Duracell batteries. "We went down to Charlotte Motor Speedway," he recalls. "They brought in director Peter Corbitt, who really knows special effects.

"We ended up hanging the cameras off the back of an insert car, shooting six little cars with six big guys remotely operating them individually, racing along behind the camera car. I remember one day, looking at the rig, and all these grown men and laughing — we got paid to do things like this!"

Fortunately, most of the commercial was done with natural light. "But, when it got dark, we had to bring in some daylight. Since we were using miniatures, we at least didn't need Musco lights — just a few 12ks.

"The trick, in car shooting, is to find the right location in relation to the sun and shoot at the right time. You have to find the right moment when the light is best for the car."

Russell has never gotten "comfortable" about shooting cars. "You can't just develop a formula and go from there," he says adamantly. "Every car is different in shape and color. Sometimes agencies will hire a director who hasn't done cars before and that person won't realize what it is that makes sheet metal look good as opposed to people. That's where a cinematographer comes in. He or she needs to scope out the car, and decide on the best time of day and location to film it."

Russell has had practically every kind of challenge when shooting cars. For a Toyota spot at ILM, he had to build a 40-foot long sky drop to cut unwanted location reflections and put in beautiful skies.

"If you are on stage, shooting cars, one of the best ways to put in sky reflections is to use huge light boxes," he says. "I've had Fisher light boxes brought in. They are 40-or 50-feet long and about 20-feet wide. That way, you can lower your lights close to the car and put the reflections where you want to accentuate the lines of the car.

"Now, of course, with the refinement of CGI, if you put something in the shot that shouldn't be there, you can always take it out in post. Although, I am not a fan of spending money in post, sometimes that is more expedient than trying to make it work at the shoot."

For a German Ford commercial in Munich, Russell shot one night on the stage and one night at an airport. "We had rain on the stage, and then we created 300 feet of rain outside. The rain stops, as a CGI sun breaks through CGI clouds.

"To get the effect of the clouds reflecting in the car and water, I had to use 10ks and 20ks shot into an overhead silk, undulating above the car," he recalls. "I photographed the car and its reflection in the pool of water, so you didn't know which was real and which was the reflection. Not until the raindrops broke the reflection did you realize that it was the reflection that was right side up.

"The whole time, I had lightning machines going as we rotated the camera. When we were outside, we had two cameras, one on a boom arm and one on the rear of the camera car. A big generator truck followed us with both a crane arm supporting three Lightning Strikes and a large light box on it. We tracked with the Ford, through the rain. By creating our own rain, we were able to keep cameras and lights relatively dry outside the path of the rain, through which the Ford drove.

"See, commercials are really mini-movies. At least, with the production values."

Lighting cars has always been a challenge. "It's harder than lighting people, lighting glamorous women," he says. "It's sheet metal. The color of the car makes a big difference. It is through experience that you learn what to do.

"Lighting a black car is like lighting a mirror. It is all reflection and you have to have big broad light sources that reflect into the cars so that you can shape it out and delineate the lines of the car.

"A light-colored car can be shot in daytime and you can let the sun do the lighting. You have your prettiest lights early in the morning and late in the afternoon. What sells a car is not only what the car looks like, but the environment it is put in."

Take the six-minute movie the agency behind the Infinity car wanted to create in 1992. "The idea was to create a video to distribute to over 2,000 targeted markets," he explains. "The concept was a formula — product plus persistence equals romance. In this case, it was the Infinity car as a vehicle for a young man chasing his dream girl through the streets of San Francisco."

The shoot became gorilla filmmaking. It was the length of about ten commercials to be shot in five days and nights. "A nightmare. Shooting a black car at night," he recalls. "Although the car was the star, the city was the mood. Fortunately, I'd spent many years in the Bay area as a lighting designer, so I knew the areas of interest like the Legion of Honor, Opera, Financial District."

At first, Russell's director wanted to shoot without lights. However, film tests convinced him that they needed to supplement what they had. "It's all about reflections and shadows, and giving them definition," he explains. "When we tested, I tried a bunch of different film stocks and underexposure techniques. No matter what, the black car, without added reflections and something to silhouette it from the background, looked rather boring.

"My choice was to go with a wide open lens and utilize available light. Fortunately, the streets were well lit. To define the body of the car as it approached the various locations, we set fluorescent lights on the ground, reflecting them into the car's sides.

"The hardest part of the spot was when we needed to shoot down to the ground or into the night sky," he continues. "I was concerned that I didn't have any bright background to separate the car. Here, we used that dreaded tool – smoke. It saved us. Smoking the air gave us light reflections in the black car's backlight.

"In this case, we wanted to see our 'San Francisco fog' as a visual, not a filter. It also gave us something to light. To do this, we overexposed the smoke about two stops. We then threw in shafts of light from Xenon's, or a 12k down the block. Of course, we never knew where the smoke was going to drift, so it was frustrating but fascinating.

"As with any other car shoot, we also had to light the city in such a way that it reflected on the cars properly," he adds. "The key to reflecting light is to have the scenery brighter than the object. You have to find a balance. If you are filming at a 1.4 (six foot-candles), the buildings have to be at least double what is on the car."

For this particular shoot one of the biggest challenges was the Legion of Honor building. "Here, we had about five hours of pre-light for 15 seconds of film. We had a crane, with one 12k for moonlight and 25 or 30 little lks throwing lights against the walls behind the columns. This let the columns fall into the shadow in the front. Once again, I made use of fluorescent lights lying in the gutters and lots of smoke drifting through the backlight, our artificial moonlight."

Ward Russell has gone all over the world shooting cars. He has done commercials in Mexico (where he always gets sick), Germany, Spain, Italy, Puerto Rico, Argentina, Japan, and Canada. Car work, according to Russell, is really international. "However, I find that the Europeans are a little more adventurous than we are," he says. "They aren't locked into the standards and practices and conventions we are.

"Most of the commercials that I did in Germany have all ended up on my reel. They have had more visual freedom in the past, although the last couple of years have seen American commercials loosening up and becoming more visually exciting.

"For example, color is really important to European shoots. I did a series of three commercials that where each turned into a different color. One was in blue. One in red. And one became night with only reflections of the city in the black car — no lights at all."

While car commercials have made up more than half of Russell's workload, during the last couple of years he has been concentrating on more people-oriented projects. In fact, out of the 68 commercials he shot in 1999, only five were car commercials.

While he maintains an incredible car reel, his general reel has become most impressive with dialogue spots, light comedy, sports, and even food spots. Occasionally, he will find time to do a feature or two. However, he chooses his projects carefully. "There is a lot of challenge and fun in the short shoot," he says. "You get a bad team in a commercial and you know you are finished in a relatively short time. With a feature, you have to keep the team together for weeks or months. That means you had better get along — or suffer."

When Russell does do a feature, it is with a great team. In the mid-1990s, his long-time commercial and occasional feature partner, Tony Scott, took on another extravaganza. *The Last Boy Scout* started out as a down and out private eye story that really turned into a buddy picture between private eye Bruce Willis and an on-the-skids football player, blacklisted because of drugs (Damon Wayans).

"One of the most challenging sequences was at the Los Angeles Coliseum," Russell recalls. "Tony conceived the idea of putting a live video feed of the action through the gigantic scoreboard so that he could see the whole shoot-out and knife fight.

"To do this, we had to be about 100 feet up in the air. We were literally filming in the light tower — although there were no real light towers in the angle where we needed to be. We had to build a 40-foot light tower on top of a 50-foot scaffold in front of the scoreboard.

"So, we had other scaffolding, a platform, and the camera equipment and lights so that we could photograph the actors in another light tower, fighting and so forth.

"Fortunately, we were shooting at night — so, if I didn't look down, I wouldn't know how high up I was," he laughs. "I have to admit, that was one of the scariest locations I've ever filmed at.

"One night, we were shooting with three cameras and we were all on the scissors lift, about 40 feet up above the 50-foot scaffolding on the tower. We finished the shot and started to get off — but someone had accidentally untied the rope that had the scaffold tied to the light tower!

Suddenly, the whole thing started to tip away from the light tower and fall backward. Fortunately, my grips saw what was happening and grabbed the scaffold, stopping it before any real danger was done.

"Only for someone like Tony Scott would I go to such lengths! He is a great guy and would never ask anyone to do something he would not do himself. In fact, he was doing a commercial with a friend of mine on the Colorado River. They were floating and shooting their way through the rapids of the Grand Canyon.

"Tony wanted a shot from water level, floating above and below the water. Instead of asking anyone else to attempt this very dangerous stunt, he took the camera in its underwater housing and jumped into the roaring river, floated through the rapids getting the shot. Unfortunately, in the adreneline rush of the moment, he forgot to turn the camera on. How could you not love this man?!"

Russell enjoys the opportunity to work with all the different pieces of equipment created for the making of motion pictures. "It is necessary to keep the audience glued to what you are presenting on the screen," he says. "I've used everything from a Pogocam to a Steadicam, a doorway dolly to a Chapman crane. In fact, I recently did a series of three commercials for 'A Gift of Giving.com' company in which we shot from the actor's point of view. We saw only bits and pieces of his body appear in front of the lens.

"To do this, we used the Bodycam version of the Doggiecam. The camera was rigged to shoot over the actor's shoulder, with a body harness supporting the rig. Although the actor had to pan the camera with his body, I had them build a remote so I could tilt the camera more than the body would accommodate. It worked out most great."

Another piece of equipment Russell developed from a director's desire to show a type of energy in a scene by holding the camera — not as a means of moving the camera, but because "you cannot hold a 40-pound camera steady," he explains. "Holding that heavy a camera for a long period of time wears out the sturdiest of operators — not to mention, it is impossible to light through the camera.

"After experimenting with several types of partially inflated toy balls to rest the camera on, the best solution appeared in the form of a small ATV innertube sandwiched between some hardware to hold the camera on. I could pan and tilt somewhat, and although it is impossible to hold it completely steady, it can be used all day long! Jimmy Sweet, my key grip (who invented it), affectionately nicknamed it the 'hemorrhoid cam!'"

Russell also becomes inventive with film stocks, as well as post-production tools. "You really have to keep up with the latest on everything," he says. "There are more film stocks than you can remember and Kodak is coming out with more every day. The major film manufacturers are desperately trying to put off that day when videotape will replace it. It is an exciting time because of that.

"When I first got into the business, there was basically only one color film stock, 5254T, 100 ASA. Today, there must be seven or eight different tungsten and daylight stocks. All of these stocks are better than older ones. The improvements in decreasing granularity and increasing the speed of the new films continue to keep film a step ahead of videotape.

"There are new ways to process film, bleach by-pass, ENR, cross-processing from positive to negative film. All of these are to give a new, different look. We have seen what can be done electronically and are trying to find ways to make films look more modern.

"The advent of the Telecine machines is putting its stamp on the look of current cinematography. With film-to-tape transfer, we are able to take advantage of electronically manipulating the images in ways never possible in film processing. Not only can scenes be made warmer or cooler and lighter and darker but also extremes in contrast never thought imaginable can be reached on film.

"Colors can be manipulated not only overall but isolated to highlights, mid-tone, or shadows. All kinds of visual effects can be added — soft effects, swing tilts, grads, and hundreds more. Almost any mistake can be corrected. The Telecine has made art out of many a music video disaster. Very few, if any commercials, are on the air today that have not had at least minor and often major alterations in the Telecine transfer.

"CGI has driven movies in the last ten years, so you are no longer sure what is shot live and what is created or composited with the computer. The number of special effects in any movie is driving the economics of transferring to video and then back again to film almost into the realm of acceptability. The day is almost here when our final timings will only happen after we have manipulated the look of our film electronically.

"In the hands of the artistic people in this business, this is a great evolution. But, in the hands of people who are not artistically trained and don't know how to work with the tools, you can kill the look of the commercial or the visual concept of the Director of Photography. A cinematographer's job will no longer end with the finish of principal photography. It will be needed for the Telecine manipulation, where the final look of the film will be created."

Many of these concepts really came up in Ward Russell's last feature, *Blackwood: The X-Files*. "It was unexpected," he laughs. "I was in the Bay area working on a commercial for Shell when a messenger arrived with a script. I told him I would read it later, and the guy freaked. He had to wait for the script – the project was so secret."

Even though Russell had seen only a few episodes of the hit series, the script read sold him. He would be able to use all the cinematic toys – and visual effects available to the industry.

"I also knew I would enjoy expanding the television format to a feature film," he says. "We were going to have some fantastic sets and challenges, and I was going to enjoy taking each one on."

Ask Russell what the most difficult shot was in the feature, and he'll laugh and say all of them. "We had to mix fake ice with real ice, we shot in below zero temperatures inside the set (when it was over 100 degrees outside), and went from the Arctic to the dessert."

Most of the feature was shot on massive exterior locations or at elaborately constructed sets at 20th Century Fox. "It was kind of strange," Russell recalls. "We were in the middle of one of the hottest summers in Los Angeles, and a good deal of the time we were working inside in sub-zero temperatures, wearing layers of protective clothing. No wonder we were sick a good deal of the time!"

That didn't matter because Russell was fascinated with making the story into a feature. "One of the first things that I realized was that everything was going to expand — what had played in costume and sets that worked on a television screen might not work when 30-feet tall."

That meant extensive meetings with the various departments. At times, it meant changing everyone's approach to the shoot. "One of the key sets was a series of ice caves," Russell explains.

"When I first saw the design department's models (made from reference photos of the real caves in Canada), they were brown and blue. The ice look just wasn't there. I was told most of the ice was canceled for financial reasons. My job was to get them to use fake ice, which could be lit so that it looked exactly like the sun filtering down through the layers in the real location."

Production design gave Russell a resin poured over sculptured forms and mounted on cave-shaped ribs. This gave him the ability to backlight through the material, creating a rich double CTB blue look — just like natural light.

"Ice was a big part of this picture, but there were a lot of other challenges. The scale of the ice fields, a cornfield and train chase, and the blowing up of the Federal Building (setting the whole story in motion) were the biggest jobs."

In one sequence, Russell had to dissolve from a prehistoric cavern to the same cave in present day as a child falls into it through a hole in the Texas landscape. "We then had to rise out of the cave (shot on stage), into the real daylight of Southern California (made to look like Dallas), and then return to it twice more after it had been transformed into a scientific research facility."

This was a major challenge since Russell had to match several locations into one seamless shot. The exteriors were done on location and the interiors on stage. The hole entrance had to be created on stage so that he could shoot in and out. "We had a sky drop hung flat against the permanents and some late afternoon sun from a 20k with half CTO to allow us to shoot in both directions.

"We had another cave shot, which began with the real ice field in Canada and an entrance to the real cave. This then continues down into the stage ice cave at Fox.

"We shot the cave on stage first, using accurate reference points. Our main concern was the ice's texture. It varied from cave to cave. We were also concerned with the shades of blue coming from it."

Production design built a 150-foot long field of real ice on one of the Fox stages. "See what I mean about having to live in the cold, in the middle of California summer," he jokes. "The field was eight feet off the ground, allowing effects to put collapsible portions of the floor in, so our heroes could rise out of and collapse into it.

"We then had movable steam hoses and nozzles for the geysers of steam. We had huge catch-alls under the set to catch the five days of melting ice.

"We had to keep the ice from melting, and see the breath of the performers at the same time," he continues. "We had water vaporized into the air through emitters to raise the humidity. Mathematical calculations determined the tonnage of air conditioning necessary to counteract the heat output of the lighting units (a lot of them)."

Russell and the team decided to go this route, using a huge Translight background to avoid CGI ice fields. "Because there were just too many of them on this picture already," he says. "Every shot involving a CGI background would cost about the same as the entire Translight. The one 40-by-80-foot structure was a savings.

"The problem was how to light it. There were seams in the photo, visible ones connecting the panels. And, the color temperature of the photo didn't even come close to matching tungsten or daylight bulbs.

"There were no 'windows' or a 'forest filled with trees' to temper the visual," he continues. "Even the jets of rising steam weren't going to be able to hide the defects."

Refusing to give in, Russell called for help. He made a phone call to Don Burgess, who had had a similar challenge on *Contact*. "We had had three days to solve a problem that had taken Don two weeks, but his suggestions were invaluable.

"We ended up putting various densities of neutral gels behind the Translight, hoping to blend the seams. We also added a layer of pale magenta gel over KinoFlos, lighting from behind. When we took another reading the next day, the addition of a layer of pale green to the bank lights (sunlight), and more blue to the space lights (ambiance), worked.

"Although we didn't completely erase the seams, we had a color match. At least the tighter, longer lens shots would work. With a diffusion net (30 by 80 feet) in front of the Translight, for atmosphere, we had a slightly out-of-focus feeling and a successful shot.

"When the Translight just wouldn't work, we had a massive green screen on tracks, pre-lit with 20ks gelled with dark green for the CGI shots."

The ice field was another challenge. "Real day exterior locations have one single sun source," says Russell. "Since there was no one light big enough or bright enough to light a 150-foot stage, we had to find a way to simulate it.

"That meant a single sun source look, which my gaffer Jerry Solomon and I created by blending little sources and diffusion. He hung 40 Maxi Brutes in three tiers, as close together as possible. The bottom tier had flood bulbs, the middle tier had medium bulbs, and the top had spots.

"By focusing them from near to far, we achieved an even stop over the whole stage. Then, key grip Jim Sweet hung a very large Visqueen drop in front. Just enough diffusion to blend 360 bulbs."

Another of Russell's challenges was a chase sequence shot in Soledad Canyon in the San Fernando Valley, with matching shots of a cornfield in Bakersfield, California. "The chase starts with Gillian and David racing their car after a train carrying questionable substances," Russell explains. The shot tracks through a tunnel and to two glowing domes in the middle of a cornfield. As the two race through the field and the domes, enemies in helicopters and "creatures" pursue them.

This night sequence involved three locations, miles apart. "We had prerig crews set generators and cable, but the Musco lights and Condors couldn't be moved until the previous night's work was finished," Russell explains. "The sequence began at a train intersection when the car drives up from one direction and the train comes, in silhouette, from another, leaving in yet another direction.

"We wanted to make it as simple as possible, using moonlight and the car's headlights. With one night to do two scenes, there was no time to move equipment from one direction to another. So, we prepositioned a mini-Musco light and two NiteSuns before dark and focused them as quickly as possible so that we could look in each direction. All we had to do now was race the sun."

Over the next three nights, Russell shot at the bottom of a canyon with a single access road. "It took three days to get all our equipment out to the location," he says. "We had to plan carefully. Once something was in place, it was almost impossible to move. Each piece had to service three locations, panning or tilting as little as possible. To make it even more difficult, first and second units were shooting at the same time."

Russell placed a Musco light along the ridge above the canyon, first. The light could reach down into the canyon from the top and light another intersection as well as the background mountain for the train and car. The second placement was a mini-Musco in the ravine above the tracks. "The hardest part was being able to light so that we could see around the curve," he explains. "The Musco backlight was our workhorse. We then filled the bottom of the canyon with smoke, and now we could see the train's silhouette."

To see the car drive up, Russell placed one 200-foot crane and one 150-foot Condor with six 6k LTM PARS on each, creating a moonlight and a spread for enough of the area.

While second unit was shooting this sequence, Russell shot the two film's stars on a close location, filled with artificial corn. This allowed the actors to descend down the cliff to the field. "All we had to do is pan a few of the lights on the crane and Condor, and add a balloon light for fill," Russell adds. "Ground fog from plastic tubes confused the issue and disguised the fact that it wasn't real corn."

The next night Russell and crew shot the actors looking over the ledge into a field that wasn't there. "We had used another crane to lower a large 30-by-40-foot green screen over the edge of the canyon. This was lit from underneath by green KinoFlos and side 20ks gelled green. It didn't matter if we saw some of the equipment in the shots, a lot of this was for CGI."

Of course, these shots were just the builds to the stars' exploration of the cornfield and the glowing orbs. "Three Musco lights and one mini-Musco gave us moonlight for the helicopter chase. All we had to add is splashes of Xenon lights for searchlights."

The domes at the end of the field were inflatable structures. "Easy to get to the location," says Russell. "We made them into huge Chinese lanterns by putting five bare 20k bulbs inside each dome.

"The nightmare was lighting the inside of those domes on the stage, not on location. "At first, we thought that would be simple," he says. "All we needed was to have the fabric glow without showing the source. We thought we could put the lights on the outside of the domes, not light with one central light inside as before. We tried strip lights on the ground.

"Help! I remember being in the middle of another shot, when my gaffer was setting this up. He came over and, mildly, said 'we have a problem.'"

On location, everything blended. On the stage, however, there were hot spots everywhere. "The inflatable domes filled the stage," he explains. "There wasn't enough room to get the lights back far enough away from the fabric. Hot spots. The only solution was putting silks between the lights and the domes. A grip nightmare! But we made it!"

Ward Russell could go on and on about the technical challenges of *The X-Files* feature. He could talk about action sequences with aliens (CGI) and without aliens. "Then there was shooting downtown Los Angeles at the Unocal Building, which we used to shoot the blow up of the Federal Building. Then there was . . ." Ward Russell cuts himself off. He's getting tired, just thinking about this project.

"No wonder I've been sticking to commercials. A few cars and a lot of the new 'dot com' spots selling sites on the Internet," he laughs. "I love doing features, but the kind we're doing today, well, they are great but exhausting. I'll stick to commercials for a while . . .

"Although, I'm not opposed to a few more challenges, and a great crew like we had on *The X-Files*."

*Many woman ACs I've worked with seemed discouraged over the years to try to move up after they witnessed how long it was taking us pioneers to get recognition. After the initial novelty of the idea wore off, no one wanted to take a chance. It is ironic, when you think about it, there are many more accomplished women working in theater lighting, accepted for what they can do not for their gender, than there are in the motion picture and television industry.*

*Nancy Schreiber*

It usually takes Nancy Schreiber, A.S.C., a few minutes to adjust when she wakes up in the morning. If there is the noise of a creaking lift and the slam of car doors and delivery trucks, then she's in her loft in Lower Manhattan.

If it's semi-peaceful, with the occasional lawn mower or road construction, then she's in her house in Santa Monica, California. And, if she looks around and sees strange windows, and hears a language that isn't her native English, she has to think for a moment longer.

In the past few years, that has really been the case — since she has been shooting very interesting and very different projects in far off places like China and Vietnam. It's a great way to travel and to work with new and exciting people," she says about her choices to shoot feature films and documentaries around the world.

At the moment, she's taking a breather — trying to get her bearings. She's just returned from Robert Redford's Sundance Film Festival, where two of her projects — *Shadow Magic* (a period feature shot in Mainland China) and *Reaching Normal* (a half-hour drama directed by Anne Heche) premiered to rave reviews. Soon, she will be on her way to Baltimore, Maryland, shooting the second *Blair Witch* film (*Blair Witch-Hunt*).

"You even get to go to such exotic places as the Caribbean, India, China, and Zimbabwe when you are shooting independent features," she says, as she runs her hand through her short blonde hair and pulls her jacket closer leaning against the guard rail off the Venice Beach Pier. She glances at the beach joggers with a bit of longing. "The problem is that you don't get to stay there very long. Schedules tend to be short and budgets tight."

One of only half-a-dozen female members of the prestigious American Society of Cinematographers, Schreiber is what might be called a movie industry enigma — a very talented cinematographer who has done more features, documentaries, and music videos over the past ten years than most cinematographers do in their careers. Yet, only a few of the projects have the "instant recognition factor." *Your Friends and*

*Neighbors, Buying the Cow* (to be released mid-2000) and the upcoming *Blair Witch-Hunt* are more "mainstream" than most.

"That's sad," she says. "The stories in the smaller projects are often interesting and enlightening and feature some of the so-called 'name' talent who want to hone their tools in often off-beat and certainly creative areas. I've done wonderful features with stars such as Jeff Goldblum, Forest Whitaker, Shirley MacLaine, Kirstie Alley, Matthew McConaughey, Jason Patric, and others.

Although the Jason Patric produced and starred feature, *Your Friends and Neighbors*, did well in wide release, most of Schreiber's projects have been the type that make the circuit, including Sundance, and are shown in art houses and often become solid video hits. "Of course I'd love to work on more films with budgets larger than four to eight million dollars," she admits. "However, there is a certain satisfaction in knowing you are being hired because you can bring an interesting quality to a low-budget — independent — and do more than a 'trendy' picture. Look at this year's list – sequels, remakes, and hero parodies. We've seen them all before.

"Now, if we could get 20 or 30 million or more to do stories like *Nevada, Chain of Desire,* or *Lush Life*, I'd really enjoy the challenge!"

Projects that make their debuts at venues such as Sundance are a peculiar breed of project. "It is ironic that there is discrimination against many of us about moving "up" if we haven't worked on mega-budgeted films before. Could it actually be any more difficult to shoot a large-budget film when one has two or three times the number of days of a small film, and all the toys and crew necessary?

"Often out of necessity, one is forced to take risks in coverage and shooting style on modest films because there is no time for coverage from every angle possible with every lens imaginable. But I'm not complaining – the scripts are often unusual and allow all involved much creativity. Many of the most revered DPs are now shooting these modest films because they want to sink their teeth into good unconventional stories."

How did Schreiber fall into this revered and often ignored world of movie production? "Funny, my mother often asks that question," she laughs. "Every downtime, she suggests I join the real world. Not too many people understand that, for us, wondering where your next job will come from or where it will take you is normal. You get to meet an incredibly diverse group of people, and learn some of the most unusual and often useless, but never dull things.

"Am I avoiding the question? Probably. The answer isn't earth shattering. It didn't come with a blinding flash. I started out studying psychology and art history at the University of Michigan. Somehow, I got involved in the underground film scene in Ann Arbor, making several short films that I produced, directed, photographed, and edited. Arty, experimental films, one slightly futuristic film based on the book *Altered States*. After all, it was that late 1970s.

After graduation, Schreiber moved to New York. She answered a small advertisement in the *Village Voice*, for a production assistant position. "I got a crash course in grip and electric," she says, shaking her head. "The film was totally under-crewed, but somehow I became the best boy electric, and was like a sieve, couldn't learn fast enough."

Schreiber's combat training led to an intimate knowledge of lighting, from a gaffer's point of view. She became the first woman gaffer in New York's NABET Local 15. "It was an interesting time," she says seriously. "I began in commercials in the era of the 'hard sell.' That meant, whatever the cinematographer might do, the product always came first and you had to see it.

"I mean, really see it. No quick cutting, no canted angles, no storytelling that would confuse us as to the product being exalted. It was smooth camera moves, warm fuzzy colors, soft light, all very mainstream and palatable. In fact, those Chinese lanterns so popular today were all the rage then, and I used them in documentaries as well.

"I worked on large commercials with several still photographers turned commercial directors, such as Melvin Sokolsky and David Langly. We did Burger King, Ivory, Tide, McDonalds. I felt I had to be perfect, working harder than the guys, being more personable, giving 110 percent. I felt like I was constantly judged. But I never stopped working.

"In New York, we never used generators," she continues. "We always tied into the main electrical panels. I was *fearless*. We would be in these funky basements, often with maintenance men looking skeptically at me. But, I would wow them with some electrobabble, and they would think I knew what I was doing.

"I remember one time, and I think, fortunately, only one time that I screwed up," she recalls. "We were shooting a Burger King commercial on Long Island and all of a sudden everything went black. I ran to the box, no voltage. Looked outside, no power. I thought I blew the transformer out on the pole! How embarrassing! Turned out, someone else had been stealing power off the same transformer. So, the electric company was actually grateful for my mistake!"

Very early in Nancy Schreiber's career, she got the job of a lifetime. She went to mainland China, with Shirley MacLaine and Claudia Weill, to film *The Other Half of the Sky*. "It was a different era in China," she recalls. "Mao was still alive, the Cultural Revolution in full force.

"I also co-gaffed the first all-woman's feature with Celeste Gainey, today a prominent lighting designer for upscale restaurants. I am still friendly with several of the women on the crew. The sound recordist was

Maryte Kavaliauskus, who is married to Fred Murphy, A.S.C., the key grip Alexis Krasilovsky is a professor, who has just published a book on women DPs. Doro Bachrach, was the Producer, and today is a well-respected Producer. Nancy Littlefield was the first AD. She went on to head the NYC Mayor's Office for Film and Television.

"I remember, they had a hard time finding a DP, but found a wiry energetic woman named Roberta Findlay, who had shot exclusively porno and was probably the only woman who had shot 35mm film. We had an enormous Arri blimp. The stock, I'm certain, was 5254. The Director was Karen Sperling, a niece of the Jack Warners.

"We built sets all over an abandoned mental hospital on New York's Ward Island."

At the same time, Schreiber was working as best boy for Bobby Vercruse (Bobby V), who started Filmtrucks and went on to buy Cinemobile. He gave Schreiber her start on larger-budget projects. "The equipment details I learned from him were incredible," she says. "He was one of the few younger gaffers who supported me, and wasn't threatened. The older gaffers were great as well. I learned a lot from people like Jack Reidel and Moe Odegaard. They weren't threatened that I might take their jobs away as it seemed some of the younger men were."

There was no set etiquette for men and women at the time. "I remember the other electric and even the grips wanting to help me lift heavy cable. I would politely let them know I was doing just fine.

"Bobby still likes to kid around, telling the story of my wearing culottes to a shoot and all the grips wanting to foot my ladder, as if I were wearing a dress!

"Actually, I was so anxious to fit in, that I dressed like one of the guys — baggy jeans, big T-shirts. I was certainly afraid to be feminine!" Of course, now Nancy Schreiber doesn't try to fit in. She is herself — long manicured nails and all!

Was it difficult for Nancy Schreiber, being the first woman in the gaffer's position? "I was certainly a novelty," she admits. "There were few women doing commercials, at least on the camera and crew side of the job. Some agencies hired us to show how 'forward' thinking they were. Others hired us just because we could do the job.

"I was lucky, I found a niche. There was even one cinematographer, Gary Young, who hired me as the gaffer and a woman assistant named Lorraine Boda. Now, that raised some eyebrows! It never occurred to me that I couldn't make it. It seemed so natural being a gaffer.

"I wonder if I had begun my career in Los Angeles if I still would be a technician. New York didn't have the same 'studio' influence and bias against anything new and different. New York seemed a much more open place for women in positions of power.

"It's funny and sad," she adds, pausing. "Most of the women DPs I met when I first started are the women who are working now. Joan Churchill in documentaries, Sandi Sissel, A.S.C., Judy Irola, A.S.C., Lisa Rinzler, Dyanna Taylor.

"Many woman ACs I've worked with seemed discouraged over the years to try to move up after they witnessed how long it was taking us pioneers to get recognition. After the initial novelty of the idea wore off, no one wanted to take a chance. It is ironic, when you think about it, there are many more accomplished women working in theater lighting, accepted for what they can do not for their gender, than there are in the motion picture and television industry.

"There are only a few women shooting decent budget films today," she continues. "It isn't that the crews won't accept and respect us. Once they see you know what you are doing, they are so loyal and enjoy the change of the dynamic. It is definitely getting better in recent years, as Sundance films that have been shot by women generate more widespread interest in 'the Industry' and more women such as Ellen Kuras, A.S.C., and Tami Reiker, have moved 'up.'

"Because I came up through the ranks as gaffer, I can talk the language. Actors, as well, seem to respond to women DPs. I am very attentive to them. I listen to any problems they believe they have with their looks, and try to gain their trust so that they are working freely with the Director, without worry. I really do look out for them. The more I shoot, the more respect I have for actors and the kinds of risks they take in their work. A far cry from the term 'talent' that was often used in commercials."

In the 1980s, Screiber might have become an "in demand" gaffer for commercials and features but her heart was in shooting movies herself. She did what many wannabe filmmakers have tired, and literally created and shot her own movie. It was called *Possum Living*, and was a cinema verite about a family in Pennsylvania who chose to be nonconsumers.

"I was intrigued at the ingenuity of the 20-year-old young woman, Dolly Freed, who along with her Dad, had created a lifestyle of raising their own vegetables and rabbits. They got wheat from the feed and grain store during the years of double-digit inflation.

"Dolly had been pulled from the school system when she was 11 years old, and taught by her father. I found her, because she wrote a book about her lifestyle and even found a publisher in New York. I was struck by her confidence and know-how after being self-taught and living reclusively in the country."

Schreiber followed Dolly to California, to appear on the Merv Griffin Show. She raised all the money and ended up distributing the film through a collective of social issue filmmakers called New Day Films, which is still in existence today.

"I worked with a very small crew, one sound, one AC, a Production Manager, a PA, and myself," she recalls. "I had minimal lighting equipment, since there was hardly any power in Dolly's home. We didn't have the luxury of high-speed stock and super-speed lenses then, either. The stock was 7247 (Kodak), and I used an Éclair NRP with an Angenieus 9.5-57 zoom."

The film went on to win numerous awards, a blue ribbon at the American Film Festival. Janet Maslin gave it a wonderful review in the *New York Times* when it played with a Lee Grant documentary on the Wilmar Eight at the prestigious New Directors-New Films at MOMA. " I made the film really as a way to show the world I could shoot," Schreiber explains.

"However, everyone now wanted to pigeonhole me as either a Director or a documentary cameraperson. This was exasperating, after all those years doing lighting on slick high-end commercials. I finally ended up shooting student films and did get some work on some prestigious documentaries such as the *Middletown* series for PBS."

*Middletown* was a project about real people's lives, a documentary to be shot entirely handheld. "We filmed a wedding of two people, both on their second marriage," she recalls. "The bride had two sons. I was sometimes assigned to the bride and to shooting other women in the bridal party. At other times, I was with the groom and the groom's party. John Lindley, A.S.C., was the DP.

"I remember on the wedding day," she recalls, "we had shot 25 rolls before noon (7:00 A.M. start). And, this was 16mm — 10-minute rolls. My shoulder was a bit red and my right hand felt like it was permanently frozen in the shape of the camera handle! Nothing like filming real life, and not wanting to miss a moment!"

It took a while, but Schreiber began shooting music videos, short dramatic films, commercials, and documentaries. "Documentaries are tough," she says. "You work a lot harder, simply because you have to do so many jobs, including carrying your own equipment.

"I really enjoy the freedom of documentaries and music videos. You simply don't have time to do things 'conventionally,' You can get away with a lot of things that grips wouldn't let you get away with on features," she says, shaking her head. "I remember hanging off the front of a car, trying to get a moving shot handheld — holding on to the ledge where the windshield wipers are stashed!

"As I get older, I can't believe how dangerous it was and how foolish I was! Safety is of number one importance! My grip friends would be horrified to learn of my escapades! I was lucky, plain and simple!"

While trying to break into the feature genre, Schreiber also began shooting startling high-end documentaries where people cared about style as well as content. One of these was the highly publicized *Amnesty International World Tour*. "This was a dream job," she says. "Again, with the Aaton on my shoulder, I recorded Sting, Springsteen, Peter Gabriel, Tracy Chapman, and Y'ousou Ndour as they traveled around the world giving concerts for Amnesty International. We all flew around on a DC-10 and the staging equipment and our gear was on another DC-10.

"I remember one day early on in the tour, looking up from my book and there was Bruce Springsteen walking down the aisle, friendly as can be. It was a privileged position, being a part of the day-to-day life of some of my rock heroes for five weeks.

"We visited and filmed in Zimbabwe and the Ivory Coast, Africa and Greece, India, Japan, Toronto, Montreal, Los Angeles, Philadelphia, as well as Costa Rica and Brazil, even Argentina. During the day, when the concert was being set up, usually in large stadiums, I was out filming around the towns and getting the local color. Sometimes, I would be following our musicians where they went fairly undisturbed, trying not to exploit their privacy. At night, I would film any local artists and any special songs our artists did.

"One such time was *The Mothers of the Disappeared*, from Pinochet's *Regime in Chile*," she adds. "There, I was on stage with Sting when we were in Sao Paulo.

"Finally, our big finale was in Buenos Aires, when we switched to tape and shot multi-camera — ten cameras, I think! Before that, it was just me, a sound recordist and Production Manager, a loader and that was it!"

That was one of Schreiber's most vivid memories. "So are some of the crazier things that I shot, when I was younger," she laughs. "I remember shooting a commercial for European National Bank, where I had to ride on a motorcycle backwards!"

Each project allowed her to refine her shooting technique, and helped her develop an eye for the unusual. "There are things that I tried on my first so-called feature, that I still use today," she says. "This was one of those 'we've got the money, let's make a movie' kind of things.

"The son of a small New York town mayor wanted to direct, so he gathered family money and set out to do a story about a 'rock-and-roll band' in a small town. It was an early super-16mm feature. It never got released," she says sadly. However, she did cement several relationships that are still alive today.

"I went on to do a picture called *Chain of Desire*, directed by Temi Lopez, with Linda Firentino, Malcolm McDowell, Seymour Cassell, and Grace Zabriskie — gaffed by the David Lee and with key grip Rick Stribling from the earlier project. (both have gone on to work with Directors like Quentin Tarentino and Robert Rodriguez).

Schreiber continued to search for a break into the world of features, taking unusual assignments along the way. One was a project called *Forever Mine,* now called *Trapped*. It was shot at a former Girl Scout camp in northern Wisconsin. "Some British investors had turned it into a studio — or what passed for a studio," she recalls. "January, in this location, was certainly a challenge! I am still friendly with everyone that was involved in the project. The Director was a lovely man named Leshic Byrzinsky.

"We had massive original sets, such as an underground mining tunnel area designed by Brian Savagar. Brian won the Academy Award as Art Director on *Room with a View*. We were always working to find interesting ways of hiding lights. Most of the time, we worked with Kerosene lamps and battery-operated quartz flashlights.

"I have to admit, I went a bit wild during the more futuristic moments," she laughs. "The hardest challenge was shooting night exteriors in the chill of the January weather. I had so many clothes on, I could barely get near the camera to operate!

Being low-budget, I was the DP and operator — which I enjoyed because of the intimacy with the project. Today, I operate, occasionally, on some projects if they are small, and I try to find a Steadicam/A-camera operator as the same person. I tend to light through the lens and often shoot the first couple of takes, then pass the camera to the operator so that I can be near the Director at the monitor.

"I remember shooting a poor-man's-process night exterior car scene inside a warehouse on this picture," she continues. "It was so cold (wind chill factor of 40 below), even I didn't complain that it might look artificial!

"We did enough wide 'pass-bys' of the car, so no one noticed we weren't outside for the tighter, warehouse shots. Brian, the designer, had a large black drum built to rotate, with silver Mylar and foil bits placed sporadically on the drum. As I filmed, looking through one side of the windows, the drum would spin. With just a little bit of light hitting the silver, you got the impression of movement through the dark woods of northern Wisconsin.

"We didn't want too many headlight gags hitting our car, as an abduction is taking place with some escaped prisoners, and we wanted the area to feel deserted and scary for the two kidnapped (or car-napped) girls."

Projects like this allowed Schreiber to develop an unconventional approach to shooting. For her, there is always a different way to tell a story. She will always try to find something people haven't seen.

"I like to work with the director, to design a visual to suit the unusual aspects of a picture," she says. "And, I try not to be swayed by fads."

While struggling for a foothold, Schreiber was based out of New York, believing that the low-budget world on the East Coast offered more interesting opportunities. "New York featured arty little 'downtown' movies, while Los Angeles tended to cater to erotic thrillers," she explains. "So, why was one of the first projects to catch the eye of film festival competition screeners an erotic drama out of New York?"

*Chain of Desire,* tackled AIDS and the sexual obsessions of New Yorkers in the 1990s. It starred actors like Malcolm McDowell, Seymour Cassel and Linda Fiorentino. "I took a lot of visual chances on this picture," Schreiber admits. "We used only low and very wide angles. Shots like this do take a longer time to light, but then you are ready for more of the day."

The film featured impressionistic sex and nudity, "people pretending to make love," she says. "But what was eye-raising might have been two men kissing, Linda Fiorentino getting it on with a painter at a church (Elias Koteas), who turns out to be married. And, a kinky Grace Zabriskie in a maid's uniform, turning on Patrick Bouchault with her ruler.

"The film was loosely based on the Schitzler play *La Ronde*, which was then made into a movie by Max Ophuls. It is a series of vignettes of couples in which one lover moves on to the next, who moves to the next and so on.

"There isn't any nudity in the film," she says again. "Yet, it seems erotic, for what is not seen but just implied. It is also a very funny movie, quirky, with a deeper message in the age of AIDS.

"I remember shooting a church scene where Linda Fiorentino has sought refuge in an old building under renovation. The Elias Koteas character is plastering the walls and sees her crying. The church had fabulous stained glass windows, and for a very short time, the sun would hit the windows with the most deliciously burnished glow.

"Often, on movies, one hears the AD saying 'we've got to go.' Well, that day, when the sun hit, it was me *screaming* 'we've got to shoot now, hurry, let's go!'"

Since the movie was low-budget, Schreiber found herself constantly dropping and picking up 12ks, "only when I couldn't do without them," she laughs. "I remember that I needed Xenon's at the large club location and couldn't afford them at this little church, so when mother-nature cooperated it was 'smoke and shoot.'

"The club location had been a famous East Village club called The World," she adds. "The only time we could film there was during the first week of production. This was distressing, as it is always better to start small when you have a new team working together. But, we just jumped into the fire.

"There were choreographed song and dance numbers for our principals and extras, who consisted of countless numbers of East Village low life, drag queens, hipsters, along with the usual assortment of SAG extras.

"There were scenes at the bar, scenes behind the stage and in the dressing rooms. The World provided a seedy decadence, which designer Scott Chambliss and I got to embellish.

"We had to return to The World on the very last day of production. During the weeks we were there, one of the owners had been murdered —right where we had been shooting! We had some difficult time getting back in after the murder, but somehow it got worked out. I remember the crew sneaking off to look at the taped off area and the bloody floor. It was really creepy, but we got our shots!

"The club was supposed to be set in the tower of the Chrysler Building," she continues. "Scott Chambliss had built triangle-shaped windows in the balcony of The World and my gaffer David Lee constructed fluorescent triangles of light to mimic the Chrysler Building.

"The Director, Temiscoles Lopez, had always wanted to bookend the opening and closing of the film with aerials of nighttime Manhattan, moving in and out of the Chrysler Building. Producer George Moffly asked me if he could find the money, would I do it. Even though I've been a daredevil, and enjoyed activities like sky diving, I had always turned down helicopter work," she laughs.

"It just wasn't worth the risk. I really didn't think George would be able to come up with the money. This was my first film with him," she adds. "Now that I've done three others, I know he must find money on trees!

"Anyway, I said I would do it if I could have Al Cerullo as the pilot. Wouldn't you know it, New York wasn't busy and we got Al.

"I felt a bit reassured that he had a double-engine helicopter. I remember it was the night before we wrapped. A summer Friday night – and it was raining. There was tremendous air traffic, not only from the commercial airports but, also, those consumer commuter planes to The Hamptons.

"Only the AC and I went up. On the first pass it was so windy and bumpy, I was so depressed. But, we went up again and I think I got the hang of the Tyler mount and the rain had died down. We did move in on a window of the Chrysler Building, which did match nicely with the constructed interior. And, we also circled around and around the top of the building.

"I also remember tilting straight down onto the streets and rooftops, seeing Broadway in a different way. When we turned left – or rather east on 42nd Street, the wind really whipped us around. Although I am proud of what I feel are distinctive aerials in an overshot medium, now that my budgets are larger, I'm relieved that nowadays we can afford helicopter operators and Skycam. Cerullo was also an amazing pilot and I was able to work with him again on *The Blair Witch-Hunt*, this time with Skycam.

High shots and rooftops were a large part of this picture. Even when Schreiber was "on the ground," there were higher challenges. "I remember we were on a rooftop in Manhattan, where we were able to nicely light our actors. But, the nearest building to our background was blocks away," she recalls. "Our gaffer, David Lee, was able to use a very long throwing PAR to get a kiss of light on the distant buildings.

"Remember, we were low-budget and didn't have Musco lights available. We had to save our Condor days for larger night exteriors. The scene looks terrific. The building is slightly cool, the actors are in cross backlight, motivated by their candles — as they talk and embrace.

"It was important for me to show Manhattan," she continues. "We wanted to see it through the windows of our 30 locations, whether day or night. And, we wanted to take advantage of our real views on this location picture — no Translight or blownout windows.

"There is a scene in Linda Fiorentino's loft, where she is walking around talking on the phone, as a tugboat goes by in the background. I gelled windows and brought interior lights up so that there was a one-and-a-half stop difference between interior and exterior.

"Another scene in Linda's loft used a very wide lens (17mm). Linda is in the foreground on the phone while Elias Koteas is in silhouette in the background.

"On *Chain of Desire*, I played around with people moving from being silhouette in front of windows or buildings, to being properly exposed in the same shot. I think I used the technique four times."

The project won Schreiber a nomination for the Independent Feature Project Spirit Award in 1994 — and plenty of great press.

To Nancy Schreiber, it sometimes feels like she has done a lot of things in her career backwards. When she finally came to Los Angeles to look for work in the feature field, she ended up shooting a picture about New York! "I really enjoyed doing *Lush Life*, which starred Jeff Goldblum, Forest Whitaker, and Kathy Baker in a story about a dying musician's last fling," she says, enthusiastically.

"This was a Showtime Movie, directed by Michael Elias, who was mostly a writer/producer from television. However, he was a jazz aficionado. He developed the script with the cooperation of Chaticleer Films.

"It was an ambitious shoot," she says. "We would often have four or five pages of dialog each day and still have to do several musical numbers scripted as an eighth of a page.

"I usually used three cameras for the musical numbers – Chris Haarhof on Steadicam, doing a wonderful job. (He was one of the amazing operators on *Saving Private Ryan*.)

"The music was done by Lennie Michaus, and was often a big band of 30 or so.

"The final party, which Forest Whitaker threw for his 100 best musician friends (knowing he was dying of a brain tumor), was shot at the Wilshire Ebell. It was supposed to be New York, so we used Translights outside.

"Anyone who has ever filmed at the Wilshire Ebell knows there are major rigging restrictions so that the architecture is preserved. In 1993, the helium balloons weren't around a lot. So, we did find clever ways of making our own pillars — part art department and part grip. Fortunately there was also a balcony over part of the room," she adds.

"I remember shooting a park dialog of Forest and Jeff sitting on the Hudson River. (We were somewhere in the San Fernando Valley.) When we took Jeff and Forest to New York for a few days of establishing shots, I had to shoot the over-the-shoulder reverse two-shot, looking into the Hudson at Riverside Park! Naturally, it had been sunny in March in Los Angeles. But, I had clouds and almost rain in New York in June!

"Ah, the fun of working in the movies!" she laughs.

*Variety* said that Schreiber gave the film a very "textured" look. " I like to think I created a look to match the intensity of the story," she says. "The subtext of the story was all about music and movement through life. To me, music and emotion can be created through color and movement. I wanted to do that with my camera."

It is hard to get Nancy Schreiber to single out a film or two or even ten in her résumé to talk about. Each one features a different approach to moviemaking — 'because we were often trying to make something out of very little, and do it in a most unusual way," she laughs.

"One of the projects that sticks out in her mind is a small story called *Scorpion Spring*. *Variety* said the project had a 'footprints of Quentin, Tarantino, Robert Rodriguez, and Sergio Leone. "It was shot on a shoestring," she recalls, "with some fine actors, including Rueben Blades and Alfred Molina.

"Although it was a contemporary 'spaghetti Western,' we tried to do some unusual things. It is all about using your eye and your brain to find a different approach."

One of the plusses in the low-budget field, as mentioned earlier, is that lack of money often forces a cinematographer to also be the film's operator. "It is often difficult to find an operator who has your eye. When I'm behind the camera, I go for interesting composition and frame in a peculiar way. It's a drag to always be reminding or correcting an operator.

"I often frame unconventionally — off center shots, no head room, dynamic composition that fits with the story."

That's a lot of what she did in her next project, called *Nevada*. "This is a woman's story," she says, "a story about a dissatisfied wife on the run, who gets drawn into the lives of the women residents of a very small California town. "Writer/Director Gary Tieche wanted the leisurely feeling of the 1970s film style," she explains. "So, we looked at *The Last Picture Show* and *Tender Mercies*.

"We found a wonderful, old, almost deserted mining town in the California desert for the setting," she explains. "Randsburg was our Nevada, with a few color changes and carefully chosen angles. To make the story work, we came up with lyrical dolly moves, long Steadicam shots following the women through their lives in this town. Again, I used close-ups and long lenses to intensify the story."

Recently, Nancy Schreiber ran into cinematographer Laszlo Kovacs, A.S.C. "He told me he had seen a beautiful film that I'd shot," she says, a little in wonder. "I thought he had made a mistake! He had seen *Nevada* on the Independent Film Channel and loved the light and color. He couldn't believe we shot the movie in 24 days!

"I'm sorry not many people saw it, because it had a great cast (Amy Brenneman, Kirstie Alley, Kathy Najimi, Bridgette Wilson). Unfortunately, there was no distribution.

"This was a tough one, 120 degrees in the shade, yet Panavision never faltered. I used the Sepia to increase that feeling of the sweltering heat in a small town in the middle of nowhere. This was a great ensemble cast of women, in a town where the men are working in the mines all week and just came home on the weekends."

Schreiber did something different, on the crew side as well. On this film, she had an all-female camera crew for the first time. *Entertainment Tonight* made a fuss over it. "Veronica Johnson was my first AC, a statuesque model — a gorgeous African American, who was great on focus. She passed away a year or so ago, at age 33, from cancer," she says sadly. "It was very tragic.

"My second AC was Aurelia Winburn, who is now a hot first in New York. And, we had Karen Chow as the loader, now an assistant in Los Angeles.

"We had to work together to survive," she says. "I'd drink eight glasses of water before lunch, and sweat it off as fast as I drank it. As time went on, we were all delirious. But it was worth it. What a great town, and a great group to work with!"

In the last three years, Nancy Schreiber has really broadened her scope of shooting. In 1998, *Your Friends and Neighbors* — came out. In 1999, she shot *Buying the Cow* — another mainstream feature, due out in 2000. And, in between, she went to China for *Shadow Magic* and Vietnam to do *Breathe In, Breathe Out*. "Don't forget Anne Heche's first directorial project, *Reaching Normal*," she laughs.

"Where do I start," she smiles. It has been a busy year — and 2000 promises to be even busier, with *Blair Witch* shooting from March until early May.

Late summer 1998, Schreiber's *Your Friends and Neighbors*, directed by Neil LaBute and produced by star Jason Patric and Steve Golin, hit the theaters. "It is Neil's bent version of male/female relationships in the vein of his first film, *In the Company of Men,*" she says. "Neil's idea was to use the same theatrical style as he did in his first film, that is, play it out in tableau situations. The action was to unfold in front of the camera."

They chose to shoot Super 35mm, allowing them to use wide lenses (17.5mm to 21mm), still being able to format for television without losing information and without pan and scan. "We also chose to make it a nondescript 'never-world,'" she explains. "This wouldn't be Los Angeles or New York or Chicago — but simply an urban city."

To enhance that style, Schreiber worked with production designer Charles Breen to control the color, keeping everything in green, brown, rust, yellow, and orange — Hopper colors.

Between searching out locations that would show the never-world city, she attended the three-weeks of rehearsals. "It helped a lot," she says. "Not only were the actors (including Patric, Amy Brenneman, Aaron Eckhart, Ben Stiller, Catherine Keener, and Natassja Kinski) building an intimacy, I was able to watch them and do a few tests at the same time. This gave me the chance to build my own intimacy with the characters, the look, and the story."

One of Schreiber's most interesting challenges was a sequence in a Los Angeles bookstore. "This was a short shoot, so we were really moving," she explains. "We had one day for two very different shots — a 360-degree Steadicam shot that ran for four minutes without cuts, and another long Steadicam shot looking up the aisles. Fortunately, that looked in a single direction.

"Jason Patric's (the swinging bachelor) character spots Catherine Keener (his best friend's girlfriend) and tries to pick her up. She ignores him and he verbally abuses her. We wanted to do a four-minute move."

The location was three adjoining rooms with windows out front and glass blocks at the end of the store. "Traveling through the rooms and turning around meant keeping all the lights above." she says. "That was relatively easy. Keeping the crew out of the shot, well, that was interesting.

"There was a set of stairs up to a small loft," she continues. "We put the monitor up there and practically drew straws for people who could be grouped around it.

"Lighting — well, that was interesting. We had two rooms that were reasonable. We were able to add some lights to the book stacks, so we could go in and out of them as Jason goes on his verbal attack. However, the third room was so small we had to keep the Steadicam outside looking in. The ceiling was so low, we saw it in the shot."

Schreiber put wall stretchers in the ceiling of the main room, putting ten PAR-56 lights with narrow 500-watt spots above. "We added a few normal tungsten fresnel lights, creating pools of light. Then, in the small room, Jeff Levy, our gaffer, put small KinoFlos on the shelves.

"We used the short, lightweight zoom (27 to 68) on Steadicam at a 3.2 stop to move through the bookstore. The hard part for operator Dave Luckenbach was keeping the lights out of the frame.

"To give Jason, who has deep-set eyes, a little more punch, we had a handheld eyelight. At one point, there was an interesting dance between the handheld eyelight and the Steadicam," she laughs. "That *was* a small room!"

Larger shots were just as big a challenge for Schreiber on this feature. In the sequence where Jason Patric and Aaron Eckhart are jogging around a track, things also were a little tricky. The location used was Patriotic Hall in downtown Los Angeles. The building almost stands alone (off the 110 freeway), rising tall into the skyline. "And, where did we decide to shoot," she says, ruefully. "The eighth floor! How were we going to rig outside those windows?!"

Since the building was very old and not in the greatest condition, it was impossible to drop anything from the roof. "So, how do you light several 360-degree passes and shoot without cuts?" she says.

"Fortunately, the ceilings were high. So, without a pre-rig day, we worked as quickly as possible, changing the lights in the ceiling fixtures to daylight 500 bulbs. Then we lined HMIs up along the upper bleachers and shot them through diffusion, keeping everything just out of frame. I then used a traveling 'bug' light adapted by Dave Azato at Leonetti Camera. This 200-watt PAR light (with a small Chimera lantern) worked great. We went off AC, for this, because we were doing so many takes over such a long period of time.

"Doing it this way, saved us from the risk of the light popping off in the middle of a perfect four-minute take or risk draining the batteries.

"Of course, we had to suspend the cable for the light across the ceiling and drop it down into the middle of the room. The only way, since the camera saw all four of the corners."

One of the things that fascinated Schrieber about this masochistic comedy was how to bring the attitude of the picture to the screen without going overboard. "There were technical challenges, mostly in where to hide the lights in our practical locations with such wide lenses. The real challenge, however, was to keep the restraint and simplicity we set, yet ensure that the audience was drawn in by the images as well as the words."

In late 1999, Nancy Schreiber got to do another mainstream picture. "*Buying the Cow* was a departure in that it was pure comedy," she says. "This was not an arty labor of love, but actually a commercial and funny film. The young ensemble of actors was amazing. Jerry O'Connell, Ryan Reynolds, Bill Bellamy, Brigette Wilson, William Forsythe, and Alyssa Milano really enjoyed themselves.

"The script is about a young man obsessed with the dream girl from his childhood," she explains. "He is unable to move on and commit to his current girlfriend when she gives him an ultimatum. He leaves town for several months and has a wild time.

"Walt Becker, the Writer/Director was open to the comic possibilities of wide lenses, swish pans, unusual places to put the camera and other techniques. We didn't go over the top visually, because we didn't want to be obvious. Yet, we wanted the camera to be playful, whimsical, and with movement — so different from *Friends and Neighbors*. We used a lot of Steadicam to keep moving.

"Lighting was naturalistic. We must have filmed in 25 bars, restaurants, and clubs. We wanted each one to have its own character and color. Even though it is a comedy, I didn't overlight the film. Nights were moody, days interesting, often sidelit without too much overfill.

"I used the Millennium camera, which converted nicely (and quickly) to Steadicam. This allowed us to ramp in a couple of dream sequences, all this without carrying several camera bodies."

Earlier that year, Schreiber used the Millennium camera for another project called *Reaching Normal*, which was a half-hour project directed by Anne Heche. The project, part romance and part science fiction, was shot for Showtime. "It's about a woman who is feeling alienated in her marriage and thinks she is going crazy," she explains.

"In reality, her extrasensory perception is surfacing. When a scientist into otherworldly research contacts her, everything goes wild. It causes a major change in four people's lives. Anne's idea was to show how sudden events can cause people to pay attention to their lives."

Chanticleer Productions (a company Schreiber has worked with on music videos and that produced *Lush Life*) backed Heche's vision of pushing the envelope. They allowed the two women to do what they wanted, including moving masters, long Steadicam scenes, cranes, dolly and hand-held.

"A shot that showed Anne's gutsyness is a huge fight between Andie McDowell (the wife) and her husband (Alan Rosenberg). It weaves through the house set, which was constructed on stage at Dos Carlos Studios. We followed a different character or whipped between characters on each take, using a different lens. Unfortunately, this was intercut in the editing room with scenes involving Paul Rudd and Joey Lauren Adams.

"Because of the 360-deegree point of view of the Millennium camera, all lights were hung above the set or outside the windows," she says. We used small tungsten units inside (Tweenies, Babies, Peppers, Kinos and so forth). Outside, fresnels (2k, 5k and 10k)."

The two used other techniques to enhance the story. "We used ramping speed changes in shots such as the one where Andie runs around in her perfectly sterile backyard, finally letting go as she splashes in the kiddie pool," she explains. "As she begins to run, we ramp from normal to slightly slow-motion, then back to normal. This was enough to show her world turning over. For the end of the shot, we used the Technocrane, rising above her as she finds some inner peace and freedom."

As if that wasn't enough work for Nancy Schreiber, between these three projects, she managed to travel to far off lands, making two very different projects. *Shadow Magic* allowed her to return to China to see how the country had changed and shoot a period piece. Set in 1902, this film is the true story of the first motion picture traveling salesman — a Westerner, hoping to entice people to watch movies.

"This is also a love story," she says. "We strove to balance the technical achievements of the time with the human drama of the turn of the century in China."

A fascinating idea in itself. Couple the challenges of the story with other complications – like an all-Chinese crew who did not speak English, the inability to work with the tools available in the States, and the tight schedule (something that she is no stranger to), as well as many major locations. "That didn't matter," she says. "The director won me.

"She is a Chinese woman who was brought up a communist, and had forsaken it for America and capitalism after her parents were sent away during the Cultural Revolution. She worked on Wall Street, and when she became tired of the financial world, she decided to show her view of China to the world through film."

Although Hu wanted to stay true to the period, she also wanted to add modern elements to the film. "Much of the story takes place in a photo studio, and Ann wanted to make those shots visually stunning. So, we used a modern tool — Mylar — to add to those shots, covering boards like modern-day reflectors, even though this wasn't historically accurate."

This allowed Schreiber to control the palette, assisting in manipulating the colors in the sets and locations as well as the costumes.

One of the most interesting challenges was working with the technical inventions of the time — the actual camera and projectors used at the turn of the century. "We had to find a projector that would fit the period — one that could give us enough light so that we could expose the film properly," she says. "The art department did a mock-up of the prop camera and projector.

"When we were shooting the 'projection booth,' we needed to find a working projector that was bright enough to project our film within the film to the 1902 audience. Our solution was to work at an incredibly low light (T1.4 rating 5279 at 500 ASA)."

Equipment to play in front of the camera wasn't Nancy Schreiber's only challenge. She had ordered what she would need before she arrived in Beijing. However, what she ordered was definitely not what was there. Instead of an Arri 535B she got a 535A, which proved to be problematic because of the complex electronics. By the end of the shoot, she was able to get a 535B. Also, "we ended up with a dolly that was halfway between a Panther and an Elemack," she says. "One wheel was broken from the beginning to the end.

"The crane was used on a mock street scene, with camels, rickshaws, horses and vendors. It had no railings or safeties. I was strapped in with a flimsy seat belt. But, it worked."

Add to that challenge the "effects" Schreiber had to use. "If you are wondering what happened to smoke cookies, when they were banned for health reasons in the States, now you'll know. China embraced their use! Ten cookies equaled enough to hold the atmosphere on our extended shots!"

Perhaps Schreiber's biggest challenge was that she never saw what she was shooting. "We sent the film back to Duart in New York," she explains. "We knew it would be weeks before we saw prints, but it was several weeks later, if not more. The material got stuck in customs! We were virtually flying blind. We saw dailies once — and the video dailies got to us the day before we returned to the States.

"Although I would have liked to see them," she adds, "I knew in my heart we were okay.

"The added challenge — oh yes, there were more — were the shots in black-and-white on Kodak's 5222, for our film within a film. I had them processed in Beijing. I needed to match the Lumiere footage and found the lab there contrasty but clean.  So the footage did need to be degraded in post."

Despite the short hours of sunlight, the need to carry most of the equipment by hand, the language barrier, tourists watching and getting in the way at The Great Wall, and more, China was a unique experience Nancy Schreiber would never have missed. *Shadow Magic* was picked up at Sundance by Sony Classics.

"Vietnam, was also amazing and exotic," Schreiber adds with enthusiastism. "It was my first 'professional' venture out with Divicam (small digital format). The Director, Beth B, is quite well known in New York circles as an artist, filmmaker, and was a Super-8mm artist in the early 1980s. I had always wanted to work with her.

"Beth bought a Sony DSR-200, which is under $3,000.00 and a little larger than the Mini-DV Palmcorders that are so popular. It was important to me to have a camera that fit on my shoulder, as I knew I would be shooting for hours and wanted to be steady, which is hard with those tiny cameras.

"The camera was terrific in descent light, but I was unhappy with low- light conditions — dusk or dark interiors were muddy and noisy. But, the experience of traveling with almost no equipment was liberating.

"The film, called *Breathe In, Breathe Out*, just premiered at The Rotterdam Film Festival," she continues. "It follows three Vietnam vets back to the site where they were stationed 30 years ago. Each of the three vets brought one of their children with them, to help them bring closure to their painful experiences.

"We started in Saigon (Ho Chi Minh City now). We then traveled north, up the coast to places like Danang and Mai Lai. (We also went to Hanoi but didn't film there.)

"It was so liberating, having the light camcorder on my shoulder," she adds. "We had a sound recordist from New York and a Vietnamese grip/electric helper.

"Often, it was like a vacation. The people are so lovely in Vietnam, forgiving and friendly. We were truly welcomed. It was overwhelming for the vets. The project is very moving and emotional. There is lots of healing, lots of tears.

"I lit interviews in black limbo when we were in hotels. But, the rest of the film was shot on the bus with the vets and their children or in the villages and former battlefields — mostly available light, with Foamcore bounce fill or sun gun as the sun went down."

Unlike many cinematographers, Nancy Schreiber has never been and will never be "typecast" into a film genre. When she isn't shooting these run-and-gun documentaries, she's doing mainstream features. Between those, she shoots music videos or quirky little projects. Most of the time, the pressure she has to handle is budget, time, and location — lack of equipment, or no equipment.

"Now, I'm facing a different pressure," she laughs, as she brings herself to the present, realizing she's about to take on a project that has that all difficult challenge — the word "sequel." "There were no expectations, except those within the production, on the first *Blair Witch Project*," she says. "No one knew how big the project would be.

"With *Blair Witch-Hunt*, there is already a buzz, and we just started shooting. The original *Blair Witch* project was filmed in 16mm black-and-white and MiniDV. After attending Sundance this year, I felt the MiniDV format lacked resolution, especially in low light. So, I opted to shoot our video sequences in Digital Beta. But 95 percent of the movie is being shot in 35mm, with a great deal of Steadicam.

"The sequel is being directed by Joe Berlinger, one of the filmmakers of the award-winning documentaries *Brother's Keeper* and *Paradise Lost*. I previously shot commercials and documentaries for Joe and we had really hit it off. There is a lot of pressure on everyone for the sequel to perform well. It has a great script, and I hope it will be a terrific film.

"One of the challenges I'm facing is blocking out the buzz. I just keep doing my job day-by-day, shot-by-shot. Just like you have to do with every project you work on."

*Every time you shoot a film, you are trying to create an experience for the audience. You always have something in mind. You aren't there to shoot the pages, you are there to let the feelings you have come out. The work is all about going for that gut level. As a cinematographer, we only have ourselves to offer. That is what makes our work unique from each other.*

# John Schwartzman

It's that once-a-year event when cinematographers and their friends clean up, dress up, gather, gossip, and, oh yes, honor their own at the American Society of Cinematographers Awards dinner. At the moment, John Schwartzman, A.S.C., is leaning across the back of his chair, watching Warren Beatty tell the beginning of yet another Vitorio Storaro story. He laughs in the right places, his mind only half in the night's events.

It's not that the evening isn't entertaining, he is really enjoying himself. It's just that he has a little bit on his mind. Like the preproduction challenges he's tackling on his latest pairing with director Michael Bay — *Pearl Harbor.*

Hollywood hype, high budgets, fast-paced shooting days, major locations, and challenging lighting jobs are just part of John Schwartzman's days. And he loves every minute of it. "I grew up on film sets," he says, in a matter-of-fact voice. "My father was one of the first entertainment attorneys. He literally created 'independent financing,' while representing clients like Stanley Kubrick, Billy Friedkin (who is sitting a few tables away from him at the awards), and Frances Ford Coppola.

"At 12, I was sent to Mississippi to get a feel of movies being shot on location," he smiles. "I roomed with one of the teamsters. I wandered around, while the musical version of *Huckleberry Finn* was being shot. Cinematographer Laszlo Kovacs, A.S.C., would give me rides up and down on the Titan crane. From then on, I knew the job of cinematographer was the best job on a set! I wanted to be one!"

Naturally, young Schwartzman wanted to get into the business. However, from a typical traditional family, his parents wanted him to be a lawyer or doctor. So, he started following their wishes, studying economics at the University of Colorado.

"My step-mother is Talia Shire, who is Frances Ford Coppola's sister," he says. "When I was home, we would spend vacations at Frances's Napa house. One Thanksgiving, George Lucas was over. It was 1981, and he was already a billionaire and a major player." At dinner, Schwartzman let out a secret. He wanted to study "the business." Since Coppola was his uncle by marriage, and Lucas was right there in the room, he took the bull by the horns and asked the two of them to write letters of recommendation to film schools.

Surprisingly, both said "no." The answer was logical. If they did it for him, they would have to do it for every "relative." "I accepted their answer, or so they thought," he laughs. "Later that evening, they were both bragging about what great *Risk* players they were. 'Let's make a bet,' I said. 'If I beat you, I get the letters of recommendation.' By 2:00 A.M. I'd invaded the Ukraine. I'd won. True to their word, they both wrote me letters."

With these heavy hitters behind him, John Schwartzman got into every film school he applied to. "The deans of the universities were all calling and welcoming me," he smiles. "At first, I didn't know where to go, but I finally settled on USC. It had a better program and reputation at the time."

Since Schwartzman's focus was always shooting, he got to do some of the best projects. He partnered with two Directors who have built strong reputations today, Greg Araki (who makes independent, edgy, movies with gay themes) and Phil Joanou (*State of Grace*). "Phil was set to direct a senior project," he recalls.

"Now, at USC, there was a written rule that no movie could be longer than 20 minutes," he smiles. "However, we found out that George Lucas, Bob Zemeckis, and John Milius all made longer projects. We figured, 'if we made a good film, who would care.' Our film came out to be 32 minutes.

"The way things worked was we would shoot the project at USC and we would give them a sound reel. They would give me the negative and I would cut it – part of the cameraman's responsibility.

"Well, we turned in a fake sound reel, and took the cut to a place called JDH sound. (I don't know if they are still in business) and begged them to mix the film for free.

"When the school got wind of what we were doing, there was a big tadoo! USC even tried to subpoena the film! It became a pissing contest between Phil's lawyers and the schools. Our platform was — 'This is our money, we should be doing what we want with it.' Since Phil's dad was a major player in the advertising world, his lawyers were stronger than the schools. We finally got the project back and it was shown at the DGA, which was a big deal every year. By the time the movie was over, we were getting cards from agents."

The school told Schwartzman he "may as well leave." He would never get the credits he wanted for the degree. He had "aired dirty laundry in public." "The bigger irony about the whole thing was that I failed the cinematography course," he laughs. "I got a C- (anything under a B was a failing grade for a graduate student).

"Seven months later, I got a call. I'd won the Nissan Focus Award for Best Cinematography of 1984 for *The Last Chance Dance*, the film that got me a failing grade at USC!"

At this time, writer Richard Martini, who had a three-picture deal at Columbia, contacted John Schwartzman. Not satisfied with just writing, Martini wanted to direct. But, the studio wouldn't let him. John Travolta's manager Jonathan Krane told Martini he should "do a shot film" to prove he could direct. "So, I got the call. Would I DP for free? He made me a promise. He would hire me to shoot when he got his first feature to direct," Schwartzman explains.

At the time, Schwartzman was DPing anything he could, and working as an electrician on films like *Nightmare on Elm Street*. He was also doing a lot of press kits, since the world of the electronic media was coming alive. "My cost of living was low, my rent was four hundred a month," he recalls. "So, I said I would do the project."

The short film, budgeted at five thousand dollars, was a hit. Suddenly, the two had a million dollars to expand it to a feature. And, that's how the comedy *You Can't Hurry Love* came about!

"At 25, I was a cinematographer! Some people were telling me — 'no. You have to go up the ranks.' I didn't know what to do.

"Again, I called on family. My uncle was Conrad Hall's doctor. With his help, Connie had just gotten over a long illness. So, my doctor uncle told me to call Conrad if I had questions.

"Why not? 'Should I become an assistant?' I asked him. 'If you want to be a DP, be a DP,' he told me. 'Hell, you are already one anyway, so why move backwards? You can always hire guys to load the camera!'

"Consequently, I've never worked as a focus puller in my life. I can barely load a Panaflex. If the threading guide isn't on the door, I'm doomed!"

Schwartzman made the decision and never looked back. Soon, he hooked up with a friend from childhood. At the time, music videos were like low-budget features. Some of the hot new directors were really pushing the envelope. "I've known Michael Bay since seventh grade," Schwartzman says. "He went to school with my younger sister. When he started at Art Center, I was the only one he knew that could shoot. So, I would do his Art Center films, which were highly polished pieces of work.

"When Michael joined the gang (and it was a gang) at Propaganda Films, I was beginning to think of myself as the new Roger Corman. I was pigeon-holed, constantly being hired for a week of reshoots, shooting handheld, chasing bare-chested coeds with very few clothes and a lot of blood on their chests! Music videos with Michael sounded great and they paid better!"

Somewhere in between all this, Frances Ford Coppola was directing *Tucker*, with Vitorio Storaro, A.S.C., as the cinematographer. Schwartzman ended up doing the video press kit, strapping on a Beta and 16mm camera. "And following Vitorio around, asking all sorts of questions," he says.

"The most important thing I learned from Storaro was to trust my eye," he recalls. " 'The light meter doesn't matter', he would say. 'If you like the way it looks, shoot it.' In fact, he would be pissed if he saw me with meter in hand!

"He also gave me another bit of advice — 'Don't try to be friends with everybody in preproduction. When the movie comes out, no one will remember you were a nice guy. But, everyone will remember the film. That lives on forever. You fight for the image you believe in.'

"He also told me something that is very hard to follow — but I try. It's more important to say 'no' than 'yes.' Cameramen are so thrilled to do what they do, they want to do everything. It is the project that you choose that's important. You can only be one person, not three people at a time. You have to turn things down."

So, with Storaro's advice in his head, Schwartzman began shooting music videos with the likes of Michael Bay and David Fincher. The projects were filmic in content, with bigger budgets relative to today's dollar. They told stories.

With Bay, he did projects for Slaughter, Chicago, Poco. With Fincher, Madonna. "And, Paula Abdul's video for 'Just the Way You Love Me,' with so many products in the shots, David and I had a great commercial product reel," he laughs. "For the video, we ripped off the best — Leslie Dektor and Joe Pytka.

"It was number one for four months. It contained everything we could think of, color temperature mixes (ala Storaro), tungsten PAR 64s mixed with daylight for a warm, backlit golden look. Things you would see in *The Conformist*. Smoke. Water. Steam.

"It didn't matter if it worked or it didn't," he laughs. "The record company had no idea what we were doing.

"Today, music videos are shot in a very deconstructed style," he says sadly. "It's a Bolex with a 22-degree shutter, doing the most screwed up parts of *Saving Private Ryan* and not understanding why.

"We were trying to be beautiful — employing brute arcs, playing with the quality of light and different tools. We'd use the Unilux Strobe, then throw up for two days because of the headaches from it. We'd vow never to use it again. The Directors paid homage to film and used videos to build their craft toward ultimately directing features."

John Schwartzman was lucky. He was able to bring this style of shooting into commercials shot with Fincher and Bay.

On one commercial, Schwartzman met Jeremiah Chechik (*National Lampoon's Christmas Vacation*). They hit it off, and Checkik told him that he would shoot the next picture Chechik would direct. "True to his word, in 1991, the script for *Benny and Joon* arrived," says Schwartzman. "There was one hitch — the studio. I was from MTV, with no studio feature resume. Hell, I wasn't even in the Union yet! Fortunately, the film's producers (Susan Arnold and Donna Roth) fought for me."

Schwartzman was perfect for the job. Chechik wanted to widen the range of the film's aesthetics. "It was going to be quick and economic, but different," says Schwartzman. "Jeremiah didn't want the lighting to get in the actors's way, so there was rarely a lamp on the set.

"For all the day interiors, we created sources through the windows. Jeremiah would get together with the actors (Johnny Depp and Mary Stuart Masterson), and they would work out the scenes. We would play with the light as part of the character. We would put a window behind, or have them stand by it, be in silhouette. Basically, we used filmmaking as a graphic art, a very classic style for someone with the MTV moniker attached to him.

"It goes back to the exercise of lighting an egg on a white sweep — front cross, back cross, silhouette. In cinematography, you have choices. You use what is right for the tone of the picture."

The film was a huge break for John Schwartzman. He loved working with the actors, and he was able to build a tableau style of shooting that really caught everyone's eye. "The shoot went fabulous," he says. "We were so lucky. The weather was great. We had rain when we needed it, sun when we needed it. Because we were shooting in Washington State (Spokane), the sun didn't go down until a quarter to 10. We could do so much.

"The location was so close to where we were staying, we would ride bikes to work," he recalls. "Each morning and evening we passed this wonderful old 1902 carousel. I would see the light dancing off the water, something like 4,000 tungsten globes bouncing off the merry-go-round.

"There was one scene, between Mary Stuart, Johnny Depp, and Aidan Quinn, where we didn't have a location. So, I went to Jeremiah. What if we did it there? It was an extraordinary accident, and it made the scene.

"Gary Sheppard, our fabulous transportation coordinator, said to me 'enjoy this movie kid, because there aren't many like this one.'"

People have told John Schwartzman that this picture doesn't look like an American cinematographer shot it. It has a European sensibility, "whatever that is," he says. "Every time you shoot a film, you are trying to create an experience for the audience. You always have something in mind. You aren't there to shoot the pages, you are there to let the feelings you have come out. The work is all about going for that gut level.

"As a cinematographer, we only have ourselves to offer. That is what makes our work unique from each other.

"Sure, when you are doing projects like *Armageddon, The Rock,* or *Pearl Harbor*, there is a lot of preplanning. However, you still have to have the freedom to create and improvise on the day you are shooting. That's what our work is all about."

After *Benny and Joon*, Schwartzman went back to doing commercials. Then, one of his best friends, Michael Lehmann (Schwartzman shot second unit for him on *Heathers*) called. He was getting ready to do another movie and sent the script over. Originally, *Airheads* was to star Bill Murray and John Cusak. By the time they were ready to shoot, it was Brendan Fraiser and Joe Montagna. "A completely different take," he recalls.

"Still, it was all studio, and my chance to do something completely different from *Benny and Joon*. I would be working with greenbeds, would be able to prelight an entire stage on dimmers, and work with a huge set — 300-by-200 feet.

"This was going to be 'Old Hollywood.' On *Benny and Joon*, it was catch as catch can. Here, I could set the printer lights and work with a lab and better understand this part of the craft.

"At the time, I believed in the movie. I'd seen it work in my head, with the original actors and the original script. If the studio had let Michael keep the *Heathers* sensibility, this story of three morons who take over a radio station to get their heavy metal demo tape played would have worked. A rock-and-roll version of *Dog Day Afternoon*.

"Unfortunately, the studio and producers handcuffed Michael. They didn't allow him to keep the *Heathers* edge. It went through such a de-flavorizing wash that we had to fight, even to let the heavy metal players wear tattoos!"

Schwartzman, gaffer Dave Dubois, and operator Mitch Dubin tried to ignore all this. They concentrated on putting the best they could on the screen. "When you have a script you always believe could be a good movie and it doesn't pan out, it's a drag," Schwartzman says.

"However, you still have to give it your all. You work as hard on this as you do on any picture. You never go into a picture thinking it is going to be a failure because it is just as hard to make a bad movie as a good one."

So, they laid out the two layers of plywood and the linoleum. They planned their shots from room to room. "We did what *ER* is doing today, only eight years before," he says. "Soft compound tires on the dolly, a hybrid, blocking long moving shots, and trying to have fun. When we finished running through the 25 rooms, then we figured out the coverage! We were going for a *Rules of the Game* style."

Schwartzman's next challenge was, again, completely different. For *Pyromaniacs, a Love Story*, he left his crew behind and went to Canada. "It was exciting, thinking about meeting 40 new people and leading them down a path to make a movie. At that time, I needed something to shake up my life. This was it. It wasn't so much about what I was shooting but getting me out of my comfort zone."

The least of Schwartzman's problems on the picture came from the location. While he was used to having tools like the Musco lights, he found himself having to create things in Canada. "That is fun, sometimes," he says. "It was the old adage, 'don't tell me how to make the clock, tell me the time.' We made it work. I didn't do anything out of the ordinary on this movie."

When John Schwartzman returned to Los Angeles, he did what he usually did – commercials. He was determined not to make the mistake he did on *Airheads* – he would hold out. But, not long enough. "I was about to lose my health plan (commercials were non-union in those days) and my wife and I were going to have a baby," he says ruefully. "I rationalized. I needed the work, when Nick Castle called me to do *Mr. Wrong*.

"I should have known better!" he says, forcefully. "I love Ellen DeGeneres. Her show was great. She is a trooper. But, it was a major challenge every day, trying to make her look like a 29-year-old woman who wasn't married and looking to find Mr. Right. She had only a five-day break between her TV show and the start of filming.

"Still, having said that and admitting it is the worst-looking movie I've ever shot, I learned more about cinematography on this picture than I ever did. I really believe I am where I am today in my shooting because of what I had to do to solve the problems we faced.

"One of the other great things about this picture was that I've never seen more people work so hard to do something as pedestrian and work together to do it," he adds. "We all had to work our behinds off, on even the simplest-looking shots.

"For example, there is a scene where a car pulls up to a curb and Ellen gets out. She walks down the street. To do this simple shot, we had to hang a 60-by-60-foot solid over the street, off a construction crane. Then bring in brute arcs and everything else we could think of.

"Every shot became a ballet of grips, electric, lights, camera, everything. If someone walked through a room, we would have silks, blacks, negative fill on the floor. Hard work.

"None of my old music video or commercial tricks seemed to work on this movie, and all of the calls I had made in the past regarding sets or wardrobe, this time, just blew up in my face! I had to figure out how to get around all these problems.

"On my previous pictures, all my talent was basically kids and they didn't really have any facial problems that I had to be concerned with," he explains. "On *Mr. Wrong*, I had a mature woman who had just finished a grueling year on the number one television show. And, instead of a well-deserved summer break, she was embarking on a 50 of 51 shooting days project, and I had to deal with it.

"I always loved shooting in convertibles, because traditionally, you need less lighting. But, here, the open-air toplight created many problems. We had to rig huge solids over the moving car to remove toplight. Then we had to rekey from a movie-friendly angle.

"Boy, did I want to do another *Benny and Joon*."

Instead, two months later, Schwartsman's old friend Michael Bay asked him to do a new picture called *The Rock*. "It was a great script about the only man to ever break out of Alcatraz, breaking back in to fight off terrorists. With Sean Connery as the man, it was obviously James Bond. And, with Michael Bay as the kind of Director who would fight for the images, we would be able to 'go for it,' pulling out all the stops. After *Mr. Wrong*, this would be a great change of pace!"

To do this picture, John Schwartzman assembled a new crew. "Well, somewhat new," he says. "Mitch Dubin would operate A-camera. I already had Chris Haarhoff on Steadicam. Then came people like Les Tomita, Jim Dunford, and gaffer Andy Ryan. I had the best of Hollywood's grip and electric and I needed them!"

Reflecting back, Schwartzman admits they were a little out of control on this one. The idea was to appeal to the MTV generation. That meant fast, super-fast, impossibly fast in-your-face cuts and moves. At times, they were averaging 50 setups in a day and a half.

"We would turn the camera on and shoot the shit out of the shots! At one point, Technicolor called. We were shooting too much film 'We can't keep up with you guys,' they said.

"Michael and I had a shorthand from years of commercials and videos. It allowed us to move faster than the studio anticipated. We raised the bar for action movies several levels. It was not just about technique and flash, it was how everything came together.

"If you took the age of the DP and the director and added them together," he smiles, "it would be less than that of the lead actor! The advantage that Michael Bay and I had working together on *The Rock* and later pictures is that we both came of age working together, first in videos, then commercials, and finally features.

"One of our biggest struggles was convincing people who had been doing only features that we, in fact, knew what we were doing, and when we said we only need this, that was all we needed.

"Remember, by the time we started *The Rock*, we had shot probably a thousand days together. Very few feature Directors do that in a lifetime. And, our careers were just starting.

"The other person who needs to be mentioned is production designer Michael White, who came up with us on music videos and commercials," he adds. "The three of us had a solidarity of purpose and understanding of filmmaking born out of experience (over 2,200 shooting days between 1986 and the start of *The Rock*, like Bay and White). We were able to accomplish so much, because we only worried about what was inside the frame lines.

"It was our intention to give a familiar genre a new, young, fresh twist, putting the camera in what seemed to be harm's way.

"Again, the commercial world gave us an opportunity to play with tools that generally didn't find their way into features because they are too expensive to experiment with.

"This film was the first time the Fraiser lens system was ever used," he adds. "The sequence on the roof of the 'lower lighthouse' was done with it. This gave greater depth-of-field when Nick dives to grab the poison visual effects ball before it goes off the roof.

"We also used it in the car chase, to get the lens close to the action. We would put the camera safely behind a car and then bend the Frasier out into harm's way, without risking an operator's life."

Yes, it took a while for the industry to accept *The Rock*. But, once the audiences got their vision and their brains back in sync, everyone wanted to be the next Michael Bay/John Schwartzman team.

Schwartzman's next break came while he was waist deep in a water tank at Sony, feeling like he was in Mexico (running to the bathroom to be sick from what he was picking up in the water), and praying for the shoot to be over. "The call I got was from Richard Donner," he says. "John Scotty, the AD on *The Rock*, suggested that the legendary director meet with me for his new project."

The meeting was supposed to be for half an hour. Two hours later, John Schwartzman walked out of Donner's office past at least three DPs waiting to go in. "I called my agent, immediately," he laughs. "'If I don't get this job, I'll be really surprised.' It turns out that Dick and my father were really good friends. At first, I thought he wouldn't hire me because he remembered me as a five-year-old. I might remind him of his age. That wasn't the case. We clicked."

Barely 15 minutes after he left the studio and got home, the phone rang. "There was this booming voice on the other end. 'Kid, do you want to make a movie with me?' A week and a half later, I was on the Warner jet with Dick, Mel Gibson and Joel Silver, scouting locations for *The Conspiracy Theory*."

One of the first discussions the group had was film format. Schwartzman had worked in Super 35mm on *The Rock* because they felt there wasn't enough anamorphic gear available. "When I saw the movie, I was disappointed," he says. "The dailies looked better than the release print. Making the Super 35mm optical caused a loss of contrast and increased grain because the optical printer focuses grain. We wanted edgy and it wasn't as edgy as we could have had.

"When Dick said he wanted anamorphic, I thought that was fantastic. I hadn't shot a movie in scope before. I was really excited. What a great experience, anamorphic, New York and Dick Donner!"

Schwartzman was in heaven! Donner gave him total control over the visuals. The young cinematographer established a look to support the story of a paranoid man trying to come to terms with what was happening in the world and his life.

"I wanted to use reflections as a motif for the schizophrenic nature of Mel's character," he explains. "Also, reflections allow you to change the nature of things. By using selective focus, you can choose to see through a window or reflect what is across the street. The character never saw anything straight on, so playing off everything worked. The idea was to create a look like Sidney Fury did in *The Ipcress File*."

Ask John Schwartzman what shots epitomize the "look" of *The Conspiracy Theory*, and he will think for a moment, smile, then laugh a little. "Working with Dick Donner is fabulous," he says. "Once he trusts you, he lets you do anything you want, and even goes beyond the norm to get everyone else to let you.

"Dick allowed me to design the main title sequence," he adds. "Titles are often overlooked in their importance. They tell the audience what kind of movie they are seeing.

"There is a scene in the movie that looks so 'simple' on the screen and was a bear to do. We were probably the first — and most likely the last — film crew to ever do this type of shot in New York!"

In the story, Mel Gibson's character exits a Barnes and Noble and buys a hot dog. A wind comes up (courtesy of a Ritter fan), blowing the wrapping out of his hand. The camera follows, calling attention to the path of the paper. "We see the reflection of a black helicopter hovering and several men rappelling down from it in a storefront," Schwartzman explains. "The men disappear into the crowd. Because there is a Rap band playing in the street, we don't hear the noise."

For this minute-plus shot, Schwartzman never shows the helicopter itself. Just its reflection with Gibson in the foreground. "It took an incredible amount of light to hold Mel in that reflection," he says. "Not only were we using Union Square (which goes totally black at night), we were also shooting anamorphic. That effectively doubles the focal length."

To maintain the deep stop (4 to 4.5), Schwartzman used two Musco lights and additional lights. "We had to have the levels so bright that I had to retrain my eye for contrast. On the screen, however, it is just the right amount of dark.

"I have no idea how Dick Donner and Joel Silver got the city of New York to let us have a helicopter hover over the middle of the city! They also got them to shut down the 59th Street Bridge for a major chase sequence. Bet that won't happen again! That's what it is like, when you are working with a power like Dick Donner."

According to Schwartzman, Donner's "power" extends past the powers-that-be in New York. "One day, when we were shooting in Los Angeles, I lost my wallet," he laughs. "During the day, I grumbled to Dick Donner that I would have to stand in line at the DMV for a new one. He made one phone call, and before I knew it, there was a teamster to drive me to the DMV. I was ushered into the office like royalty, and less then ten minutes later, I had a new license! Ah, the power of Richard Donner!"

Of course, the use of that "power" and "energy" comes with major consequences when anyone is working on a Dick Donner film. "Couple that with Mel Gibson's sensibility, and everyone has to watch their backs!" he laughs. "Dick is the original bad boy. Give him an inch, and you are dead (in a good way, of course). No one is exempt from his way of keeping a tough shoot light — practical jokes."

You'd think the first day of shooting would have taught John Schwartzman to watch his back. Right. "We were on Riverside Drive (between 83rd and 92nd Streets). (Which Donner got closed to traffic, of course.) There must have been several dozen electricians using every light available in the city. We had Mel and Julia Roberts, 50 atmosphere cars, and a great crew.

"It was the last shot of the evening, and everyone was still fresh. An FBI car pulls up to the curb, the actors do their bit, and Dick yells, 'cut!' Then, he turned to me and says he thought we should do it again — the headlights weren't the right 'dimness.'"

Schwartzman's heart started beating fast. He didn't want to disappoint Dick Donner. What had he done wrong? "I had been knocking them down with spray. I gulped — the first shot, and I had made it go wrong. Then, I looked in Dick's eyes. There it was — that twinkle. Suddenly, the crew cracked up. I had fallen for one of his pranks! I was 'in.'"

Being "in" with Donner now meant watching his back. "You'd think I'd learn," he laughs. "When a crew starts a picture, Panavision will give out a certain amount of special — numbered — hats. The cinematographer always gets number one. Dick got number 20. He wanted number one.

"When we were well into the picture, it was my birthday, and we were really pushing it. Suddenly, Dick told one of the crew to take me into a near bar for a Cognac – on him. 'You'd better give me your cap, though,' Dick said to me. 'Those guys have been getting their fill of movie people — you don't want to advertise you're with this crew.'

"So, I took off my prized number one Panavision hat. And, I handed it to Dick. We had the drink, and I returned to the set, calmer and happier. Dick handed me my 'hat,' and we went back to work.

"It wasn't until weeks later, that I really looked at that cap. I now had number 12 — and Dick had the baseball cap he had coveted. I'd fallen for a Dick Donner prank, again."

John Schwartzman is extremely proud of the work he did on *The Conspiracy Theory*. "The story doesn't work, completely, but the motif we set — reflections — does. Wherever you look, the visuals play out in reflections – in water, sides of cars, mirrors. It was a wonderful exercise – in keeping up with Dick Donner, and keeping a consistency in theme."

So, how does Schwartzman follow this one? "Answering a call from Michael Bay, what else?" he laughs. "He said he had a 'summer movie' called *Armegeddon* to talk to me about. We met for lunch, and he told me it was 'an action film about an out-of-control comet about to collide with earth. To save the world, scientists need to implement a plan they were developing at NASA, a plan that didn't exist technologically.'

"His idea — fly a spaceship into the comet, land, and plant nuclear bombs that would split the comet in half! A pure Michael Bay concept! I knew we would be able to take the style we created on *The Rock* even a step farther."

While Schwartzman worked on the last stages of *The Conspiracy Theory*, Bay and his crew started to work on the clearances needed to get the cooperation of the United States government and NASA. "Michael likes to do what he can through the lens," Schwartzman says. "That meant taking our crews onto launch pads, with shuttles, and into the famous white room and the Orbiter Processing Facility."

The moment John Schwartzman finished *The Conspiracy Theory*, he embarked on the most expensive 'test' ever done. "We were going to use it in the movie so that really didn't count as prep!" he swears. Why the rush? NASA does only one night launch a year, and Bay wanted to get everything out of that launch he could.

"We had to know where to place the cameras and what to capture," Schwartzman explains. "The first step was to know the equipment, so my first assistant Richard Mosier worked with Panavision to find a way to tie the Panaflex cameras into the launch computers."

In total, the crew ran 13 cameras, everything from 1200mm anamorphic to 28mm and running between 24 to 120 frames. "We placed them about 150 yards from the launch, well within the restricted three-mile zone.

"We had to set them up 24 hours before launch. You should have seen the amount of cables and connectors, not to mention the time it took to hook up the software," he says. "To protect ourselves, we even brought in refurbished 65mm camera batteries for better voltage.

"The biggest nerve 'challenge' was — did we get it right? Once everything was in place, nothing could be touched or moved. The area went into 'lock down' until after the launch. Even NASA people can't go into that three-mile zone. We were a bit 'nervous.' Would the equipment stand up to the elements and perform after that time period? Would the shot be ruined by condensation on the lens?"

Everything worked for the day launch. The dry run gave them confidence. "Of course, we would have an added 'challenge' when we went back for the next launch. That one was at night."

Schwartzman had NASA's 40-10k Xenons to give him about 200 foot-candles of available light. "That was prelaunch," he says. "However, right after the burn starts the light goes from 200 foot-candles to 18,000! The rockets sent the levels up six stops!"

To do this, Schwartzman worked with NASA's hard data, allowing him to find the point where there would be 12,000 foot-candles and at what point there would be 9,000. He then looked at Red Huber's photos (The *Orlando Sentinel* photographer who shot stills of every launch). "This allowed me to see where he put his exposures," he explains. "By counting backwards, I could figure our f-stop and exposure."

NASA was amazed at the footage he captured. This opened the doors. Now, Bay, Schwartzman, and crew had "the run of the area."

Schwartzman's favorite shot (NASA area) is actually a recreation. Done in Florida, at the Kennedy firing room, which is the room that overlooks the launch pad, it is when the button is pressed to send the shuttle off. "I talked to the people who were in the room to get a sense of what a night launch looked like. Then, I recreated it. This was one place where we couldn't go for real."

The real room is huge. "No television screens, just large windows looking out at the pad, which is close to three miles away," he says.

"I rigged Condors with eight Dinos outside the windows and ten Lightning Strikes for launch fire. We couldn't use radios in the building. The signal might have interfered with the launch. So, we shouted down stairwells to the guy on the dimmer board," he adds. "It took 70,000 watts of Lightning Strikes power to simulate the launch light, by the way.

"As we left, one of the men that does this for real (they were in the shot on film), said he thought he was sitting in the middle of a real launch — we had really captured the reality."

NASA even allowed the crew into the Orbiter Processing Facility (where the shuttle is readied), which is a cross between an operating room and a hangar. "It was a challenge for lighting," he says. "Available light wasn't great – very little. Fortunately, our liaison talked them into allowing us to pre-rig the location.

"The challenge was being able to rig it so that we could do Michael's constantly moving shots. We had to do wide angle and up-close-and-personal on the shuttle being readied.

"We brought the Technocrane so close to the wing of the Orbiter that the guy in charge of security was a little nervous," he adds. "'Touch it, and I'm out of a job,' he'd told me. I didn't know that replacing one tile cost a million dollars!"

So, what does John Schwartzman do for an encore? "Take on a movie that was harder to shoot than *Armegeddon*," he laughs. "*EDTv* might have looked simple on the screen, but Ron Howard's version of making an every-man famous by putting his life on television was a major, and I mean major, challenge! Not only were we going to light for a shot, we would also have to light for two video cameras that fed images to a truck — that sent them to monitors in the shots!"

*EDTv* was the ultimate homage to the 'making of' movies. This was a return home, of sorts, for Schwartzman — after all, he did start with "video press kits." "Except, we were shooting film and video simultaneously," he says. "A film runthrough, change the lighting, then come back for video would be too time consuming and too costly. Everything had to work at the same time."

Schwartzman wanted to do video as video — rawness, iris changes, an unself-conscious, invisible, and texture so that the audience would be aware of the video. "We wanted to see the video operators in the shot, so the audience knew it was real, but they couldn't shoot the film equipment. To make this work, we needed video operators who could act, not actors who could learn video equipment."

Equipment was then a challenge. The video part was the first problem. "We thought about using the Sony Zero-Lux," he says. "But, they were designed to work without light. Put light in during the day and you can see through the women's clothes! Not for this kind of movie," he laughs. "We ended up using the Betacams with digital, extended clearscan hyperhad fronts and standard Beta backs.

*You can make something dramatic with simple lighting — if you try. As much as I enjoy the toys of today, what really gets me is when I walk on a set and there is a flag to flag off the shadow of the flag from the first flag. You know what I mean. At one point, it gets out of hand.*

*Dean Semler*

It's a beautiful California winter day — wet and cool. Dean Semler, A.S.C., stands in the living room of his Palisades Highlands house, enjoying the rain as it washes the Santa Monica Mountain range above. It is a pleasant change from perpetual sun. And, since he's not scheduled for an "Exterior - Sunny Day" shot, let the water wash away the smog. Although he enjoys this getaway high above the city, he is looking forward to a few weeks of escape — a return to his native Australia.

"We haven't been to our house in two years, I hope it's still standing," he jokes, as he strolls down the center hallway, nostalgically pointing to pictures on the wall. "We live several hundred yards off this beach at the end of a cul de sac," he explains, as he stops in front of a black-and-white photograph of the Australian shoreline. Beautiful houses dot the hills above a smooth white beach, leading to a sparkling ocean.

"It was a gorgeous day when I took that photo," he says with a smile. He points to two little specks in the otherwise placid water. "Perfect timing. There's a swimmer out enjoying the water. And, there's the shark that caught up with him a few minutes later and ate him," he adds with a straight face. He walks away from the photo, a twinkle in his eye. "And, if you believe that . . . ," he continues, a twinkle in his eye and a laugh in his voice.

Actually, his story explaining a few nicks in the beautiful photograph is a perfect reflection of Semler's sense of humor. His low-key, relaxed approach to his life and his work is evident. This is a man content with the direction both have taken, confident that, for the most part, the choices he has made have all moved him along the path he is destined to follow.

One of the few cinematographers in the business who has tackled a variety of genres, he has done everything from simple period pieces and complicated road pictures, out and out comedies involving challenging special effects and intense personal dramas, to pictures shot on the water or with pigs, bulls, horses, and other beasts. Despite that, he still follows the philosophy that less is more and simple is better.

Walk onto a Dean Semler set and two things strike you immediately — there is ease and quiet around the camera. And, there are as few lights exposing the story as possible.

Semler learned both these principles early in his career as a news photographer and, despite all the toys available, he still employs only what he has to and when absolutely necessary.

Born in a little country town called Renmark in South Australia, whose principle support came from growing wheat, fruit, and making wine, his father worked as a welder to support the family. "I joined the railways in 1960," he smiles, as he settles into a deep couch, glancing once more at the vivid cloud-filled sky outside a huge expanse of window. "My father felt it was safe and secure — a government job. I'd make a good living, and the family could travel anywhere in the country for free."

For a while that life was interesting. However, he wanted a taste of something different. When a Rupert Murdoch television station opened several hours from his home, he applied for a job. "And I got it!" he laughs. "Why, I have no idea to this day.

"Television was new," he says. "No one really knew what they were doing – it was a process of teaching yourself and each other as you went. There were so many possibilities."

Semler found himself watching everything that happened. "I spent the first year in the props department," he says. "Then, I jumped at an opportunity to operate a studio camera.

"I remember the first day I was going to do a live shot. I was so scared," he laughs. "I put my eye into the eyepiece and listened to the countdown. When the red light came on and the Director pointed to my camera, I froze. All I had to do was a super on a card advertising the 'two and six at Woolworth's.' What a rush! To this day, I still feel a sense of excitement every time I step on a stage or begin to shoot a film."

Three years of live television was a magnificent training ground for a young kid. "I consider myself very fortunate to be a part of the birth of the Australian television industry," he says.

While working in the studio, Semler used to watch the three news cameramen (Brian Bosisto, Pat McEwen, and Trevor Rose) come in at the end of each day. "They would be carrying their Bell and Howells and a few 100-foot rolls of black-and-white (16mm) film. There was something about it that fascinated me. I wanted to be one of them. I wanted to know more."

This inspired him to buy an 8mm camera and begin to make his own home movies. "Silly little documentaries," he smiles. "You know, things like 'a day in the autumn hills.' After a while, I put in a proposition to the bosses to let me do a film on the running of the studio. They agreed, and gave me a 16mm camera and 200 feet of film. Wow!" he laughs.

The studio must have liked what they saw, because at 20, Dean Semler was given a position as a news cameraman. "We were little one-man bands," he recalls. "We each had a tiny little mini-van that was bright blue with a fluorescent yellow NWS9 sign on the side and a blue flashing light on top. We thought we were the bees knees," he recalls, fondly. "It was great!"

Besides the obvious adventure and fun of the job, this became a great exercise in discipline for young cameramen. "Learning to tell a story on film, was a great lesson. I also took great pride in being able to edit the stories in the camera because the Bell and Howell had no flash frames. And cuts could be made while shooting.

"The other challenge, of course, was economic," he adds. "We had to be able to tell three news stories on a 100-foot roll."

From here, Semler joined the ABC affiliate in Sydney (1968), having had several wonderful years learning the trade in South Australia. "At the ABC station, I did a year of news, then another year of 'current affairs.' I was then offered a position at Film Australia, which was then the Commonwealth Film Unit. The chief cameraman there was Don McAlpine, A.S.C., I was now introduced to color and 35mm shooting.

"You may think that a government body run by public servants would not be the most exciting place to make movies, but in the nine years that followed, I had some of the most truly wonderful and rewarding film experiences of my life. It was a huge cross-section of filmmaking, from cinema shorts (15- to 25-minute movies) that were extremely visual to ethnographic filmmaking, working alongside anthropologists, both with the Australian Aborigines and the hills tribe people of New Guinea. They were unforgetable experiences.

"This was also where I shot my first drama," he adds. "This then led to my first feature called *Let the Balloon Go*. Boy, were we babes in the woods!"

While Semler was working for Film Australia, a commercial director approached him. He had seen one of the young cameraman's cinema shorts. "He asked if I would like to shoot a commercial with him on the weekend," he says. "I had nothing to lose, so I sneaked away from my government job, and shot a Mobil Oil spot.

"I remember riding back on the plane after the two-day shoot, and I was asked to invoice the company," he says. "So, I did. A hundred dollars a day for two days. When I looked at the check, they had paid me for a third day (a hold day), plus a travel day. I'd never earned money like that for such a short time."

After nine years at Film Australia, Semler decided to go freelance. One of his first independent jobs was second unit for Don McAlpine, who was shooting a feature called *The Earthling* with William Holden and Ricky Schroeder. "It was my first taste of Hollywood," he recalls. "I remember Don pulling me aside after my first dailies screening, and reprimanding me, in a nice way, because I had filmed scenic shots of Sydney, ones that I found fascinating and 'different.' But the producers wanted the 'big beautiful postcards.' I had failed to do that!

"However, I shot quite a few sequences with William Holden's double through the mountains, and dog attacks. I soon got the feeling and an understanding of what a second unit really does."

In 1980, he got a call from a Director by the name of George Miller and Producer Byron Kennedy (George's partner). "Evidently, they liked some of my documentary work," says Semler. "The last thing they wanted was a cinematographer who would say, 'I can't shoot that,'" he explains. "They wanted to get as much action as they could, as long as there was daylight. I think they were looking for 'the bold and the beautiful,'" he jokes.

Semler was anxious to meet with Miller and his partner. He was a fan of the first *Mad Max* film. "I don't know what I expected," he laughs. "I guess I thought I'd be meeting a couple of guys in jeans and T-shirts. You know, film types. Wrong. Their offices were in a very mainstream high rise. They both had suits on and George even wore a bow tie! I knew these guys were serious."

Semler and Miller clicked. He met with star Mel Gibson. And, before he knew it, he was in the thick of shooting *Mad Max 2* (released as *The Road Warrior*). "It was an incredible shoot," he recalls. "George taught me an enormous amount about shooting action. We did things like shoot at 22 frames-per-second, instead of 24 frames. This would put a little 'edge' on the movement.

"We also kept the camera moving and shaking, particularly during simulated travel. With George, you could never shake the camera too much. If you were 'timid,' he'd come along and shake the camera for you. Just a kick of his foot would do it!

"We had no video split during this shoot, so the bonding between operator and Director was very important — it was a knowing, an understanding.

"We shot from sunrise to sunset every day. We shot through sunrises and sunsets, overcast, bright sun, light rain, always aware but never letting the conditions control me. On this film, you never heard 'let's wait for the light.' We shot some wild and dangerous images.

"I remember one shot where I was laying over the front of a truck that Mel was driving. The road was very rough, and the camera mount was very primitive. It was a simple bungie cord holding a 2C Arri, which I was attempting to operate. The object was to get Mel in a mid-shot, driving as the bad guy, played by Vernan Wells, smashed through the window.

"I tried looking through the eyepiece, but the movement was so violent I had to stop because my eye was being cut. So, I closed it off and just aimed it in the direction of the action. And, I guaranteed George at the end of it that he had some exciting footage. I don't know how much, but he definitely had some.

"When we saw it in dailies, there was an enormous energy, created by the violent camera moves. It set the tone for the rest of the film."

For *Road Warrior*, Semler's key grip Graham Mardell 'invented' a crash camera to get into the action. "In Australia, there was a legendary bushranger by the name of Ned Kelly," he says. "He would wear a steel drum over his head and torso that protected his body, so bullets wouldn't get him. It had just a slit for his eyes so that he could see. We adapted this idea for a crash box. We put an Arri camera inside two torpedo-nose cones shaped like an egg.

"I then set the camera into a car tire. That way, I could adjust it like an egg in an eggcup. We would lock it off, cover it with bushes, and set it right in amongst the action.

"Years later in Canada," he adds, "I needed the same kind of shots for another picture. This time, I went to our producers and asked them to have a housing made for it. They came back with this incredible egg made out of pressed steel — about ten thousand dollars worth! It was an expensive Ned Kelly, but it worked great!"

Not long ago, Semler was setting up another adventurous shot. While deciding what kind of equipment to use, one of the crew suggested he get a "Ned Kelly." "Who knew, 14 years later, my torpedo-covered Arri would get such a reputation that American crews would want to use it?! An interesting way to memorialize an Australian bandit, wouldn't you say?"

One of Semler's favorite shots on *Road Warrior* is a long shot at dusk as Mel Gibson carries the cans of fuel up a ridge, with the compound lit up and active in the background. "The compound was all practical lights (250- and 500-watt photofloods)," he explains. "I lit Mel in the foreground with a mini-brute with half blue gel and full spun on the doors. Just the softest amount of fill, to bring out detail.

"It was high on a ridge, so I had a tiny little Honda 5k generator thumping away. Since there was no sound, we didn't have to worry about the noise."

Another classic shot, which became the poster, was of Mel Gibson standing in the middle of a roadway, as "we pushed in to Mel in his classic Mad Max pose," he explains. "It was a late afternoon shot, and I managed to hide a maxi-brute with half blue gel just off the side of the road in some bushes to give him a hard sidelight."

Semler never stopped shooting — even when he ran out of sunlight. On the last day of filming, the sun had gone down — and there was still one more shot to go. "We weren't about to keep the cast and crew for another day, so it was get it — or else," he says. "The shot was a wide shot with the tanker down below and the last of the marauders riding into the foreground, surveying the scene and riding out again.

"The only chance I had of pulling off the shot, as the sun had already set and we were in magic hour, was to pull out the fastest lens, which was an Ultraspeed (Panavision) T-1.1, and push the stock one stop.

"Fingers crossed (figuratively), we shot — and I trusted the stock and the lens and the lab. It must have worked, because the shot is in the movie!"

Long after it's release, *Road Warrior* is touted as the most copied film of the 1980s.

From *Road Warrior*, Dean Semler went on to shoot a period film called *Kitty and the Bagman*. "I am really proud of this picture," he comments. "The film was set in the 1920s – so there was electricity. It gave me great opportunities for lighting. We had wonderful sets, everything from prisons to nightclubs and period streets.

"In the nightclub interiors it is the first time I ever used the practicals on the tables to light the sets," he says. "I worked closely with the set-dressing people to give me practicals that worked both to light the actors and as props at the same time."

In 1983, Semler got a call from Director Russell Mulcahy. "He wanted me to shoot a film called *Razorback* — the story of a pig that terrorizes a town. He was looking for the boldness of *Road Warrior*," Semler explains.

"Russell was straight out of directing some of the most innovative music videos," he adds. "He had a real eye for visuals. And, I think we both stretched ourselves to the limits in shooting *Razorback*.

"Besides having to deal with animal viewpoints and movements, I had great opportunities to do some creative lighting," he adds. "I remember having a 16-foot diameter moon made up for a night desert scene. The grips set it, and I had it frontlit with one 5k, with half CTO. It was ready to go for a shot to be done in the wee hours of the morning.

"Well, by the time we got to it, the real moon had risen behind it. So, I was now faced with a shot with two moons in it. He didn't want to take his down, and I wasn't going to take mine down. So, they are both in the movie!" he smiles.

Semler says that *Razorback* is one of his favorite films. "There was a scene in a courtroom, for example. I put one arc light blasting through the window. It gave the room a great contrast, lighting one side and keeping the other darker. By adding a blind to the window, and a wind machine to the blind, it created a very dramatic shadow effect — and the arc light was cut on and off of the faces inside the courtroom.

"An effect that came out of sheer accident, I guess, was used in lighting a dry creek bed at night," he adds. "The bed was filled with dead trees. Spooky dead trees. And my gaffer, Johnny Morton, had an arc on a Condor. He was lowering it down when I noticed the shadows stretching across the creek bed. What a great effect.

"So, we used it with Gregory Harrison laying in the foreground. It added some menacing feel to the shot.

"You can make something dramatic with simple lighting — if you try. As much as I enjoy the toys of today, what really gets me is when I walk on a set and there is a flag to flag off the shadow of the flag from the first flag. You know what I mean. At one point, it gets out of hand."

Semler spent the best part of a year working on some high-quality television programs for Kennedy/Miller in Australia. At the same time, the producers were developing the next in the *Mad Max* series.

"Now, not only did we have to top the success of the first film, we had to top ourselves," he says. "More action. More valleys, canyons, and mountains. More massive interiors. More of everything.

"We were fortunate that Production Designer Graham 'Grace' Walker was as creative as he was," Semler says. "He could turn 16 beer cans, two rubbish bins, and a mudguard from a car into something fantastic."

"*Thunderdome* was rich with characters," he recalls. "There was one shot where a wonderful old actor by the name of Frank Thring, who played The Collector — a large man with white pasty skin — is sitting on his throne.

"We were shooting in the location which is now the Olympic stadium, and I had a hot spot on his head at least four stops over. I sent the gaffer up to check the overhead light, and Frank looked down at me, his face sweating. 'Come f... art!' he said. 'Let's just get on with it shall we?'"

From there, Semler went on to shoot *The Coca Cola Kid*, the story of a salesman from Atlanta, Georgia, who brings the product to Australia. "It was pretty straight on," he comments.

Shortly after he teamed up with Director Joe Sargent for *Passion Flower*. "It was a movie-of-the-week set in steamy Singapore. In Australia, television movies were shot in 16mm, because of the PAL system. This was my first experience in shooting 35mm for drama for television."

Semler really enjoyed *Passion Flower*, not only because he was shooting another period piece, but also because the locations were so lush. "And, Joe Sargent was incredible," he adds. "There is something about Joe, he's so damned fast. And, that's not because he drinks coffee all day! He is fast and good. Scenes that I thought impossible to do — period, Singapore, tourists everywhere — would be wrapped by 3:00 P.M. He is a wonderful planner.

For Dean Semler, one of the memories that really stands out from this film deals with "product placement." "Singapore Airlines was part of the deal," he recalls. "They wanted to show off their new high-top jumbo jet. And, I had to find a way to show it off.

"The airport runway was large, and there was a wonderful access road parallel to it. Flowers and trees bordered it. I got this idea to track with the plane as it landed, through the trees and flowers.

"The problem was – there were no insert vehicles in Singapore. And, there were no large American cars, like a big Cadillac, available either. So, we had to settle for a BMW!

"We took the trunk off and the 2C was mounted in the back. I operated. My focus puller got in with me. And, Mervyn McLachlan, my key grip, drove. And, off we went. The jumbo lands at about 170 miles an hour and immediately begins to slow down. We 'tried' to keep up. I was concentrating on keeping the plane in frame and staying as tight as I could on the zoom.

"I managed to stay all the way in at 250mm for a short period. The trees and flowers were whipping by. It was fantastic. Finally, we came to a stop. I jumped out, excited. 'How fast were we going?' I asked. 'About 200 clicks,' I was told. We had hit about 120 or 130 miles an hour.

"Suddenly, our silent excitement was broken by this RRRRRRRing and SCREECHing. . . Up came our 'police escort' on their little Kawasaki bikes. We'd gone so fast, we'd out run our police escort!"

Now, Dean Semler became known for another kind of shot. More commercial shots — for speed and motion. "I got a call from a man named Jim Money — a Director for a company called Challenges Accepted. He wanted to do a commercial for GM. It would be a traveling shot as the hero car drives toward us at 40 miles an hour, a reveal of the interior, to see that there is no driver. But, also showing all the luxuries of the inside of the car. And, the car driving away from us in the end. All, in a 57-second continuous move spot.

"We cut a hole in the roof of the car," he explains. "That went over really big with GM! The location was a dry lake bed.

"We had the Louma crane mounted on the back of a pickup truck. The key grip (Graham Mardell) guided the camera through the hole in the roof with two inches to spare on either side, traveling at speed over rough ground.

"We had the driver set the car on a straight course, I got on the operating controls, using the Louma crane video (which was really bad), with my head in a black bag.

"'I can barely see the car,' I said. 'I see it. I think I see it. I see the highlights. I think I can find the hole in the roof. I found it!'

"The crew was so excited that they got the shot, no one yelled 'Cut!' If we weren't on a dry lake bed, it probably would have gone off the side of a mountain!" he laughs. "The commercial was so successful and unique that Louma put it on their show reel. In fact, I think it might still be there today!"

Semler went from shooting on a dry lake bed, to shooting on real water – with more than a few complications. *Dead Calm*, starring Sam Neill and a young Nicole Kidman, was his first feature with Phillip Noyce directing — and one of his most interesting experiences.

"Think about one boat on calm water, the camera on the shore. Add a second boat on the water, and keep them both in their relative positions. Now, add a third boat. And, try to maintain their positions, fighting currents and wind. Now, really complicate it and put the camera on the water as well. That was *Dead Calm!*"

Fortunately, production found an area in Australia, called Hamilton Island – a honeymoon resort of sorts – that sported calm water and beautiful horizons. "Still, we often had three different call sheets for each day," he says. "There was the one that gave us optimum shooting on calm water in good weather. One for bad weather, another for storm sequences. And, one when it was too dangerous to go out. So, we would go into the studio for cover."

The studio had a tank big enough to hold one of the boats. "No water, just on hydraulics," he recalls. "Funny, I could be out in choppy water and nothing bothered me. Put me inside on the hydraulic boat, and I would start to get a little seasick!" he laughs.

Semler recently looked at a copy of *Dead Calm*, and still smiles at the little continuity difference he finds in one of the most challenging shots. "This was the scene where Nicole is on the radio talking to her husband," he recalls. "It was a huge emotional scene. She was really working hard. We were tight on a 180mm anamorphic lens — not much depth of field. Not only was the boat moving, so was she. That didn't leave much of a margin for error in focus.

"I started shooting the scene at f2.8/4 and found that we were finding difficulty keeping focus," he explains. "So, I said to Nicki, I'm going to pour a lot more light in, you okay? She said yes. I lit the shot up to f16.

"Now you will see in the cut, the different size of the pupils in her eyes — from the earlier takes at 2.8 wide open to the cuts at f16. They are tiny black dots. I notice them every time, although most people wouldn't."

Semler's next adventure was a John Milius project in the jungles of Borneo. "People would say how did you cope with the jungle and swamp and heat and mosquitoes and snakes?

"What swamps?" he laughs. "We were at a five-star hotel. We drove down a paved road. Then, we jumped off and we were on location.

"There are a few shots that really stand out in my mind," he says. "One was the night sequence of the Japanese invasion. I had brought Brute arcs and tungsten Maxi-Brutes (at no simple effort) to bounce into a 30-by-30 frame we had made for us. My idea was to shoot a mixture of tungsten and daylight into the cloth to get the right color without using a gel.

"We had a beautiful soft bounce about two stops under. With great effort. Guys had to lay cable through the mud. We had to struggle to get the brute arcs in.

"Then, John Milius showed up. 'What's this? Too much light.' He wanted them off! What was I going to do? So, I had the props guys mount military flares on 20-foot poles and run behind the camera. Sometimes, simpler is easier!"

That same year, Semler got to fulfill every young boy's fantasy. "Dirt, hats, horses, gunfights, and an incredible cast," he says. "*Young Guns* was a dream. It was my first taste of New Mexico, and a wonderful challenge. I really enjoyed Director Christopher Cain's vision, and saw many opportunities for drama, emotional and visual, on this picture."

Despite the small sets and challenging locations, Semler continued to keep his lighting as simple as possible. "Often, it was one light through a window," he says.

Semler has a bone to pick with people who make Westerns. He learned something very important on this picture. "Everything is dirty," he says. "That is the Western environment. However, most people don't take that into account. Watch a Western. The guy gets off his horse and there is still a crease in his pants. He comes off a dirty trail and goes into a saloon for a drink. Take a look at that glass after he pounds it on the counter. Do you see the dirt of the trail on it? That's not real."

*Young Guns* was fun. A lot was going on. "How could you not enjoy this?" he says. "I remember one day when this scruffy young guy came up and gave me a big hug. I looked down. He was — well — a cowboy. It was Tom Cruise. I asked him what he was doing there. 'Emilio's going to shoot me today,' he says. Take a look at one of the showdowns. That's Tom Cruise as one of the fallen victims. Emilio Estavez was a good buddy. He'd invited Tom to New Mexico for the day. See, everyone wants to do a Western! How can you not enjoy yourself!"

Semler went from one Western to another. When he finished *Young Guns*, his friend Simon Wincer was starting a television mini-series called *Lonesome Dove*. "I don't know why people advise against feature cameramen doing television work," he says.

"I had a lot of opposition to shooting *Lonesome Dove*. They think if you are shooting television, you are never going to get a feature again. That's bloody ridiculous. You are still shooting. This project got me into the DGA (he directed as well as shot second unit), and allowed me to work with some incredible actors."

It also allowed people to see how Semler worked — quickly and economically. After doing a lot of pictorial material, he was given work with the principal actors.

"The day I was to shoot with Robert Duvall, I planned everything carefully, as always. I got to the location, and the first AD said Duvall was in a foul mood. That's just what I needed. It seems that he thought he had the day off. He didn't find out he was working, on the second unit no less, until someone informed him at 11:00 P.M. the evening before.

"When he turned up on the set, he was a real pussy cat. He was great. I had him in and out in a matter of an hour, in three very simple shots. He couldn't believe he was finished!

"*Lonesome Dove* was a wonderful picture to work on," he adds. "It was kind of ironic, as well. Here we were two Australians, filming an American classic. Director Simon Wincer was great. And, I learned a lot about planning and about how Hollywood works."

Dean Semler was being introduced to everything about making movies in America. *K-9*, the cop and dog adventure introduced him to another phenomenon, the animal handler. "Karl Miller was incredible," he says. "Production had built in safety contingencies in case something went wrong with the dog. But, we didn't need it.

"As long was the crew was respectful, didn't talk to the animal or distract him, it went great. There were no problems working with the animal. In fact, I introduced Karl Miller to George Miller later on. And that was the beginnings of *Babe*. I had worked with George on the *Babe* screenplay and it seemed Karl would be the ideal man to talk to if animals were involved."

Where Semler did learn his lessons was on the locations. A man from the make-do with what you have and don't spend a lot of money school, he faced a challenge on a dark landing strip where a semi-truck is to meet a helicopter. "It was a big area to light," he recalls. "I was reluctant to spend money. I went to Jim Brubaker, Production Manager, asking if we could bring in a couple of Condors. We couldn't light from the ground.

"'Get a Musco,' he said to me. 'You need two?' I shook my head. Too expensive. 'Not really,' he came back. 'Think of the cable, the crew, and the time. 'It's cheaper to get it in fast and go,' Jim told me.

"That was a good lesson. There have been times when I've tried to save money and it has backfired. He was right. Sometimes, it is better to spend the money and get the shot than try not to and waste the time."

Late in 1980, Dean Semler got the call that was to kick his career in an unbelievably different direction. "You never know what can happen when you meet someone on a project," says Semler. "It was on *K-9* that I met Chuck Gordon. He had done *Field of Dreams*, and when Kevin Costner was looking for someone to do his next project, and I think Chuck recommended me.

"Kevin liked what I had done on *Dead Calm* and other projects, and sent me the script from *Dances with Wolves*. I thought the project was phenomenal, and a big thing for Kevin to take on.

"I think, what he was looking for was a cameraman who could be there with him at the end. To be there, emotionally. He knew he was going off a big diving board no one had dived off before."

Semler admits that *Dances with Wolves* was a difficult shoot. The conditions were a challenge. Since it didn't get dark until late in the evening, the hours were long. "I remember grumbling to myself about having to drive to location at 5:30 A.M. Then, I got out there, and saw the sun coming up over the prairie and all the buffalo coming through. I would have gotten up at 3:00 A.M. to see that!

"Kevin was indeed a strong Director. He was careful and sure and knew exactly what he wanted," Semler says, strongly. "And, above all, he was incredibly generous with his acting experience in guiding the American actors."

Ask Semler what the quintessential shot is from this Academy Award winning picture, and he is very sure. It is a late afternoon shot where Kevin Costner and a group of Indians are riding toward camera. "We pan to reveal Graham Greene in the foreground, racking focus to him. This emphasized a wonderful emotion in the character," he says.

"Shots like these rely heavily on one member of the team – the focus puller," he adds. "And, we had one of the best in the business. Lee Blasingame was phenomenal. He would place horse droppings on the ground for marks, because we couldn't use sandbags and regular marks. They would be in the shot. He needed references at certain distances to give the horse riders more freedom. This way, they wouldn't have to hit a precise mark.

"He heard I was doing another picture. This time, *The Power of One* in Africa. He asked me if he could, no he begged me to let him go along. I asked why. 'I'll get bigger marks,' he said, deadpan!" Semler interjects with a laugh.

Despite the logistics, Semler found *Dances with Wolves* a simple project to shoot. The less-is-more theory really prevailed. He was able to find the right light at the right time of day, and use it to the best of his ability thanks to Kevin Costner's trust in his judgment.

"I remember one of the shots that stays in a lot of people's memories," he continues. "It was a night shot of Kevin dancing around the fire. We wanted to see him, the fire, the fort in the background and the prairies stretching off to the horizon. By placing the Musco off to one side, I was able to highlight the fort and the prairies, but not an overall moonlit wash. Rather, I used the Musco to spot certain sections and let others go dark. This gave more modeling to the shot. I then used the firelight only to highlight Kevin."

One of the most difficult and more than a little dangerous sequences in *Dances with Wolves* was the buffalo stampede. "Kevin wanted to create something not seen for a hundred years, a real stampede — guns blazing, Indians chasing," he says.

"We had about three to four thousand buffalo for several days. Now, they are territorial animals. They know they are supposed to be somewhere at certain times of the year. The valley where we had driven them was not where they were supposed to be. So, they were restless already. Add the trucks and equipment and people — it was something.

"On the day of the shoot, Kevin's Producer and close friend, Jim Wilson, was in a helicopter, hanging back, having just driven the buffalo over the ridge that fed them down to our cameras. We had nine cameras rigged — including the old Ned Kelly — and here the people came, riding bareback, guns blazing, hanging on by just the muscles in their upper legs. Kevin in the middle of it.

"He wanted to do this shot himself," Semler continues. "No stunt doubles. This way he had the experience but more, there was no question that this is Kevin Costner in the middle of the herd. It enabled us to get in so close, using a 1000mm or 1200mm lens.

"Suddenly, Kevin gets hit by another horse and comes off. All Jim Wilson could hear was 'he's down.' Norman Howe, Kevin's stunt double, rode into the herd and checked him out. Kevin immediately got back on his horse and we continued shooting."

Of course, in addition to the footage Jim Muro got on Steadicam, Dean Semler had to get into *Mad Max* mode. Next thing people knew, there he was strapped down on the back of a pickup, handheld camera near the ground — shooting hooves and dirt flying at the lens. "I wasn't going to let the others have all the fun," he smiles. "My key grip Bear Paul created what we called the 'scrotum' camera. A camera in a brown sack that I could hold close to ground and get incredible shots."

Semler went right on to other projects — shooting a Western comedy called *City Slickers* and a wish-filled drama called *The Power of One*.

"Working with John Avildsen on *The Power of One* in Africa and Zimbabwe was a very different but also enjoyable experience," he says. "John is a former cinematographer and was head of the camera local in New York. He knows cameras and lighting intimately. He is a master of running multiple cameras.

"We could be inside, on a character at a desk. He could place cameras where you would have no idea there were multiple cameras on the shot. It was a matter of position. Move a painting up, a vase to the left, even move the set around — and suddenly, several cameras had optimum location for multiple coverage."

During rehearsals Avildsen would go out with the actors and shoot the picture, including coverage, on high 8, and then edit it in the evenings. This would enable him to see the movie before he even shot it.

There were a few bumps in the road on *The Power of One* that caused Dean Semler a little concern. "One interesting piece of creativity happened out of necessity," he recalls. "We were on a location called Fothergill Island. We needed a shot of the Armin Mueller-Stahl character and the young boy, taking a donkey and cart across the plains with wildlife behind.

"The problem was — it was a quarantine country. We couldn't get the donkey in! 'No big deal,' I said. Make a cardboard cutout of the donkey and put it on the cart in silhouette. Walk the two past the cutout, and have the big elephants (including the king with huge tusks) in the background.

"It still looked phony. So, we hooked a tail to the 'donkey' and had a props man hiding behind it, pulling the tail with a string. It looked great — except the poor prop guy was terrified. He was dangerously close to the elephants!"

The end of *The Power of One* was a challenge for Semler. With a Director who was master of fight scenes (Avildsen learned on the *Rocky* pictures), he knew the big confrontation would be something. "Five cameras looking 180, wide, superwide, tight and whatever else. Shoot several takes, move around to the other 180, and repeat the choreography. No big deal," he smiles.

"Now, the lighting. I thought we would do it with firelight. Since, it was supposed to be an African village. Then, the effects guy from Britain had an idea. He came in with this 'canon fire' that shot 15 feet in the air. I got excited. I would have loved to use it. However, it wasn't going to work. The fire blazed so hot we couldn't control it or flag it. And, anything that got close was in danger of being burned. So, the old standby worked — flicker boxes around the ring. Simple, right?"

Of course, when Semler finished the project, it wasn't really finished. "I'd gone back to Australia for a rest," he recalls, "when John called. 'Come over and shoot a sunset,' he said. 'All the way to Africa?' I asked. This was Hollywood, they wanted their cinematographer to finish the picture.

"A few days later, I got a call from the production people asking what I needed. I told them a camera out of London, an assistant. They wanted to know why I couldn't use one out of Nairobi. I said I wanted to make sure it worked and we'd get what we wanted. Then, there was the principals, wardrobe.

"I didn't hear for a week. Then, John called. 'Well, mate, we're going to shoot in Los Angeles. After all, this is where the actors live. You want to come over?' Sure, I said.

"So, I arrive, and we go to the location, which was to substitute for Africa, in Palos Verdes. 'Where is the sun going to set?' John asked. 'I did a fair calculation, and measured. 'About here,' I said. 'No, I want to know exactly where,' he came back. John Avildsen is a stickler for exact measurements, you know. He wasn't satisfied with 'about here,' so he hired an engineer who plotted it out — exactly.

"We put three marks in the ground. The grips then built a ramp off the peninsula so that the actors could walk into the sunset.

"Comes the day of the shoot, and the actors walked the 100 foot flat path. I'm behind the camera. The sun is going down — it's going down — whoops! It's over the center of the platform — and still got a long way to go! It's going to miss! I managed to slide the camera over and get the actors to walk a diagonal and get the last 35 seconds of the sun.

"Before we left, John saw this little interesting road, and had the actors walk down it.

"You aren't going to believe this — but, John was just getting into the digital mode. And, I'll be darned — all that work for the real sunset ended up on the cutting room floor! He used the little road and a digital sunset – he liked the 'look' better! He could create the exact sunset he wanted and digital trees and sky and . . . "

In this same period of time, Semler did a completely different project. "Cowboys and comedy — an interesting combination. Put Billy Crystal and a great cast into it, and call it *City Slickers*," he says.

"We had a great pro in the cast — Jack Palance," he adds. "We could be out in the hot New Mexico desert, the sun blazing. Just before the word 'Action,' he would tilt his head back and lift his eyes up and let the sun hit his face. Not a blink out of him. This is a professional actor who learned through the Hollywood system. He knows that camera and lighting are his friend."

Semler really learned to respect an actor's creativity one day on the set of *City Slickers*. "I know, they are all talented," he says. "But, sometimes I just don't know how they can pull off their performances.

"We had this one scene we called 'best and worst day,' where the three lead actors are on horses, riding down a dry creek bed, telling their best and worst. It was four to five pages of dialog. Behind them, the rest of the cast, chuck wagon with a cook, and 150 head of cattle.

"In front of them, in the narrow creek bed, the Shotmaker running on batteries for sound, Steadicam, lights on the back of the Shotmaker, the Director with video, assistants, sound and stills, grips, lighting. Maybe a total of a ten people. Not to mention wranglers walking with the Shotmaker, holding the horses' reins because they were literally touching the car.

"Then, behind, a thousand feet of cable to the generator, because the batteries on the car weren't enough for the two 4k HMIs we shot through frames for the hats — and then 30 students pulling all the cable back to the generator. Despite all this, the actors gave a consistent performance, take after take! That's something else!"

While Dean Semler was shooting *City Slickers*, rumors began to circulate about the Academy Award for *Dances with Wolves*. "It was a wonderful experience, and I loved receiving it," he says. "But the impact really didn't sink in until I was back in Australia, scouting a location sometime later. I stopped at a station for petrol, and when I went to pay, the guy refused. 'Not you, mate. This one's on us. We are so proud of what you did for our country.'

"Later on, I was scouting in the outback and stopped at a cattle station ranch. It was late in the day, just about time for that incredible red sunset, when the manager's three sons returned. You know, the tall, lanky, hard working guys with dust on their faces. When they took their hats off, the white band of clean skin showed.

"They invited me up on the verandah for a beer. 'You're the bloke that did that picture dancing with wolves, aren't you? I got a bone to pick with you.'

"It was the first time ever someone had something bad to say. It seems that they'd seen it at a small theater, and one of the boys had a criticism. 'Those buffalo — they were wearing ear tags, weren't they?' he said, looking at his other brothers. 'Yes, they were.' I said. He gave his brothers a smug look. 'There ya are. Told ya.'

"Oh, well, if that was the only criticism!" Semler laughs.

Semler went on to a very different project – a period piece in real locations with opulent costumes and floppy hats – and magnificent sets by Wolfgang Kroeger. "One of the main challenges of *Three Musketeers* was working in historical buildings that we had to protect," he says. "Some of the sequences were done at the Hinterbruel, where the Germans developed the V2 rocket during WWII. It is a series of tunnels beneath the earth, about five-feet to six-feet high and maybe four-feet wide leading into open caves and underground waterways. Lit, basically, with real firelight, provided by special effects."

In 1994, Semler signed on to do another adventure, with one of the stars of *Three Musketeers* in the lead. This time, Kiefer Sutherland was joined by Woody Harrelson in a fish-out-of-water story. "Shooting horses racing down the main streets of modern day New York City at night was interesting for *The Cowboy Way*," Semler says.

"We wanted to try to shoot everything with available light, but horses absorb the light and cars reflect it," he says. "A little tricky. I used the new Kodak 5298 and pushed it to 1000 ASA. Even so, I needed to bring in other light sources for the horses. Cars have headlights — horses don't."

For Dean Semler, the most fun of shooting this picture was working in the train tunnels below Manhattan. "I got to drive the train," he says, like a kid in a candy store. "For 20 minutes, I was doing what my father thought I would do for a living! Only, instead of Australia, I was driving it through the tunnels in Manhattan!"

From there, Dean Semler went on to one of the biggest pictures he's ever done — another Kevin Costner project, "that I felt was *Road Warrior* on water," he says about *Waterworld*. "When we first discussed the project, I said to Chuck Gordon that we should double the schedule, whatever time it would take on land — double it."

In reality, the project took 166 days to shoot. "Not bad, after all, we were in Hawaii for six months. A great place for a location!"

For Semler, the biggest challenge was shooting the hero trimaran. "This was three narrow pontoons and the rest was trampoline," he explains. "Whenever we were to shoot on it, we would have to crisscross specially designed platforms, not only for walking but for laying down track or hooking up lights.

"Each morning, Kevin Reynolds would take us through the scene and work out where the camera was going to go. It would generally be Steadicam — operated so admirably by Mark O'Kane. Then came the job of laying the platforms across the boat or along the edges of the boat for the camera to move on or lights to be locked down on. We would go out to sea and hope that the weather was in our favor.

"I had only 100 degrees of horizon, so we were constantly fighting the sun. In the morning we would have frontlight with green/blue water, midday we had the sun directly overhead with dark water, and later in the afternoon the sun reflected in the water like silver.

"I tried to compensate with a light barge of 4k PARs and 12k HMIs, bringing it in as close as possible. However, the barge would drift with the currents and the wind and it became unreliable to light this way. So, all I could do was place the Hydroflex 1,200 watt PARs on the trimaran and, bring them as close as necessary to the actors.

"They were designed for underwater, but I had to use them because of the constant sea spray. It was a challenge and a big jump from a 12,000 watt HMI to a 1,200 watt HMI but it seemed to work."

In 1999, Dean Semler teamed with Phillip Noyce again. This time, to bring the best-selling book, *The Bone Collector*, to the screen. "After a lot of film tests, we finally end up with Fuji 8571 (500 ASA)," he says.

"It was hard, shooting Denzel Washington flat on his back in bed for five to six weeks," he explains. "As most people know, the most difficult lighting job on a person is when they are lying down. Add to that, the dark face and the light sheets, and, well it was something."

Another challenge for Semler was the need to show time ticking away visually. The story is all about trying to beat the clock. "Phillip was a stickler for time on this," he explains. "It wasn't just sunrise, it was five minutes before sunrise or five minutes after.

"So I had to try to create a time of day on the set to within minutes. This proved extremely difficult, as the stage in Canada (Montreal) that we had, the set built on was quite small — for what we really needed. The set was a good size, but there was very little room outside for the models of the New York buildings that were up to 25- or 30-feet high. And, the cyc that ran behind it. Also, we had trouble getting light into the windows at the right angle, without hitting the models.

"We also had to have indications of the life outside the windows," he adds. "When we were using the scaled down set, for example, Bear Paul would make up little cardboard silhouettes like a 'vicar' pacing in one window. Or, we would have a 'Mrs. McCallister' in her apartment window having tea. We even had little chimneystacks with smoke. Life outside the windows to help create the illusion.

"On several occasions, we used blue screen outside the windows. And, there were plate shots used, particularly when we were looking down so that we could see vehicles in the street. I think it all blends pretty well."

In the year 2000, two Dean Semler projects will be released. *D-Tox*, a thriller starring Sly Stallone, is about a cop whose fiancee is murdered and he falls apart and tries to commit suicide. He is convinced to check himself into a detox center in the middle of the Wyoming plains in winter, run by an ex-cop played by Kris Kristofferson. Here, he finds that the killer is among them.

"The biggest problem was the five weeks of nights in blizzards," he adds. "I used the new Kodak 77. It worked great — both in the stark snow conditions as well as in the monochromatic interiors of the detox center where no primary colors existed, neither in the sets or wardrobe. But it still picked up the hues of the subtle colors."

As Dean  Semler relaxes back and looks at the sun peeking over the hills after the day's rain ends, he sighs. He'll be home in a few days, after a few more pick-ups for his last project. "*Nutty Professor 2: The Klumps* introduced me to a whole new way of shooting," he says with a smile. "I have enormous respect for Eddie Murphy playing his multi-character roles and also for those geniuses that do special effects, like John Farhat who did this picture.

"We have come a long way since the days of simple effects. Putting five Eddie Murphy's into a shot is easily possible, thanks to the technology of today.

"We had to adapt to a whole new way of shooting on this picture," he explains. "We would come in at our morning call and prepare like hell. While Eddie was in makeup (it took three to six hours to put the prosthetics and costumes on), we would be setting lights and readying the cameras. We would then see dailies and have lunch and come back ready for Eddie.

"Once we had him, we would do everything we could with that one character in that one day. If it meant having two or three mini-sets ready on that same stage, we would have them prepared. This is the only way we could work — given the amount of time and effort it took to get Eddie in and out of his brilliant but complex makeup."

Dean Semler settles back and thinks about the difficult shoot he's just finished and smiles. "It's going to be great to get home for a few weeks," he says. "I want to see the house and the beach and everything. I wonder how different it will be."

When Semler comes back to the States, he will be preparing for a sexy romantic comedy called *The Breakers*, with Sigorney Weaver and Jennifer Love Hewitt, and Gene Hackman

Semler has done action, romance, drama, and comedy — virtually every style of film imaginable.. "The last thing I want is to be pigeon-holed. I love all the different genres. And, after all, isn't variety the spice of life."

*The language of any particular film is determined by all the decisions and choices made from the time the first word goes on the paper, to the screening of the answer print. The cinematography is an important part of the language. Photographing a movie means understanding that particular language.*

*Dante Spinotti*

It was a bold move, but in 1998, Dante Spinotti, A.S.C., bought a house in the Santa Monica area of California. The kids, his treasured motorcycle, some of his wife's favorite furnishings, all have arrived. Although they visit their ancestral home in Italy as often as possible, the work is in the States. He wanted his family with him. The demands of the movie industry have finally made California their second home.

Originally from Tolmezzo (Udine) in northern Italy, Spinotti had to travel to Milan to find a way to participate in any area of filmmaking he could find. "At the time I got interested in the world of filmmaking, about the only type of work in Milan was television movies, documentaries, and travel logs," he explains, as he paces the hardwood floor of his new home. Outside the back window is a quiet yard, with a little guesthouse, which will be constantly occupied, as family from Italy comes to share his new adventure.

"My father gave me a camera when I was ten. I caught the magic of the darkroom," he explains. "I started developing pictures myself under my bed, closing the windows. That went on for a long time.

"I really liked taking still photos. Soon, I became the soccer team's official photographer. At 12, I knew where the main action was and how to capture it on film."

Soon, the locals began praising his work and the very young still photographer had a one-person show.

"My family really didn't know what to do with me," he admits. "I wasn't very interested in studying Greek or Latin. None of the traditional careers seemed to be for me. I started going to the local theater with a friend. What I saw on the screen sparked my interest."

It was quite evident, young Dante wasn't going to "conform." "So, they sent me to an uncle who was in Nairobi, Kenya," he says. His uncle was a Director/cinematographer with East African Film Services. "I was barely there three months when he gave me a movie camera. 'Why don't you go and cover Jomo Kenyatta's release from prison for UPI,' he told me.

"I soon found myself in the Kenyan countryside. We traveled by night, got where we were going in the morning. There were a lot of other photographers around, most of them English and veterans.

"I was 18, and thought I knew something. I was soon fighting the crowds, shooting with an Eyemo 35mm spring load black-and-white newsreel camera. When the material was sent to London's main UPI office, the response was, 'they are a little repetitious,' Nevertheless, the coverage was bought."

Dante Spinotti was finally a working photographer. Over the next few years, he helped his uncle do projects like the East African Safari as a boom operator, painter, driver, P.A., and cameraman.

Moving into motion picture photography was a natural progression. At the time, Italian filmmaking in Milan relied on short contract jobs. "Mostly television projects, and a few commercials," he explains. "I came back from Kenya because things were slowing down there due to the coming independence in the country."

Spinotti began doing anything he could to learn the craft. "One of the good things about working in the television industry in Italy in the late seventies was that it was state-owned. You couldn't be fired. This allowed me to experiment and even make mistakes without fear."

He began working on historical and cultural projects, documentaries, and features for television. In 1980, he went freelance and moved to Rome. "There were different projects available, but I consciously tried to chase quality stuff. I wanted to make little movies with a story that meant something."

Spinotti's first picture was Sergio Citti's *Ill Minestrone.* "We needed to conserve every penny, so we shot it in 16mm as a three-hour television story. We cut a regular feature out of the material and enlarged it to 35mm.

"The beginning was tough, as a freelance beginner in the Italian film industry," he adds. "The hardest part was to do work that could be seen and recognized."

It was Italian Producer Dino DeLaurentis scouting for new blood who brought Spinotti to the attention of the American filmmaking scene. "He was looking for technicians around the world, mostly Italy and England," Spinotti recalls. "He wanted to stay away from the 'mainstream' film makers for his new North Carolina facility. He thought bringing key personnel in from out of the country would keep the material fresh and help in training locals."

In 1986, DeLaurentis paired Spinotti with a hot new young Director by the name of Michael Mann. The story was called *Manhunter.* "Actually, Dino wanted me to do a project called *Tai Pan,* and even sent me to Italy to meet with the Director," he comments. "However, the Director thought I was too inexperienced to do such a big project. So, Michael Mann's *Manhunter* was my next project. It was a really dark story about a serial killer."

From the first day of prep, Spinotti realized making movies in America with a Director like Michael Mann was completely different than working in Italy. Although he did projects with top Directors back in his home country, there was a slower go-with-the-flow attitude. "Production in Europe was smaller," Spinotti comments. "The crews were limited to 40 or 60 people. American projects were three times as big. Just the logistics were an organizing problem.

"In America, there was a lot of preparation. Visualizing, pre-rigging, and pre-lighting were the key. Michael knew exactly what he wanted and how to use cameras. He would, at times, want different speeds in each camera, giving the editor a way to put the elements together in a strong and emotional way."

It is difficult for Dante Spinotti to pick one shot from *Manhunter*. It is more about sequences and the elements that made them work. "I remember one shot where we were running down small roads through heavy vegetation," says Spinotti. At the end, the idea was to capture the police as they rush at the camera. It was a scene where the 7th Cavalry arrived.

"Michael and I were in the trunk of a running car with two cameras. It was the middle of the night. We had no idea where we were going. For lighting, all we had were the headlights of the car and a few lights inside. We needed to get shots of Bill Peterson and Dennis Farina, so the hero car was running a few feet away from our feet.

"We wanted a kind of energy and punch, so we shot from the back of the car, using the sharp curves in the road. It was a big scene, and really gave the audience the feeling of a 'punch in the stomach.'

"Cinematic language is fundamental to moviemaking," says Spinotti. "You have to have an open mind and be willing to work endless hours and deal with difficult logistics. But, it is worth it."

Spinotti's next project was completely opposite *Manhunter*. *Crimes of the Heart* starred Sissy Spacek, Jessica Lange, and Diane Keaton. "It was an eight-week shoot, difficult because of location and because we wanted to pay extremely close attention to our actors. We had three wonderful ladies — the first time I was dealing with major female stars.

"The house was another character in the story. Ken Adam designed it. He constructed a house on the location, not on stage but inside a real town. Director Bruce Beresford created small drawings to document each day's setup, showing us the charm, drama and romance in the life of these three Southern ladies.

"Ken allowed for our challenges by giving us walls that could be cut, stairs that could be moved, and a lot of windows where we could get light in. It was charming and very real.

"I remember one scene where we were to shoot Jessica Lange and Sam Shephard returning from a night at the river. We needed to capture them arriving at the house in the morning sun. Jessica gets out of the car and Sam picks her up and carries her inside.

"We were hoping to shoot early in the morning, about 7:00 A.M. or maybe, 7:30 A.M.," he continues. "I wanted the beautiful sunlight through the trees to show the ex-lovers coming back after spending the night together.

"Unfortunately, we weren't able to get the shots at the optimum time because Jessica was then nursing her two-month-old baby. So, we added a little kick by wetting down the area and using as much of the sun as we had at about 10:30 in the morning."

Although Spinotti did several fairly successful projects after *Crimes of the Heart*, the film that he feels was one of the turning points in his career was *Beaches*. It was a major studio project, with major stars, and a Director Spinotti fell in love with.

"I was just back from shooting a commercial in Dallas, and I was enjoying a little of the California wine. Okay, I was drunk (a little)," he laughs. "At some point, my agent unexpectedly called. The head of production wanted to see me at the studio."

Does Dante Spinotti remember what the conversation was about? He says he doesn't. Pretends he was too drunk to care. But, it really is bravado. He's Italian. It takes a lot to get a strong Italian drunk. "Whatever I said, they liked me," he adds. "And I was to go to work right away.

"The first thing we did was some tests on Bette Midler. This didn't go well. She showed me some work that she liked. I saw a lot of light on her face. I wasn't thrilled with what she showed me."

In her straightforward manner, Bette Midler told Spinotti she didn't like what she looked like. So, "I bought myself a Kodak book on 'how to light a beautiful lady,'" he smiles. "It took a $1.50 to show me how to make her look great."

Beauty lighting is one of the most difficult cinematic tools. There is a fine line between camouflaging the flaws and making things look so unreal no one will buy what they see. "*Beaches* had several challenges, besides lighting Bette and Barbara Hershey," he says.

"There were times when the actresses wore hats. Other times, when they were on the beach. And, times when it was hats and beach and water. Then, there was the challenge of keeping Barbara fascinating and still showing that she was dying.

"At times, the costumes didn't work with the location," he adds. "They would look great in overcast weather, but . . . So, I asked first AD Benjamin Rosenberg to ask Barbara to wear his sweater. It really worked against the gray of the beach and the blue/green of the ocean."

For Spinotti, one of the most enjoyable parts of making this movie was working with Director Garry Marshall. "When you work together with a group of people for three or four months, it becomes a part of life, of a group of humanity.

"Having a Director who cares for his people is wonderful. It becomes a creative family. After a while, I even began to enjoy his good-natured barbs, as he maintained I couldn't speak English. He would counter my broken English with his trademark mumbling.

"Garry had strong rules," he adds. "'Dante, the faces aren't lit enough,' he would say. In the moments of comedy, he wanted to see things."

It is a completely different approach from his next Director and project. "Paul Schrader wanted to make Venice look dangerous and Byzantine," Spinotti recalls, as he thinks back on the first days of production on *The Comfort of Strangers*. "That was going to be a challenge to focus the look of Venice into one of it's less known characteristics. We needed to keep it that way, even when it was not.

"The other challenge was our visual interpretation of the story itself. Taken from a Harold Pinter play, the story leans toward what I find most interesting in projects, people and their way of making it through this life they are given. And, getting into the dark side of that life."

To bring the waters and the character of Venice into the complex emotional value of the picture, Schrader chose locations carefully. "We then found ways to enhance the emotions and the danger, by how and where we placed the camera," he explains.

"I remember one scene where we were introducing our hero couple (Natasha Richardson and Rupert Everett), as they go out to dinner. Instead of doing the ordinary, putting the camera at eye-level or in the normal position, I suggested water-level seen from inside the canal and from a boat would be more interesting.

"Especially, when we went under a bridge that opened the scene. At that point, we reveal the other side of the canal. At the other end, we put a lot of smoke and backlit it with deep yellow light, reflected in the canal.

"To make the shot, we created a plastic box that allowed us to put the camera literally one inch higher than the water. As the camera looks down the canal, we can see the danger level of it, the Byzantine images in it and the characters' weird relationship to it."

Spinotti enjoyed shooting in Italy, but by this time (1990), he was much in demand in the States. Director Herb Ross was the next one to nab him to come to America and, this time, do a political drama exploring the corruption in politics.

"*True Colors* was interesting," he comments carefully. "The story was typical of two friends who take different roads. They eventually were facing off. What I enjoyed most was the intensity and method of Ross's approach. The film was filled with a political feeling.

"We wanted sharp and pale at the same time. John Cusack's eyes had to be strong. His intensity complete.

"There was a scene at the pool, where John is waiting for his best friend's wife," he continues. "He is laying on the diving board, with the camera overhead looking down. I had two underwater HMIs under the flat board at water-level, giving the shot a green glow. Then, two sidelights to rake his body. She reaches him at the pool, and the whole scene is lit from the pool with the underwater green gelled HMIs, which delivered a wonderful sensuality."

In 1990, Michael Mann offered Spinotti a film called *The Last of the Mohicans*, a mythical historical/adventure/romance. "It was set in a late 1700s and early 1800s landscape, nature, and a wonderful script," he says. But, the production was long delayed, and Director Garry Marshall gave him the opportunity to join the Cinematographer's Union in Los Angeles.

By 1991, he was in the enviable position of being caught in a bidding war between Directors. Marshall really liked his casual but specific approach to lighting and called him to do a picture titled *Frankie and Johnny*. Later, Michael Mann wanted him to do the now active *The Last of the Mohicans*.

"Garry Marshall and I were really getting along, and I had promised to do yet another project with him, when Michael called me back," says Spinotti. "I had no choice but to turn him down."

But, as is normal in the industry, things changed. Spinotti found himself, at the end of *Frankie and Johnny*, available, and after four weeks with another cinematographer, Mann made the offer for *Mohicans* once again.

"This time I jumped at it," Spinotti recalls. "It was a chance to do candlelight and bonfires. The period was simplified and strong. Everything had to be surreal and powerful to render the period.

"There was a scene where Hawkeye walks into the fort to meet his love," Spinotti says. "In the middle of the siege by the French army, we wanted to see these lovers. To enhance the bonfires, we simply put Dino lights through diffusion, far away. It gave us the extra kick and made Michael's long lenses really gritty and strong.

"There is also a scene where they are in the infirmary," he recalls. "There is a clear exchange of love looks between the two characters. It is a dramatic situation, where he is talking to her as she works on a patient. As he walks in front of her, he looks at her with the camera staying with him.

"He is now in profile and she is right in the middle of the shot, in a very specific place. She can't be looking anywhere but at him. You can't escape the face and the expression of a woman falling in love.

"This is one of the things that I like about working with Michael Mann," Spinotti continues. "He is a master of a very unique and strong cinematic language. He is always deep into the material and the intensity of making films, a master of the sequence of emotions. He knows exactly where all the ups and downs are in a story and the specific camera compositions.

"There is a final scene in *Mohicans* that takes place on the ledge of a cliff," Spinotti continues. "The ledge was in North Carolina. The young Mohican backs to the end of a black rock, just before he is going to die, killed by Magua's famed knife. Michael shot low-angle, with a slow Steadicam moving along the rock's edge. The slow move of the dark rock in foreground renders the moment suspenseful and intense when we got to the very edge of the precipice."

The teamwork between Mann and Spinotti was quite evident to the motion picture industry in the States and abroad. In 1993, Spinotti won the British Academy Award and was nominated for the A.S.C. Award for *The Last of the Mohicans.*

From *Mohicans*, Spinotti did another project in Italy and then, in 1994-95, he signed on to do a Michael Apted film and a classic Western, with a twist, directed by Sam Raimi. All were character-driven psychological stories, with a different edge to each.

"When I was working with Michael Apted and we began discussing *Blink*, for example, I realized that this was a story told from a woman's point of view. This woman (Madeline Stowe), blind in the beginning, regains her eyesight after a bad accident." Stowe was an important element in the project, so important that she spoke to Apted about using Spinotti as the cinematographer. It was her feeling that he would bring a certain look to the most stunning element of the story, the look and feel of a woman regaining her sight in her late 20s.

"Many of these shots were from her point of view," explains Spinotti. "Does she or doesn't she see the murder?

"The idea was to make the eye (cornea) the 'camera.' To do that, we needed the eye to be the lens of the camera. Clairmont designed a set of lenses for us. They had a single element (later called 'Blurtars') that limited the sharpness of what the lens saw.

"We created a soft side and sharp middle. By adding distortion filters on the left and right as well as the top and bottom (in the matte box), we could control the distortion in motion. We sometimes used the slant lens to add distorted vision to the shots."

Spinotti did a second film with Michael Apted that year. *Nell*, starring Jodie Foster, was completely different. "It had a strong story set in the forrest of North Carolina," he recalls. "Jodie wanted us to shoot in 1.85 to achieve intimacy and naturalism, but I thought the anamorphic would really tell the story. Michael wanted to include the landscape and the dimensions of the location in many shots."

Spinotti was undeterred. He remembers waking up at 2:00 A.M. one morning, determined to find a way to convince Foster to go anamorphic. "I'd seen a movie in a small Arizona theater a month before," he recalls. "It was a small screen, and the picture was grainy and gray. My fear was that this would happen to us. I wrote her two pages of notes and convinced her anamorphic was the way to go."

Not too long after, Spinotti teamed with yet another different Director. Sam Raimi's *The Quick and the Dead* was their tribute to the Sergio Leone Westerns. "Sam would story board each shot in a precise way," Spinotti recalls. "It really helped eliminate cuts and gave us reference to really dig into the characters.

"Production designer Patricia von Brandenstein gave us an incredible set (the Western town), allowing me to create atmosphere, such as inside a saloon, where all we had was candles and lanterns with a gray and overcast exterior. Because of our work together, I was able to put lights in to allow me to show Sharon Stone's eyes, bright and alive, in the dim locations."

Late in 1995, Dante Spinotti and Michael Mann re-teamed for one of the year's most talked about pictures, the pairing of Robert DeNiro, Al Pacino, and Val Kilmer in a real-life story set against the backdrop of Los Angeles. The film featured over 100 locations, and mostly night shooting. "For *Heat*, Michael Mann used every tool imaginable, from visual effects to color, set design, costume, and editing to enhance the story shot in the anamorphic format," he says.

Because of the variety of tools, as well as the way Mann worked with actors, allowing them to move within a shot, it was always more important for Spinotti to light a whole scene rather than a specific shot. The big robbery was multiple cameras, and the final fight at the airport was so complex it necessitated extensive interaction and cooperation with airport personnel and the various airline companies.

"This was planned carefully. One of the most complex sequences was the armored car robbery," Spinotti recalls. The scene starts with a truck rolling under freeways and hitting the armored car in the middle of the street. Mann and Spinotti refined their approach during a full rehearsal, which included crashing trucks and other pieces of reality. It was eventually shot in a single take, with 18 cameras.

The logistics were some of the most difficult Spinotti and the team had ever faced. It took long conversations in preproduction to lay out camera positions. "We even had two full rehearsals before we started to shoot the crash.

"Michael gets really involved with everything," Spinotti continues. "Before we could run even one of the 18 cameras, we walked through our paces several times. Michael then reviewed them again during the rehearsal."

Because the crew was not allowed to mount equipment on the actual freeway (in Los Angeles), the grips built a platform in the "V" of two off ramps. "We put a camera and crew up there, then added a little camouflage."

Mann also placed cameras below roadlevel, "in storm drains," Spinotti laughs. "They provided great low shots as the action came over the screen."

In reality, this was not the most challenging shot in *Heat*. "I don't think the company has ever taken on as big a shot as the final chase at LAX," Spinotti comments. "We began by following two of our characters across the runway. To do this, we used a huge section of airport near the hangars.

"One of our first challenges was to balance the sodium vapor lights," he explains. "We used Dinos (on dimmers) with CTS gels (all the Dinos and 9-light Maxis available in California, at the time). And it gave us just enough backlight for the three cameras."

The final fight required the cooperation of airport personnel. Michael Mann's reputation and determination had won. Airport authorities allowed the biggest lighting setup ever attempted on an approachway of a working airport. It took 26 Dinos on three different dimmer boards to accomplish the basic lighting.

"We rigged them on Western dollies, shrouded by tents so that the lights wouldn't blind incoming planes and control towers," Spinotti explains. "We would keep the Dinos on the far side of the runway, always shooting across the landing, away from incoming planes."

Mann decided to cover the scene with long lens ECUs and Steadicam moves. This allowed Spinotti to control the Dinos with the dimmer boards as the cameras made their moves. He could shut lights off when they were in the shot and turn them on when they went out of the shot.

Originally, Mann wanted to cover the scene with special runway lights that were created for the shot. However, when he saw the test on the real runway lights, he realized they could green screen them in where they had to be seen.

"It was easier to photograph DeNiro with motion-control equipment and, after the scene was edited, go back to the airport to shoot the plates of the approach lights at their full intensity," Spinotti explains.

In late 1996 and early 1997, Spinotti took on two other U.S. projects for a small company called New Regency. *L.A. Confidential*, with Curtis Hanson directing, was completely different from the quirky *Goodbye Lover*, directed by Roland Jaffe.

Did Spinotti know that *L.A. Confidential* was going to get so much attention, including the A.S.C. and Oscar nomination for 1998 as well as the British Society of Cinematographers and Los Angeles Film Critics Award?

"They were both small and interesting projects," says Spinotti. "I really liked the two Directors and saw very different possibilities for each picture."

One of the most important lures for Spinotti was the way this young company viewed the involvement of the cinematographer. "They are much more cooperative and supportive," he explains.

*L.A. Confidential* was, on the outside, a very moody piece. "It has a 'what you see isn't what you get' quality," he explains. "The film is set in the 1950s, a time that might appear to be innocent, but is really brutal and corrupt. It is this brutality that will destroy the city.

"To show this, we had to set up a visual dichotomy," he explains. "We created a seemingly beautiful world, bringing back the Los Angeles that is busting to be 'the' city. In the opening, for example, we wanted to give the audience things to think about. We presented hookers as movie stars, and showed the corruption below the surface of glamour.

"Curtis suggested production designer Jeannine Oppewall and I look at Robert Frank's stills," he adds. "Frank had a style that captured the Los Angeles of the period that we were going to create. His photos were intellectual, evocative, real but poetic. He had a dry approach that really focused on storytelling.

"What I saw showed me the camera style that would fit this picture. He dutched the angles slightly in order to wipe away the reality of the situation. He would direct the audience's mind into his reality. He could tell the audience what he wanted them to look at, focusing on precise elements only."

To do this, Spinotti chose Super 35mm (giving him the ability to use spherical lenses) but still release the print in an anamorphic ratio. "This way, we could use the spherical lenses to give the film a more photographic look. We could carry a deep focus and keep the still photography quality as a reference."

Spinotti has a few favorite "still photograph" shots, from *L.A. Confidential*. "There is a scene where several young men are being interrogated by a young policeman." Spinotti wanted to involve both the police officer and the suspects in the same "photograph." "So, I worked with production design to use two-way mirrors in the interrogation room," he explains.

"By choreographing two scenes (the one inside the room and the one outside, where other officers are watching), we could see one scene through the mirror and the other reflected in the mirror at the same time. The challenge was to find camera angles that kept the different levels equal in the shot. We also had to compose all the shots for inside the room, and be able to move the mirrors on gimbals to keep proper light levels for balance in each shot.

"One of the things that helped was giving the two-way mirror a more equal ratio between transparent and reflective side. "The higher ratio (60) was on the viewing side, instead of reflective," he explains.

"By adding Kinoflo lights to the practicals outside the room, on the reflective side, we achieved a better balance, with the inside usually lit by a single practical bulb.

Another of his favorite sequences was one that was chosen for "lack of light." In recreating the old Victory Motel, production built a slightly sleazy location that was in a hilly hideaway, but close enough so the dirty cops could use their "interrogation techniques," without being caught.

"We chose a location where there were old oil pumps," Spinotti recalls. "The mechanical movement added to the mystery. The tension was even higher, as we played movement of the character to the street, against a single oil pump and single street light.

"We then composed the shot so that when the cars rush down to the end of the street, the white headlights and red roof played against a single street light."

The lack of light heightened the tension. "When two of our guys go into the building to hide from the bad guys, they close the windows, even put mattresses against them, to protect themselves.

"That was blackness. I still had to get light in, and still keep the feeling."

To do this, Spinotti used a depression in the earth outside the motel to put a Condor with one 20k-source light. Production design added a high street lamp with tungsten light in another corner of the building.

"We then had shots fired — giving special effects the chance to blast little holes in the walls. This let just enough light in to see patterns of light (enhanced by more dust). Just the right amount (even underexposed), to just see the actors."

When the "good guys" and the "bad guys" get outside, Hanson used a Western confrontation look, substituting police cars for horses. "We started tight on the landscape. We then see a street lamp on a wooden pole and the lone oil rig — then widen to show the movement of the rig and we see headlights appear over the crest as the big red lights of the police car come into view, creating small clouds."

By putting PAR lights on a Condor out of frame, Spinotti was able to emphasize the car lights. He still kept camera straight at the horizon, then used a dimmer to raise the backlight as the car approached. By adding dust as an accent, he had the classic silhouette for a "showdown."

*Goodbye, Lover*, on the other hand, might be set in Los Angeles as well, but that was about the only thing these two New Regency films had in common. "I was going to turn the project down, even though I enjoyed the script," Spinotti recalls. "I needed a break. Then I met Roland Joffe, and I had no choice. His energy and love for the business was infectious.

"We were on the same page from the moment we began. Both of us wanted to expose the elements of the amoral/moral side of this city with as much energy as possible. That meant camera movement. A lot of it."

One of the ways to do this was to carry the Technocrane for the whole shoot. This enabled Spinotti and crew to use the three-way head to dutch many of the angles and even do whole scenes in one shot. "This allowed different angles, especially on the actors' faces."

Again, what you see is not always what you get was a prevalent element of this production. Instead of using the camera to focus the audience's attention on elements, he often used colors to depict the mood and the nuances of a sequence.

"The church was yellow and gold and blue," he explains. "Patricia Arquette's apartment was white and yellow and orange. We used colors to emphasize the dialogue and story development."

When Spinotti and Joffe began discussing this dark comedy, the idea was to start each shot with a visual twist. The opening, for example, begins in a church, as the choir sings in the main part of the building. Hidden from the worshipers, in the small organ loft, Don Johnson and Patricia Arquette are making love.

That included adding a little "God's light," via a window at the top of the church location's alter. "We could open it a little and bounce the light off a 45-degree wall we painted white," he explains. "By putting HMI PAR lights outside, we had the surreal 'God's light,' needed, coming from the sky."

For a broader part of the sequence, Spinotti had a six-by-six frame designed to carry vertical blinds. By directing the light through the frame and creating the angle with the blinds, he was able to control the light to his advantage.

Once the lovers decide to join the congregation, Joffe and Spinotti wanted to keep the quirkiness moving. That's where the Technocrane helped. "Originally, we were going to use it to carry Don and Patricia down the aisle, collection plate in hand," he says.

That was too "normal," so Joffe upped the anti. "Now, the shot was to start on the plate, widen and arm out to the front of Don and Patricia, as they walked side by side. Halfway down the aisle, we had the arm swing the camera up, directly over, then behind the two actors.

"It then arched across and over the worshiper's heads, settling in the middle of the center aisle, looking at the front of the church. Complicated, but viable because of the Technocrane. It had a wonderful color progression and enhancement, moving into bright red and white."

Spinotti finally took some time off, after these two back-to-back pictures. He finally decided to move his family to Los Angeles. Within weeks, he received his green card and an invitation to join the American Society of Cinematographers — and both an A.S.C. and Academy Award nomination for *L.A. Confidential.* The Curtis Hanson movie went on to gather other awards, including the Los Angeles Film Critic's Best Cinematography Award and the British Society of Cinematographers as well.

Barely settled into his Santa Monica house, Spinotti got another call from Director Garry Marshall to shoot *The Other Sister,* a challenging comedy starring Diane Keaton. "Some of the most charming shots in the picture follow Giovanni Ribisi (the retarded love interest of Juliette Lewis's also retarded character) in his travels across America to reach her in San Francisco," says Spinotti.

"All of these shots were done near Van Nuys Airport in Los Angeles," he says. "In one, Giovanni walks away from a lonely deserted gas station (probably located in some Midwest plains) at dusk and asks for a lift on the nearby road.

"We did this with one single handheld shot, taking Giovanni from the rundown gas station in the middle of nowhere, lit by a single fluorescent tube against the background of faraway hills and a wonderful nostalgic pink- gray orange sky. The truck that picked him up on the road had a light box on top, controlled by a dimmer that was hung off an off-camera Condor.

"As the shot was being executed, special effects personnel were rigging a different situation behind us," he adds. "The camera would be looking down over a street lamp into a snowy street.

"This street was to be lit by the street lamp, with snow flakes picking up the glow of the light. Giovanni, again, was trying to get a lift from another car.

"We had a second camera covering his expressions from the ground level. This carried a tight, long lens, keeping the romantic snowflakes falling around him. A few yards away, another set was being prepared. This time, with heavy rain falling.

"That's the magic of cinema — a long dramatic trip, told in six shots, made within a limited area."

As soon as Dante Spinotti finished shooting *The Other Sister*, he began a scout for the long "Untitled Michael Mann project" that eventually took on the title of *The Insider*.

"This is a movie that relied on strong dramatic storytelling through very exact atmosphere," says Spinotti about the movie that tackled the indictment of the tobacco industry. "No frills. No action. Everything was focused into bringing tension and intimacy of camera to the faces. The environment, costume design, every detail was selected by Michael Mann to dig deep into the drama visually."

Spinotti and Mann tested light angles, intent on making the faces provocative and intimately intense rather than pleasing to the eye. This meant using the full potential of the film latitude, and, in some cases, manipulating the practical sources (like in hotel rooms and houses) as the only light in the scene.

"Michael called this 'pseudo cinema verite,'" says Spinotti. "One of the first lighting setups was with Lowell Bergman (Al Pacino) and Jeffrey Wigand (Russell Crowe). It happens in the hall of a big old hotel in Louisville, Kentucky. It was built in the early 1900s, with heavy, rich decoration, stairways and columns. Bergman is waiting, sitting on a leather chair at the base of a column.

"The camera starts a slow panoramic shot, tight on a golden leaf decoration on the top of a second column, looking down wide on Pacino.

"We had a four-by-four mirror hidden somewhere, reflecting two strong low sun effects, hitting the floor at the base of the column and touching the lower half of Pacino's face from a three-quarter rear angle. Two 4k HMI PARS were actually hitting the mirror. We had two more 4k PARS creating another sun effect on the higher part of the hall.

"The ceiling of the hall delivered a small amount of fill light, to give the ambient shadow information. We then put tungsten KinoFlo single tubes, hidden behind the counters, lighting the activity around the hotel reception area. Pacino's face is lit only by the bounce of the newspaper he is holding.

"We had hot kicks on the marble floor, created by brightly over-illuminated faraway corridors. The scene is dark, suspended, crisp, very tense for the two main characters when they first meet."

Dante Spinotti has come to believe that each movie speaks a specific language. It is as if one film speaks Spanish, another English, another Italian. "The language of any particular film is determined by all the decisions and choices made from the time the first word goes on the paper, to the screening of the answer print.

"The cinematography is an important part of the language. Photographing a movie means understanding that particular language."

Not long after finishing *The Insider* (which won him both an A.S.C. and Academy Award nomination for best cinematography), Dante Spinotti found himself wandering the streets of Pittsburgh, on a lonely Saturday night. He was about to photograph his next project, *The Wonder Boys*, starring Michael Douglas. The story is a Dante-esque experience (i.e, *The Divine Comedy*) of a man trying to find and answer to his life struggles. "And, I had no idea of how to photograph it!" Spinotti admits.

Spinotti went to a local Cineplex to see *The Wizard of Oz*. After the picture, he bought another ticket and literally theater-hopped for an hour or two, taking a look at five movies. "I found that the perfectly lit and composed shots left me with little emotions," he says. "I now knew that I was going to break those rules on this picture."

Spinotti and gaffer Jay Fortune designed a new style of strip lights that could be used on location. They would deliver a harsher, more directional, and wrapping quality. He then talked with Director Curtis Hansen about shooting the project handheld. "There is a scene where professor Grady Trip (Douglas) has to take his preferred student out of the classroom down into the street, to be taken away by the police for some misbehavior. He then engages the woman he loves (Frances McDormand) in a dramatically funny conversation.

"A finely operated handheld camera under torrential rain really adds tension to the shot," he says. "The sequence brings the audience closer, as if witnessing the event on the street with the film's characters. We added little or no light to the actors or the rain. I felt that the close relationship between the actors and the camera really rendered the soul of the scene in a pseudo neorealistic way."

There was a flip side to this style of shooting on *The Wonder Boys*. The city of Pittsburgh had a major role in the story, as a city with a very successful past in steel and coal — a past that is long gone, and so is the heart of the city. It mirrors Grad's search for identity. "To show this, we set up a series of five car sequences that, throughout the picture, happen at night and dusk.

"We decided to shoot them on stage."

Spinotti loved the idea of bringing the stunning urban landscapes, some industrial and some river, some with imposing steel mills, into the car windows. "We started shooting plates at 6- or 12-frames per second to make the nocturnal landscape really glow," Spinotti explains.

"Shooting on stage also presented the Director and actors the advantage of working away from the prohibitive climate and weather conditions in Pittsburgh's winter.

"It was a joy to put this material together at Cinesite, the Kodak special effects facility. Matching and playing with the exterior lights on stage (and adding snow or wetness even digitally to the car windows) rendered these scenes very believable and the stage lighting very controllable for the proper effect.

"We are beginning to witness a change in technology, affecting the way films are made," he adds. "These changes will affect the intimate language of filmmaking. Again, interpreting the language of the project in view of these technological potentials is the challenge that cinematographers will face in these very next years."

*There is reality, and there is film reality. . . . To get the real look, you have to reinterpret it. If you take the light off a painting — say it was about a woman sitting alone in the restaurant — and try to keep the same feeling of loneliness, you can't use the same frame. The painting isn't widescreen. So, you have to get the feeling in the 1:85 wide screen format.*

*Ueli Steiger*

It's a warm California winter day and Ueli Steiger is enjoying a rarity these days, a little downtime between film projects. His hardest decision is, at the moment, does he stay in Los Angeles and work on a few creative projects for his house in Silverlake or take a fast trip to his place in Switzerland. The warm winter weather is enticing but so is the crisp snow and clear cold air halfway around the world.

Unlike most Californians, Steiger doesn't run from the "real cold" of winter. Wearing several layers of clothes to combat the chill in Zurich is natural — a lot more natural than the multilayers of insulation he had to wear when he guided the complicated winter night shoots in New York for *Godzilla*.

"Shooting on the streets of New York is always invigorating," he admits. "But, that's work. You can't play like you can on the slopes in my native Switzerland. There is something about the weather, the terrain, and the people that keeps drawing me back, so I can gather more energy to work."

Born and raised in Zurich, Ueli Steiger wasn't your average Swiss teenager. He spent time looking at the world through the lens of an 8mm camera. Steiger and friend Walter Christen would make "weird shorts" with his father's Bolex. "They were filled with in-camera effects — single frame to double exposures," he explains.

Okay, so they were a little different. They did show his creative side. Enough to get Walter into the film academy in Vienna. Steiger, too, wanted to get into the movie business but didn't really know how. So, he did what he could to "get the ball rolling" — study English literature and the history of art at the University of Zurich. And, he kept making phone calls, determined to find a break into the creative world of making moving pictures.

"My first job was a cable boy on a live variety show similar to Ed Sullivan," he recalls. "Although my job was to take care of the cable behind the camera, I learned so much about television and production in general. Mainly, I learned that I didn't want to end up in television," he laughs.

After three years of doing any job he could in the TV industry in Switzerland, Steiger was accepted to the London International Film School. He joined an adventurous group of students who also wanted to study film.

"In London, you rotated jobs every term," he explains. "You work with a group of six people, doing different exercises and types of films. First term, it is a short black-and-white silent. Second term, everyone directs his or her own short. Third term, it is a documentary. Here, whoever pitches the best idea gets to direct.

"One of the most wonderful parts of this experience is that it is truly international," he says enthusiastically. "Because there were students from all over the world, we got to experience different cultures and points of view while we were learning our craft."

Steiger's fourth term was "esoteric and artsy," he admits. "I co-wrote the project with a friend from Venezuela. We brought all the different departments together, shooting the project on 35mm black-and-white stock. We even had the music composed for the film.

"It ended up being a nice piece called *Zape'*. A love triangle set in exotic locations," he smiles. "We shot near the school, making the green houses and a sandy beach near London look like the tropics. The project was accepted into the London Film Festival in 1980."

It was now time for Steiger to go back into the real world. He decided to return to Switzerland. "It was time to get serious and earn my own living," he recalls. "Boy, was I nervous! And, of course, that's when one of my first breaks came along!

"I got a call from a friend back in England. She said a company was calling around to schools, looking for an operator to work for free on a no-budget project sponsored by John Schlessinger. At first, I wasn't sure, but I finally decided to explore the possibilities. I called her back and left for England that day."

Steiger met with the group of Oxford college students. He realized he was one of two people involved that knew anything about film. The others had a theater or business background. But, it was a shot. "The director was Michael Hoffman, and the actors were students by the name of Hugh Grant, James Welby, Helena Bonham Carter and Imogen Stubbs. A young woman by the name of Rachel Portman (who won an Oscar for *Emma*) did the music. Back then, we were all in our twenties, naïve, and fascinated by the business.

"Interesting, how everyone in the project that was later picked up by the BBC, made it," he adds. This was the first of many pairings between Steiger and Hoffman. "He used the project as a vehicle to move up in the industry. Through it, Redford's Sundance picked up his script, *Promised Land*. Michael brought me into the mix.

"We really enjoyed working together. Michael wanted me to shoot the project (cross-financed through Sundance on a relatively comfortable ticket of four million in 1986). The producers, however, were only willing to let me do second unit. I had no feature credits."

At the time, Steiger was back in Switzerland with his own production company. He produced as well as shot commercials, documentaries, and small features. By keeping his overhead low, he was able to travel to places like New York, Idaho, and Utah. "Well, from Switzerland that was different. I also went to Africa, Kenya, Zimbabwe with my documentaries. It got me out in the world.

"It was comfortable and creative," he recalls. "I remember the day when my partner Thomas, Mike, and I were sitting on the balcony of our flat in Zurich, enjoying a few days of quiet. The phone rang, and it was Rick Stevenson from Los Angeles. Redford had just green lit *Promised Land*. I was off to the States for a picture."

When Steiger arrived on location in Salt Lake City, he started to prep for second unit. At the time, it consisted of car shots and drive-bys in the desert.

"Two weeks before the production was slated to start, they got a first unit DP," he says. "So, I did two weeks of second unit. Then, on that second weekend, the DP was let go. The producers asked me to cover the weekend on first unit. I never left. It was my first Director of Photography credit — one of the classic filmmaking breaks."

Gaffer Bill Schwartz was the only crew member to stay with him. "It was a difficult position to be put in," he admits. "Yes, I'd prepped the film. I'd set some of the shots up. But, someone else had done them. Now, when I was brought in to finish, I had to balance my ideas with those of the first unit, so everything would match. Thanks to Bill, I was able to make the transition. That relationship was what made the project go as smoothly as it did."

Steiger's favorite shot in *Promised Land* comes from the second unit. It was the second day of shooting and the image that became the movie poster. "Meg Ryan and Keifer Sutherland are on their way home, both kind of low members of society," he explains. "He's run away from his home, she is a 'free spirit,' into rock and roll and fun. They are married — after three days of knowing each other.

"The film is very much about the American Dream that never happened," he continues. "We chose to do the shot in the Bonneville Salt Flats. We used a Ford Ranchero pickup truck that we converted. Basically, I was strapped down on the back in the coldest day I've ever experienced. The wind chill factor was horrible — and we were going over 80 miles-per-hour.

"Eugenio Zanetti, who later won an Oscar for *Restoration* (Mike Hoffman director) and was nominated for *What Dreams May Come*, was our production designer. The car we shot was a 1948 Chevy. Eugenio had the roof cut off and replaced with a pink tarp. This allowed the daylight to come in through the tarp. It was really great to shoot. We had the pink on the faces – and pink is Meg's color.

"In the scenes Meg Ryan and Kiefer Sutherland drove the car off the road and onto the salt flats. The idea was to show freedom while they were running away. This was the first time I'd seen a desert like this, and I kept turning in circles, taking it all in. That's the feeling I wanted for the characters to experience.

"We had them driving through the landscape at about 55 miles an hour. To shoot it, we had to go faster to overtake them, circle them, then slow down, during the 360. We got this incredible white landscape, the moon, the sun, and their eerie vastness of space."

Two years later, Steiger was given another wonderful opportunity. He was asked to shoot a picture written by Rupert Walters (who wrote several of Mike Hoffman's films), to be shot in Canada called *Some Girls*. It was a light, mystic comedy, with more than a few "magical moments." Unfortunately, MGM changed hands and the new owners shelved the project. "Still, Sheila Benson of the *Los Angeles Times* liked it and wrote a great review. And, through that, it got seen in Los Angeles." This buzz lead to Steiger's next teaming.

The film was, for Steiger, very colorful, in an extremely controlled visual style. The locations were picked for their gothic environment — architecture and art. "Eugenio had these incredible sets built on stage, because we just couldn't find the interior location for this three-story Montreal mansion. He created a gothic building, mixing gothic and art nouveau. Even the light fixtures were moved from hallway to hallway, so we had the same style.

"Okay, they were moved because we didn't have enough!" he laughs. "It was a tight budget! We even had the wall panels rearranged to make the rooms look different," he adds, getting serious once again.

"This was a visually stunning film, with a slight mysterious feel for this American boy who experiences a completely different world," he explains.

For Steiger, there were many mysterious moments. "We had scenes where the camera sort of floats on it's own," he recalls. "There is a sequence where the grandmother Lila Kedrova (Oscar for *Zorba the Greek*) is dying. Two of our characters are to drive her back to the hospital she had escaped from earlier.

"Before they leave, we used the camera in a sweeping move to see her closing the curtains, basically closing the house. We came up with a simple rig of remote head with a short crane to fly the camera fluidly, creating an ethereal feeling for her final goodbye."

From this picture, Steiger went on to work with a Hollywood maverick and icon on *The Hot Spot*. "I almost fainted when I got the call in Zurich from my agent," he laughs. "Dennis Hopper! I took the next plane in, stayed on the couch at Eugenio's house and ran for the Monday meeting."

Hopper thought *Some Girls* was one of the best lit projects he'd seen that year. He tracked Steiger down. Hopper needed a DP to replace Haskell Wexler who had to leave the project two weeks before shooting the title sequence.

"I went to Dennis's house in Venice. I was so nervous, I almost forgot what buttons to push at the security panel. For a minute, all I could do was just stare at his face. This was Dennis Hopper! Finally, we talked for about 15 minutes — about Jennifer Connelly (who had been in *Some Girls* and was to be in *The Hot Spot*). I left, on a high. I really had no idea that I would get the project, although I really wanted it."

When producer Paul Lewis called to ask him what equipment would be needed for the title sequence, Steiger told him an Arri III, "since sync sound wouldn't be needed. I hung up, thinking, 'Why is he calling me?' Not long after, I got a call from my agent. 'You might have the job. Don't answer the phone for a little while!'"

This was Steiger's second break. Hopper worked differently from anyone else and it took a little getting used to. "Wc had about ten days to get into the production," Steiger recalls. "But, nothing really prepares you for working with Dennis. He does the unexpected. The conversations are about anything but the work. He lets that happen.

"There was a sequence out in the desert, the opening sequence, where a guy comes out of nowhere on his way to nowhere. He's searching for something in life. He ends up getting stuck in a village, with a woman who keeps him there by concocting things to hold onto him. It has the haunting 50s movie feeling — a classic film noir's color.

"I thought it would be really interesting if we saw the car going through the desert, as if someone else is watching it. That meant moving the camera a little independent of the car's movement.

"To do this, I had the camera pan in the opposite direction, in a wider shot. I added a heavy coral filter to get that hot, hot, hot desert feel — although we didn't keep it on for the whole picture. I did this without checking with Dennis. It was something he expected me to do — get the shot the way I thought best."

Fortunately, Hopper loved the sequence, and this cemented the relationship between the two. It allowed Steiger to continue to be as creative as possible on his own.

"The sets and locations were really important in this picture (as they usually are)," he recalls. "One of the most important was the car sales lot — a big exterior showing finance office and sales office.

"We had this wonderful mural with an armadillo, a woman's figure (with Virginia Madsen's face) of the wife of the owner (and the woman that suckers him into staying) in the background.

"Would you believe, we were into shooting, and I still hadn't talked to Dennis about his 'feelings about the look.' I just heard that he liked what he saw.

"He is very visual, so we had to prepare for everything — wide shot, tight shot, Steadicam. I would set up a shot, showing him what I would do using the video assist and a zoom to show different sizes. I would then discuss it with script supervisor Marita Grabjak. She would go to Dennis, and using this wonderful deadpan face, clearly outline the shot.

"He hated lists. She would write his decisions, and come back to me. We would work it out so we could do what he wanted, but  shorter. We both knew he had a tendency to cover things in long takes, ending up with a film that is too long and difficult to edit down.

"One of the most valuable things I learned on this film was just how much you need to know to get a director to accept your point of view," he says, quietly. "It is all about shorthand and doing what you think is right. I understood just how much the cinematographer is the center of communication for so many things. So, I make a point to be as accessible as possible.

"In this film, everyone would come to me. Transportation, for instance. They would ask where the trucks should be parked. I would know the direction Dennis would want to look. If I hated it, I had them park in that place. By the time Dennis arrived, the next morning, the trucks were in the spot where he wanted to be. He would grumble, knowing it would take too much time to move the trucks. 'Just shoot the other way,' he would say. I got the direction I wanted, without telling Dennis I thought his choice was wrong!"

Obviously, Steiger did something right. He is the only cinematographer who has done two films with Dennis Hopper. The second was the 1994 road picture, *Chasers*. "The only time I had to talk with Dennis was the 45-minute ride to the location," he recalls. "And, I had maybe five minutes of his attention."

Before shooting the second Hopper film, however, Steiger did his third project with Michael Hoffman – the cult comedy that really caught the eye of a broad spectrum of audience, *Soapdish*. "That was a blast. Stylish and artsy. I was scared to death going in!" he laughs. "This was a major studio picture with big big stars!

"Comedy is a lot harder than most people think," he says adamantly. "It is probably the most difficult thing to do. You are not only shooting performance but you also have to keep with the rhythm of the joke both on the set and in the camera. Often times, you are flying blind. You don't always know how it is going to come together. It's all about rhythm."

With a cast that ranged from Whoopie Goldberg to Sally Field and Robert Downey Jr. to Kevin Kline, Steiger had a varied pallet and movement that didn't stop. "We had to find a way to get everyone into the scene, keep the rhythm, and make the shots work," he says.

To do this, Hoffman and Steiger sat down and watched soap operas to see how they were lit. "Of course, we couldn't do that for our film, because they really are a bit hard lit. The pace of the shooting on a real soap dictates that the lighting designer must light the whole set for multiple cameras.

"We had to create the feeling of a soap opera, but be very kind to our actors. We needed to figure a way to shoot the shows, the corridors, makeup rooms, and offices, with an interesting look that was also flattering to the actors."

Steiger had the stage at Paramount where *Hunt for Red October* had just wrapped. The first challenge — how to put the sets in. "Eugenio and I walked around and realized there was a pit in the middle (the water tank for *Red October*)," Steiger comments. "In the scheme of things, isn't the soap opera on the lowest level of the industry? What if we put the set in that pit and built everything around it? This way, we would always see the soap in the background. Eugenio felt that was a wonderful way of interpreting the story.

"By building the offices above, with gigantic windows looking down into the soap set, we were able to keep the image of the emotional content of the story in most if not all shots," he continues.

"The lighting for the actual soap was rigged on a system of trusses that could be lowered and raised on chain motors. When we looked out offices onto the truss work — depending on where the truss was located — their angle and level would give us the feeling of being on the first or second floor."

Steiger's favorite shot is a one-take scene, where Robert Downey Jr. and Carrie Fisher (as the casting director) with Whoopie Goldberg (as the head writer) are desperately looking for an actress in the group of extras. It ends with Downey saying "let's make her a mute, then we don't have to pay her so much."

"We shot it racing through the corridor on a dolly in front of this group of five people with a 10mm lens," he says. "The 10mm is the widest lens you can actually use on people crowding a camera.

"I didn't tell the actors what lens, because they would freak. They just did their thing and we caught all their nuances on the screen.

"A shot like that is so dynamic because it makes all the movement look twice as fast. The corridors go by quickly and the actors are still in the shot and framed just right."

On this picture, Steiger admits that he learned a lot about lighting women. "It is my responsibility to make the actors look good. It's a glamorous business, so it is the most important thing. We had three divas, and they all had to look great — and still fit into the shots.

"Whoopie's ebony tones needed to be lit brighter," he explains. "It was usually one stop more and a different color. We put a straw on her. She looked good lit a little warmer.

"Now, Sally Field needed a specific direction of lighting to bring out her eyes. Sally could not take any other light from any other direction — no top or sidelight.

"This meant doing complicated rigs, tracking in front of her through a corridor with practical lighting that had side and toplight. With dolly moves, we would have three grips with sticks and flags just outside the frame line taking off light on her.

"Then if someone else was walking with her, we would have a key or a light on the camera to light her. And, we would often have a black flag over her head, close to frame line. Complicated.

"When she was with Whoopie, we needed a second light to bring Whoopie up. This couldn't hit Sally. Every shot with Sally and Whoopie was an elaborate setup — sometimes switching keys if Sally looked to the right or turned to someone else. It was dimmer off and another key light on, so light was always on the front.

"Gaffer Jim Grce and I would work with Sally's makeup artist to find just the right mix. Sally was very aware of what she needed, and extremely helpful. Sometimes, she would even stand in for herself.

"This was a great experience — working with an actress who knew she needed to be lit carefully and was willing to pay attention to our needs as well as her own. She knew makeup and lighting were going to take care of her, if she cooperated."

Following *Soapdish*, Steiger did a film called *Singles* (Matt Dillon, Bridget Fonda, Campbell Scott). "It is still as popular today as it was when we made it," he says. "It is constantly on cable. It is also all over Europe, playing over and over on German television.

"It was another great experience," he says, "Thanks to Cameron Crowe and Producer Art Linson. At first, Warner Bros. wanted us to shoot in Los Angeles. However, I knew we really needed the grunge scene in the real Seattle.

"The look really came from the location scout," he says. "Cameron Crowe and I visited the different Seattle clubs. We really researched the club scene. However, I realized we couldn't use the actual clubs. They looked great when we visited but they were dark and small. We would have a hard time getting the equipment in. And, if we used the lighting of the clubs, it would just be dark. Too dark.

"There is reality and there is film reality. We had to make the reality on the screen look like the real clubs. It is like a Director showing you an Edward Hopper painting and saying that is the look.

"To get the real look, you have to reinterpret it. If you take the light off the painting — say it was about a woman sitting alone in the restaurant — and try to keep the same feeling of loneliness, you can't use the same frame. The painting isn't widescreen. So, you have to get the feeling in the 1:85 wide screen format.

"I could walk into a room with a great ceiling. The Director might say it was beautiful. I would say, we would never see it. To get that ceiling feeling into the shot, we would have to re-interpret what made the room interesting – the height. I would have to take the ceiling and put it on the walls. That way, we could see the character."

For the grunge clubs, Steiger had to come up with something more interesting. "That's why prep time is so valuable.

"In one of the scouts with the Director and Production Designer Stephen Lineweaver, we found a big industrial pier and a loading dock that wasn't being used. It overlooked the bay," Steiger recalls. "The area was large. We could see Seattle through the open hangar doors. And, we could bring all the elements we liked."

Production design took bits and pieces from the real clubs — the idea of a car as a bar, oil barrels dividing an area, the stage. "We kept the original metal hallide lighting, which was orange, and added stage lights with simple colors.

"There is a great opening shot establishing location. We shot dusk for night as Kyra Sedgwick and several key people enter the club. For a few seconds we see outside — the water and Seattle. You know the backdrop is real, not a Translight. You know you are there.

"If we had used a real club, it would have been a dark interior," he adds. "So, despite having everyone signed off on the club, I took a step back offering a fresh perspective. I knew what I would see through the lens. I also knew that sometimes you have to stamp your foot to make things right. Even if it means more work and more money."

Then, in 1996, came the housebound comedy about every young person's dream — to trap their parents into feeling the way they felt when they are under *House Arrest*. "I called the story family therapy with a twist," Steiger laughs. "To try to stop his parents from splitting up, a young boy traps them in their basement, determined to get them to battle it out and 'save their marriage.' When neighbor children hear of this, they add their parents to the mix, and it's the kids in control, for a change."

Working with kids wasn't the challenge. For him, that is as hard or as easy as the crew makes it. The problem was shooting 60 pages of script in one room. Immediately, Steiger nixed the idea of using a real house. Production design created the three-story house on stage. Two main sets with a living room, a den, an entrance with staircase and, more important, the kitchen with two different exits to the garden and garage. And the all-important basement entrance.

Looks like he got everything he wanted — except that he had the challenge of making 60 pages look fresh — and cutting from above to below ground all the time. "See, I told you comedy is the hardest thing to shoot!" he says.

Since a lot of the action took place at the kitchen door, this was one of Steiger's key elements. "We had a staircase with the door on top. We had the gate with a quilt over it. We had to see into the kitchen, but the sets were separate.

"The only thing that we could do was put a mock-up of the kitchen at the top of the stairs/basement set so that we could shoot from the staircase into the kitchen and the reverse," he explains. "We could then shoot from the staircase into kitchen from a platform with the mock-up that was elevated about 15 feet.

"The biggest challenge here was matching the lighting and backdrops of the windows with the real kitchen set. Then, we had the additional challenge of finding a way to move from one set to the other for reverses within this same scene.

"That meant we had to be ready to light on both major sets at the same time," he adds. "This brought in the lighting budget. And the producers. It was expensive to light both sets and keep them lit!"

Everything was controllable, until the material got out of control. "At one point, this comedy really escalates into a brawl," he explains. "I got the bright idea of doing a split screen of the parents screaming at the kids, and the kids screaming back. That meant putting the sets side by side and tying them together with a wedge of a wall."

The shot began at the top of the basement stairs on the basement platform set, shooting down. It followed the adults up to the gate. Then, Steiger used the wedge that was positioned in the matte box to move halfway through the wall, getting to the split screen. "That way, we saw both warring parties at the same time," he explains.

It was literally a wipe in camera. "Just one of the challenges of comedy," he laughs. "And, I love it."

Of course, that was nothing compared to the challenge of Steiger's next project – the modern-day version of the horror-comedy, *Godzilla*. "How do you shoot a star that, at rest is 200-feet tall, running over 400 feet — and never on the set?" jokes Steiger.

When he read the script, all he could think of was "how are we going to do that?" Meeting with director Roland Emmerich and Dean Devlin helped a little. They were well organized, and had a strong concept for this 100 million dollar plus project. "We decided to shoot the film on Super 35mm, because in post you have the ability to do pan-and-tilt and reposition the frame. Like, when we had an imaginary *Godzilla* in frame, we could cheat a little with visual effects. If he looked better bigger, we could tilt the frame to give more headroom.

"Super 35mm was used on *Independence Day*, and it was a format that Roland liked — and so do I. It makes the shoot easier, especially with multiple cameras — a lot of them. You can get the equipment — the lenses are lighter. And, on a digital film the loss of image area is not really a factor."

For Steiger, the advantage of Super 35mm outweighed the disadvantages. He will fight for it over anamorphic any day.

Scope is what he needed on this picture, especially since he was lighting a creature that wasn't there. "The first thing that gaffer Jim Grce and I had to decide was just how far we had to throw the light," he explains. "I mean, we couldn't always light the 200 or 400 feet, so we had to find a place where we were comfortable.

"Then, we had to work on the shots (and there were a lot of them) in the rain. What would be from rain birds, what would be wet down, and what would be CGI rain. Pardon the pun, but there were a lot of monster decisions."

One of the biggest challenges was a shot where Steiger had to light Madison Square Park between 23rd and 25th Streets in New York, from Broadway to 5th Avenue. "It was the shade of the Flat Iron Building, one of the oldest and once one of the tallest buildings in Manhattan," he explains.

This is where the crew chasing *Godzilla* hoped to trap the monster, by setting out bate — a ten-foot tall pile of dead fish. "It was quite a sight," Steiger laughs. "Dead fish, Manhattan's sophisticated crowd watching us from the edges, rain birds, rain, wet and cold!"

It took over 250 teamsters, almost 90 electricians, more than 30 grips and three full camera crews, as well as a special effects unit. "Without *Godzilla*, which we kept having to impress on the crowd, determined to see the star!" he chuckles.

Steiger and Grce had determined that they would use 20 stories as an arbitrary height for their lights. Anything over that, CGI's problem. "Here, that meant covering four blocks in every direction," Steiger says. "That meant driving Musco lights in, augmenting them with about 80 Maxi-Brutes and every other light we could muster.

"We also had 1k nook lights on the concrete walls, mobile Xenons on Humvees, crews with lights off the rooftops, and Lightning Strikes to simulate transformers blowing — as well as flashlights in people's hands — and one of the Musco lights moving in the shot.

"I had never done a shot as large, or as technically challenging – or as wet," he says. "We were walking around with boots, rain coats, and hats – and still got wet!"

As with many of the shots, Steiger combined crane moves, Steadicam, and handheld. "That was a logistical nightmare on many shots," he says. "Since a lot of them were in water, we knew we couldn't use the Technocrane for many of them," he continues. "It doesn't work when wet. So, we had a major grip challenge. We had to use what we could when we could – and protect everything at all costs.

"With the Steadicam, we thought we could get away with covering the equipment carefully and sending a grip in with a little flag. But, key grip Tony Marra found something in testing — the rain can go sideways. That took something to solve.

"We still wanted the Technocrane for a lot of shots, so we had a rain cover designed for it. This cover fit the retractable arm and solved the crane problem. We then had it, when we really needed it — if we could afford the cost and have a place for the additional crew it required."

For Steiger, who has been able to use a few toys on each picture, having to fight for many necessary tools was a big challenge. "I won the battle for the Technocrane, even though the zoom control went out on the first test. Then I had to do battle for the Akela. We needed the 80-foot reach and remote head for several shots."

This tool was key to one of Steiger's most creative shot designs. "I wanted to reveal *Godzilla*'s giant footprint in the sand," he says. "Sounds simple. However, you have to remember that the thing is over 30-feet long.

"What I wanted was to move along like a Steadicam shot, then at a certain moment, boom up and up, making the audience think they are seeing the shot from a helicopter. This revealed the 45-foot long and 20-foot wide print."

Steiger got a demo reel and showed it to Emmerich. "He loved it, and agreed to ship the crane to Hawaii. Of course, we got there, and then we couldn't find the crane. How could you lose that large a piece of equipment????"

Next came *Bowfinger*. For Ueli Steiger, this project was a little like *Soapdish*. It was a film about the film industry. "It's a film about people who are deluded about their talents," he says. "And, by sheer determination, they finally succeed. Eddie Murphy is a great *Bowfinger*. Through him and those around him, we learn about these types of people and even started to love them."

Steiger says the film is not exploitive. "Even though the lead actress played by Heather Graham sleeps with everyone to get there," he insists. "She is a naïve character who wants something badly.

"Part of the fun was in making fun of ourselves, our business," he adds. "In the picture, Steve Martin and company go out to get 'the best crew they can pay for.' And, where do they find them? On the Mexican border, of course!

"A lot of the film takes place at Martin's house, which is small and serves as his cutting room and studio. The living room has corners and nitches, which double as a stage. He preps there. He auditions there. His office has a Murphy bed, which he uses when he seduces Heather's character."

The exterior set was a real bungalow in the heart of Hollywood. Production Designer Jackson DeGovia built an interior on stage at Universal. We had decided to go naturalistic with a natural look," says Steiger. "Hard ceilings and low ceilings. This left us with no option but to light through the windows and with practical lights already in the frame."

This was a big challenge for Steiger and gaffer Jim Grce. "We had up to eight actors in the small set at one time," says Steiger. "This meant wide-angle lenses. We couldn't light just the room and one actor, as we often do. If we lit the walls, we would have to relight the people. And, we didn't want to fly the walls.

"We tried to light through the windows. And, still give the shots some dimension. We didn't want to make it look like an overlit comedy. We wanted contrast and darkness and still see comedy.

"That's what director Frank Oz wanted as well," he smiles. "At one point when we were out on a scout, Frank and I were talking about kitchen toys – one of my passions. I had ordered a Vita-Mix. He threatened to take it away from me if the film looked like a brightly lit comedy!

"I've still got it," Steiger laughs. "So, I guess Frank was satisfied!"

Steiger's next project was an even wilder comedy. "When I got the call to do the sequel to *Austin Powers – The Spy Who Shagged Me*, I wasn't sure that I wanted to do it," he says truthfully. "I saw the poster. I hadn't seen the first picture. Did I want to do this?

"I told director Jay Roach 'I just finished another comedy.' I wasn't sure. He asked me to read the script. It was strange. Was it funny? There were so many locations, and so many complications. And, not that much money.

"Then I had a really good meeting and thought, 'why not?' It was work. And, I would be in at the beginning. Once I committed, and put myself into this film's frame of mind, the buzz started. It seemed that everyone but me had seen the first *Austin Powers*, and was a fan."

Once Steiger watched the film, he felt a lot better. "I have a lot of respect for Mike Myers," he says, sincerely. "He is the driving force behind the pictures and has created all the characters. They are completely camp and way out. That's what makes it special.

The *Austin Powers* look would be interesting to capture. It was bright and filled with pastels. "A new approach for me," he says. "It's the most lit film I've ever done. It's colorful. I drew a lot of my decisions from what I learned on *Soapdish*.

"On that film, I did a lot of tests on color. That helped me understand how to light walls that were saturated with color. It's different and difficult. You have to light all the walls separately. You can't bring lights through the windows to do that.

"You have to light each wall to key, so the color will show. In Austin's pad, for example, the walls are in the 1960s colors. To see this, Jim Grce put special lights on each wall. Each had its own light, like we would have for a character.

"If we didn't do this, they wouldn't read. If the red wall wasn't lit, it would become ugly. And, this was a film about vibrant colors."

From *Soapdish*, Steiger also learned to light women. "We treated Mike Meyers a little like we treated Sally Field, special lights from the front. In every scene, there would be a follow spot. That was a challenge, especially in his pad and in the dance sequences. These were really important, because we wanted him to 'pop out' of the shot. In wide shots, with a lot of people for example, we wanted the eye to go to Mike.

"If you watch the movie on laser disk or DVD, you can see that follow spot in the shot!" Steiger admits, *Austin Powers* was a big challenge —almost as difficult as *Godzilla*.

"Without Jim Grce I wouldn't be able to do these pictures, or be where I am," he says enthusiastically. "For a cinematographer, the crew is paramount. You can live or die through the crew. They do a lot of the work for me.

"When I first came to the States for *Hot Spot*, I hired my first crew out of L.A. I was nervous, I admit it. I didn't know anyone. I was new to the business here in the States. I knew it was critical to find a good assistant, gaffer and key grip. The last thing I wanted to do was go for big names who could be assholes to me.

"In 1988, I met Robbie Mueller at a symposium in Switzerland. He was there to talk about *Barfly*. He had used a new fluorescent system that his gaffer invented. It involved a little tool we all now use — a Kinoflo. I asked Robbie what to do. He suggested I talk to the inventor of the new 'light.'

"So, when I got to the States, I called Frieder Hocheim. He told me he was 'getting out' of the gaffing end of the business and was going to build these fluorescent lights. He suggested I talk to his best boy — he was great. That best boy was Jim Grce.

"It was the best introduction I've ever had! Jim's been with me ever since. And, when he is 'lured away' by someone else, I feel it. I'm thankful to have Jim — key grip Brian Reynolds, Tony Marra and the rest of my crew.

"Crews are underestimated," Steiger says adamantly. "They are very important. I know my crew is overqualified, but they have stuck with me. They are not 'blue-collar' workers. They are my partners in crime — and they have value."

Steiger's partner in crime, Jim Grce, went with him when he chose his next project. *The Visitor*, due out in 2000, is a time traveling comedy. "It is a medieval story that ends up in contemporary Chicago," he explains. "It then goes back to the 15th century."

The film, originally produced by John Hughes, is a French production. Based on the 1993 French release, it has the same Director and a star that is as big as Jim Carey is in the States. "It is the most popular film in France," says Steiger. "The Director wanted to do an American version to see if the story would translate. It's fast paced — and funny.

"We have a knight and his valet, transported to contemporary Chicago. The first time he sees a car, he tries to kill it. He's never used a toilet – knows nothing about today's world.

"The medieval part was shot in Shepperton, England," he adds. "We were there for a while. They shoot a little differently than we do," he sighs. "For one, there is no key grip. And, that's a problem. If I ever do a project there again, I will bring Tony Marra with me. I can't do without him!

"We had a few really big scenes, like one in the big hall where the knights gather. It was a wedding banquet. We lit it with real fire and real torches. The special effects department built additional torches, and we had this wonderful light for the period."

Steiger is anxious to see what the American audience thinks of the French sense of humor. He enjoyed the experience. But, he's not one to dwell on a project. At present, Steiger and crew are prepping *Metal God* to star Mark Wahlberg. "I'm going to need earplugs for this one," he laughs. "This is a little bit of a rockumentary. It's based on the biggest slam rock bands of the 1980s. In it, Mark plays the lead singer of a tribute band in Pittsburgh. They do a smaller version of a popular metal band.

"When the lead singer of the real band is fired, he replaces him. It's a journey, of a man who gets lost in the world of rock-and-roll, but without becoming a heroin addict. And, how he finds himself, and goes home, more confident in himself and the world around him.

"I'm looking forward to doing fast-moving cameras and rock-and-roll lighting. Check with me in a few months," he laughs, reaching for one of his kitchen toys. He's going to need the energy of that Vitamix.

"By then," he smiles, as he gulps a health drink, "we'll see how my crew helps me pull this one off!"

*Lighting is the most important tool for the cinematographer. Lighting creates mood. The mood places the audience into the story. You laugh. You cry. You feel happy. You feel sad. This is done by us — cinematographers — mainly with lighting.*

*Vilmos Zsigmond*

Stand silently in the middle of Vilmos Zsigmond's, A.S.C., house and close your eyes — you can almost feel and hear the ghosts of "old Hollywood" emanating from the walls. The multi-level home, a curious blend of Italian and Southwestern architecture, nestled in the Hollywood Hills once belonged to silent film star Pearl White. Open your eyes and there is no doubt, another Hollywood icon has taken residence.

Scattered among the tasteful decorations are memories of Zsigmond's incredible cinematic career. What isn't displayed in this wonderful old home adorns the walls of his second mountain retreat — nestled above the crashing waters of the Pacific Ocean, off the Cabrillo Highway in Big Sur, California.

Regrettably, Zsigmond doesn't spend enough time in either location these days. When he isn't shooting a big-budget feature or a major commercial, he is off to his native Hungary, to New York, or other locations — passing on the knowledge he has gleaned over his career — teaching young cinematographers to shoot film. It is his way of giving back to an industry that took him in and made him a star some 40 years ago.

It is impossible to talk about every film in the distinguished career of this multi-award-winning cinematographer (Academy Award, British Academy Award, Emmy, and A.S.C. Award — A.S.C.'s Lifetime Achievement Award for 1999, as well as several nominations). But getting him to look back over the years at the films that stick out in his mind is a lesson in creativity, perseverance, and the pursuit of excellence — in a very challenging and politically charged industry.

Vilmos Zsigmond arrived in the United States in 1956, right after the Hungarian revolution. The only work he could get was in the commercial world, "where there was room for experimentation and for the learning process that I had experienced before I could tackle the big jobs in Hungary," he says without rancor.

Zsigmond's work in film really didn't begin until he was 21 years old. This is when he started film school in Hungary. There, he learned techniques like classical lighting, captured in the old movies. It was backlight and crosslighting, a signature of the time. Zsigmond quickly worked his way up the ladder of success, becoming one of the top ten cameramen in the Hungarian film industry.

"Then I came to America and became one of ten thousand and one," he laughs. He faced several problems, the least of which was learning the language. He began shooting educational films on 16mm and finally got into documentaries. It was a way to learn English and the language of American film at the same time.

In the mid-1960s, he graduated into the mini-feature of the day — the commercial. He began working for a company called FilmFair, making many "beautiful commercials," in a style that is still his trademark.

"Whatever is beautiful in life is what I like to shoot," he says. Zsigmond has never distinguished between the "beauty" of a feature film — one of his favorite is the dark rainy days in *McCabe and Mrs. Miller* − or the "beauty" of story and location of a commercial — an early spot done for Hunt's Tomato Sauce, for example.

"The commercials became little slices of life, ala Italian neo-realism," he comments. "The idea was to become intimately involved with the lives of the people — the father, as a basketball coach or wearing a hard hat, showing his frustration with his work and his joy with his players. Bad mood. Good mood. It didn't matter.

"We even followed a construction worker as he leaves the factory and buys flowers for his wife. He walks through cheers and jeers from the crew and a traffic policeman on the corner as he carries the flowers home. We then see him greet his wife, as she prepares a Hunt's dinner."

Even though the agencies wanted the "big" commercial, they were reticent to spend money on large casts. So, Zsigmond found a way to capture the crowd by "stealing" the background with long lenses — lighting shots in what has become known as his "molding beauty" trademark.

"The shots had to look better than real," he recalls. "I couldn't do what old Hollywood used to do, lighting from any place, not caring if the movie looked like it was lit. I did what critics called 'poetic realism,'" he explains. Using the same techniques of the old masters in painting (Caravaggio, Rembrandt, De La Tour), he would light "natural" but better. There wouldn't be the double shadows from two windows like in "real" life.

Another commercial that sticks out in Zsigmond's mind is one for Chicken-of-the-Sea tuna. "This one was a challenge," he says. "We had to have this young woman swimming in the ocean. Of course, we couldn't shoot it at the ocean, because the woman would drown. Not to mention, it would have been a difficult shot.

"So, we had to build a tank at the studio," he explains. "We had to bounce light into a big white surface and reflect the sky into the water. Quite a challenge, to make a tank look like the ocean!"

something out equally, then it becomes a boring composition, because it isn't interesting."

*Hired Hand* put Zsigmond on the map because it was a Western, a big thing at the time. "A Western, with a lot of candlelight scenes," he explains. "I had done a lot of these in Hungary, because, often the part of the country we were shooting didn't have electricity.

"This made me study about exposure and how light illuminates people from a kerosene lamp. This allowed me to develop a good sense and feel for natural light."

*Hired Hand* also allowed him to be daring. "I remember one day we had this major storm, with a lot of lightning," he recalls. "Peter and crew wanted to shoot it. My question — 'How do you catch lightning on film?' I suggested something simple — set up the camera and wait. When the lightning struck, that would be the cue for the actor to walk in from the frame line."

Years later, on *The Ghost and the Darkness*, Zsigmond faced the same situation. "But it was a lot easier. The lightning was going off every five seconds, so we didn't have to wait for it. And, the film was fast enough that we could catch it as we were rolling. What a difference," he says.

After *Hired Hand*, Zsigmond began working on another "little" Hollywood film that has become legend in the industry — for pictorial creativity, sound as well as performance — *McCabe and Mrs. Miller*. This was a daring picture — for one thing, this was the first time film that was flashed in America. "It was a look that made you feel like the film was made 100 years ago," he says.

"Flashing," he explains, "is altering the contrast of the film. American films, at this time, were done in Technicolor. In Europe, there was a more pastel look. When Robert Altman and I discussed this picture, he told me he wanted a 'different' style. He already knew about flashing and agreed that we should test it.

"Up until then, flashing was done by still photographers. It was called 'latensification.' They preexposed the film, when shooting under dark conditions. This helped with the exposure. There are three different approaches to flashing," he continues. "Flashing can be done in an optical printer. The film can also be exposed normally and then sent to the lab for flashing.

"Some years ago, Panavision created the Panaflasher. That allows us to create this technique in camera, adjusting how much flash or even adding color."

When Zsigmond is asked about this groundbreaking film, two subjects come up – this flashing technique and the use of the zoom lens. "It was new," he admits. "And it was a challenge. To hide the zoom, we usually changed the focal length, while moving the camera."

There were other challenges on *McCabe and Mrs. Miller* that got Vilmos Zsigmond's adrenaline charging — "and they had nothing to do with camera," he laughs. "Actually, we rather enjoyed doing things 'improv,'" he says a little dryly. "Altman is a great improviser. During the first few days of the shoot, he would 'create' different approaches on a moment's notice. He would show me how he wanted the camera to move — always move. After a few days, he would let me do what I wanted.

"Which was fun," he smiles. "Warren Beatty and Bob Altman didn't consider the script 'final.' They were always finding 'possibilities' in our great sets (designed by Leon Ericson). This gave the company of actors unlimited choices. We never knew what we were going to shoot from day to day. The actors loved it, and I was always challenged to find ways to shoot what Altman came up with. Our crew had to be fast, to keep up with our shooting schedule."

Zsigmond learned a lot about making films, and about human nature on *McCabe*. "I also learned about Hollywood's sense of humor," he laughs. "I remember it being right before Christmas, and I had to leave the location to catch my plane to be home in time for the holiday. Director Robert Altman didn't mind. 'I'll operate the camera myself,' he told me.

"Well, I got back after Christmas, and we were looking at dailies. When we finally got to the last couple of shots, I almost fainted. What I saw on the screen was not usable. 'You can't be serious, this has to be reshot,' I said to him. Then I saw the look on his face, and that of the rest of the crew. They all broke into laughter. They had 'shot' footage especially for me, with a shaking camera, badly composed, which was not in style those days.

"Robert Altman has a 'strange' sense of humor," he says. "He is a wonderful man and a very talented Director."

When the film was completed, it was shown in a movie duplex in London. "*2001* was showing in the other theater," Zsigmond recalls. "After the two finished, Robert Altman ran into Stanley Kubrick. Kubrick told Altman he loved what he saw on the screen. 'That camerawork was wonderful. How did you do it?' Kubrick asked, assuming that Altman handled the camera the way he did. 'I didn't do it,' Altman answered. 'I had a Director of Photography.' Kubrick was astonished. 'Do you trust him?' Altman laughed. 'Of course, I trust him! That's his job.'"

Ironically, the studio hated the images. They had no idea what Altman and Zsigmond were doing. However, the critics loved it. His unique approach to making this picture won him his first British Academy Award nomination for the year 1972. (Along with two other projects that he'd shot — *Images* and *Deliverance*.)

*Deliverance* was another groundbreaking film that has become a cult classic. "I really liked and loved working with John Boorman," he says. "I had never done an adventure story before, and this was something exciting. We were planning to shoot a lot of stunts using stuntmen, but we knew the actors wanted to do their own. That meant we (Boorman and Zsigmond) would be getting into the rapids with the camera and making it real.

"The challenge was how to make the trip down the river exciting," Zsigmond says. "We shot different tests on the river, like shooting from boat to boat. We also tried different angles, different camera moves.

"We finally came to the conclusion that the most interesting shot was when we put the camera lens close to the level of the water and followed the canoes by panning the camera," he explains. "By using the camera lens in this manor, we felt we were really with the actors and did most of the river sequence this way.

"We were very lucky with the weather," he adds. "The sky was cloudy most of the time." For Zsigmond, this was the simplest way to shoot the picture. He didn't have to wait for the sun and the lighting matched all day. "It would have been more of a problem, if we had had sunlight," he says. "That would have made the look too cheerful, like a National Geographic movie.

"I really liked the green of the river and the trees, the waves and the sky. Add to that, the blacks and grays of the shadows. We didn't have to worry about the warm sunshine or the blue of the sky to destroy our simple color palette.

"Fortunately, this was made independently. We had the luxury of being able to wait for a cloud to cover the sun when we had sunshine," he adds. "If it were a studio picture, they would have been pushing us to finish. Warner Bros. trusted John Boorman and left us alone."

Even with "waiting for the light," Zsigmond and crew came in under schedule. "It can be done, when you have the cooperation of everyone," he says. "We had a great Director, actors who really worked hard at making the parts real, and a crew that believed in the picture. That's what made it all work."

In 1973, Vilmos Zsigmond shot two other pictures that have made a significant mark on movie history. *The Long Goodbye* was another pairing with Robert Altman. "Robert said he wanted to 'do something different,'" Zsigmond recalls. "I'd heard that before. Every Director wants to 'do something different.' However, this time, he really meant it. Robert wanted the camera to move — all the time. Up. Down. In and out. Side to side.

"For me, good movies are ones in which people don't know the story is being shot by a camera," Zsigmond says. "That's why I avoid the crane, unless it is necessary. I want to avoid making the audience know that they are watching a movie.

"Robert wanted the opposite. I was against it. But . . ." he smiles. "He was the Director. So, I went along.

"Unfortunately, we had a beginning operator. I didn't like how he was handling the shots. So, I complained. I told Robert I would take care of him on the 'difficult' shots — I would operate. He wouldn't have that. 'I want him to learn,' he told me. He 'loved' the way it looked. He liked the idea of images that weren't perfectly composed. 'When you are standing there, picking up your award,' he told me. Of course, the film wasn't even nominated, even though the critics loved it. (The National Film Critics voted it Best Cinematography of the Year.)

"Unfortunately, we often find that critics go for something that is new – not necessarily good — but new," he adds, ruefully.

Zsigmond's next picture was exactly opposite in experience. *Cinderella Liberty* was a great picture, to him, because of the actors. "And the locations," he adds. "I love stories that tell about people. I don't always like special effects."

For him, the way to shoot a movie is to support the story. At times, he has found pictures can be shot "too beautifully," to the point of overwhelming the story. "This was a beautiful movie in that it was not flashy, but more realistic — like the Italians were doing at the time," he explains.

It is also a testament to Zsigmond's desire to be a minimalist in lighting. "There are a lot of kitchen scenes between James Caan and Marsha Mason," he says. "The production designer, Leon Ericksen again, was a genius. He gave me a lot to work with. I could do things like put a single light bulb over the center of the kitchen. And light with only that bulb. All I had to do was put a little hair spray on the camera side of the bulb, to dull the flare off the lens.

"This way, the actors could walk around the kitchen with one shadow," he continues. "They could walk from bright to shadow as they would in a real kitchen. It's a technique painters use in their paintings — only a little more difficult to do with real lights. It is something that can't be done with a lot of movie lights. Put in a lot of light, then you have to have flags to flag the flags, and it still wouldn't look — real."

Of course, Vilmos Zsigmond admits that, at times, he tried to get a little too real. "Well, the shot looked great when we were looking at it – and it would have on the big screen," he laughs, as he recalls one of the opening shots in this cult film. It is the crucial shot where the two star-crossed lovers meet for the first time.

"It was in a bar, which we built in an empty building on a Seattle street," Zsigmond recalls. "Director Mark Rydell wanted the shot to be dark – this was a bar, where sailors come to dance with local women. Caan was to enter the doorway, look through the bar, and into the next room, where there is a brightly-lit pool table. Suddenly, this woman in red (Marsha Mason) enters the shot. She is going to be the only person in the bar that James Caan's character sees. She becomes his obsession.

"Okay, so he wanted it dark," Zsigmond laughs. "I rigged two number two blue photofloods into the ceiling of the bar, then turned to him. 'I'm done.' 'Get out of here,' he said. 'You have to be kidding!' I said, 'trust me. You wanted dark.'

"Well, we shot the scene and Mark loved it. A few days later, the studio called. The bar shot was unusable. 'You have to reshoot it. That scene won't show in the drive-in theater!'

"I couldn't believe it. 'Mark, are we shooting this movie for the drive-in theater?' I asked him. 'I thought we were making pictures for real theaters.' Of course, I had a feeling that they wouldn't see anything on the screen. But, I was determined — we couldn't be shooting for the drive-in! That wasn't what making movies was about.

"Finally, it came to a showdown. We got a local drive-in to let us run a test. During the intermission, when everyone was going for popcorn, someone announced that a 'local production company making a movie in Seattle wanted to test something on the screen.'

"The lights went down and the film ran. We could see nothing on the screen. Of course not. They were projecting at, maybe one foot-candle; of course nothing showed on the screen. People started honking their horns. I knew it, then.

"My great dark scene was going to be redone. For the drive-in theaters! (The scene was not reshot. It is still in the movie!) Thank heaven we don't have those drive-ins around any more!"

After *Cinderella Liberty* and *The Long Goodbye*, Zsigmond went on to do a series of films that were good work — but nothing that really stands out in his mind. "Except *Obsession*, my first time working with Brian DePalma," he interjects. Done in the mid 1970s, when American crews began to travel all over the world, *Obsession* was shot in Zsigmond's favorite city — Florence. "How can you not get beautiful pictures in a location like that?" Zsigmond says. "Of course, Brian had to challenge me in ways no cinematographer could imagine.

"He, too, liked to move the camera. Only, his favorite challenge was using a 360 — actually as many as he could get away with," he laughs, "to tell the story.

"In *Obsession*, we have several of them. All are important to the story – and were a challenge to create. They were done on real locations, so we couldn't light from bridges or parallels. And, hanging lights in homes on location was oftentimes a problem.

"The first one takes place during an anniversary scene. Cliff Robertson and Genevieve Bujold are dancing around and around the floor. At one point, the camera catches and then focuses on a little girl, as she descends the stairs and Robertson picks her up. He continues to dance around with this child, who bears a striking resemblance to her mother.

"In the second 360, Brian wanted to show a time lapse. To do this, we began on a mausoleum that looks very much like a famous church in Italy. This is where Robertson's wife is buried.

"The first time we go around the camera pans through an open field, then through the monument and a match-dissolve. We then see the same area with buildings and a park. We find Robertson, standing beside a more modern car — 15 years older.

"To do this, we built the mausoleum in two different locations," Zsigmond explains. "We did the 360-degree camera move with perfect precision and paned across the monument with the same speed, and from the same height.

"It was a clever way to do a time lapse — and, fortunately, we had a day that was overcast, so the light wasn't difficult to match."

The third 360 in the movie was another challenge to Zsigmond from DePalma. "This one was done at an airport," he explains. "We bring Cliff Robertson running in one direction, gun in hand, and Genevieve Bujold getting out of a wheelchair from another direction — in slow motion. The two meet, hug each other, while the camera circles them around in slow-motion. What an ending!

"Now, today, we'd use handheld with battery packs or Steadicam. However, in the mid-1970s that equipment wasn't available. So, we had to wind the cable around the tripod, and unwind it, as the camera moved around and around — ending the shot before the cable ran out."

An interesting challenge for Zsigmond's creative juices. And, an easy one, compared to some of the projects to come. At this time, the world of special effects was beginning to grow in Hollywood. Although he had the ability to use the technique on a few films, he was not a fan. As with many cinematographers, he would rather be able to control the shots by doing as much as possible in the camera.

However, although he may not be a big fan of special effects films, he did shoot perhaps one of the most well-known, and certainly well-received, groundbreaking pictures in that genre — at the time — 1977. The project was directed by a young man by the name of Spielberg and produced by a woman by the name of Julia Phillips. "I really don't consider *Close Encounters of the Third Kind* a special effects movie," he says. "At least 90 percent of the picture was what I like to do, a people story. Only the final sequence combined real action with special effects.

"One of the things that I learned on this picture was how important it is for each and every person to know how to do their job," he adds. "Special effects are so precise, you can't not be right there all the time. Everyone, from Director to actor, and cinematographer to effects crew has to know exactly what to do and how to do it."

For Zsigmond, one of the most important lines of communication in a special effects film such as this was working with the production designer (in this case, Joe Alves). And, with Doug Trumbell, who did the special effects. "With *Close Encounters*, there is a build to the story for the 'close encounter,'" he explains. "Emotionally, the lighting had to work for the story. We had to build to a light show.

"When the door of the spaceship opens, we wanted a blinding intense light emanating from the ship. At first, we didn't know how to do that, because scenes like this simply hadn't been done before."

Zsigmond and the lighting crew experimented on the set. They had to rig a lot of light inside the space ship. "It was not enough to put 10,000 bulbs in," he says. "We also needed some HMI spotlights that would create the chard of lights through the atmosphere we created with light fog.

"Even that didn't work," he adds. "Then, someone had the idea that this wasn't working because the mirrors were too perfect. If we broke the mirrors, that might work. We got out hammers and broke them apart. That gave us the light effects we wanted!

"Sometimes, you go into a project not knowing. And, the answer comes — often from unexpected places."

In 1978, Vilmos Zsigmond added another film icon to his growing resume. It won him the British Academy Award and an American Academy Award nomination. "*The Deer Hunter* was wonderfully directed by Michael Cimino," he says. "We shot very long scenes — and I mean long scenes. The wedding sequence, for example, lasts 30 minutes on the screen. The idea was to create a real Ukrainian wedding in America, so people would learn about their ethnic culture.

"When you really study this wedding, there is not a lot going on. But, what is really happening is that we are getting familiar with the characters. Getting intimately involved with their lives is far more important than the action.

"For the Vietnam part, we wanted realism — explosions, torture, cruelty to men by men — just like being in the war — any war.

"I remember one scene when they are playing Russian Roulette," he continues. "There is only one light source, a shaded light bulb in the middle of the gambling hall. We made it look like this one light is actually lighting the whole scene. This made the image full with shadows, real and frightening! When Christopher Walken dies in his friend's arms, everyone in the cast and crew was crying.

"Robert DeNiro's performance was so powerful, amazing, and unbelievable. We felt we were experiencing the real thing."

The power of this movie has lasted — for audiences — and for those behind it. Even though Zsigmond has gone on to do a series of big pictures, *The Deer Hunter* remains on the top of his list. "To me, it is the finest movie I've done in my life," he says adamantly. "Michael Cimino's directing inspired the whole company, and selecting an incredibly talented cast made this movie a memorable classic."

There is also a scene just before the boys go to Vietnam. "In the bar, one of them is playing Chopin on the piano. You sense this maybe is the last time they are together. The music, the lighting, the acting and the camera all blend together. Then, a long dissolve to the Vietnam War, end of part one."

In 1979, several projects later, Zsigmond made another of his "favorite" films. "One of the things that I really loved about doing *The Rose* was how much I could add to the story with the lighting," he says. "Lighting is the most important tool for the cinematographer. Lighting creates mood. The mood places the audience into the story. You laugh. You cry. You feel happy. You feel sad. We — the cinematographer — do this mainly with lighting. Of course, the Production Designer is our closest ally in this creation."

Although the story of *The Rose* is based on the life of Janis Joplin, the title was created because her family would not give the production company permission to do her story. "By creating a fictional character that was a lot like Joplin, we had the freedom to use more lights and create lighting effects."

Zsigmond used a whole range of techniques in the rock-and-roll story. One of the most important things for him was the juxtaposition of wild concert footage with the quiet of the limousine. "The lighting was different but the characters meshed into each element," he says.

"Both the Production Designer and Director (Mark Rydell) encouraged me to not limit my lighting — to go as wild and do what I wanted," he continues. "I wanted to get great concert footage. I needed great camera operators who would improvise a lot besides following a plan by me and my Director."

For Vilmos Zsigmond, the ultimate emotional moment, where lighting played a major part is at the end of the picture. It is also his favorite sequence. "It begins with Rose, stoned out and at the end of her rope, in a telephone booth begging her manager for help," he explains. "Suddenly, a helicopter swoops down, picks her up and flies over to the stadium.

"The final concert was at a stadium in Long Beach," he recalls. "We had about 12,000 people, for only two hours. So, we had to get everything as quickly as possible — and that included the helicopter shots." To do this, Zsigmond called on his friends. Cinematographers like Haskell Wexler, A.S.C., Conrad Hall, A.S.C., Owen Roizman, A.S.C., Laszlo Kovacs, A.S.C., and others pitched in on cameras. Their instructions – get great footage. "I wanted them to improvise, as well as follow the plan Mark and I had," he says.

The sequence began with a helicopter-to-helicopter shot. Then, after she lands and descends from the helicopter, Rose is picked up by a Steadicam that takes her through the crowds, into the stadium, and onto the stage. "We needed to catch everything, quickly," he recalls. "We'd paid these people something like a dollar or two, to be there. They wanted to see Bette Midler sing. But, once she'd done a few songs, they weren't going to stick around."

To make the shot more impressive, Zsigmond had the not-so-captive audience fill one side of the stadium, letting the other be dark. "That was easy," he says. "To add to the pressure, we knew we could do the shot only once — because the emotional impact was going to be supported by light — follow spots, and expensive fireworks.

"As she gets out of the helicopter, we see a collection of lights flashing — spelling out 'Rose.' Once she gets on the stage, an expensive one-time-only burst of fireworks — again spelling 'Rose' went off. We couldn't set the fireworks and pop them off again.

"This scene was so strong, because it was done with lights," he emphasizes. "Take the lights away, and it wouldn't have been as good. Even with the camera moves and the music, it still wouldn't have carried the emotion it did. It wouldn't have said what Mark wanted."

Vilmos Zsigmond was going from one huge challenge to another by now. His next project, the much maligned and talked about Michael Cimino epic, is *Heaven's Gate*. The buzz was starting, while the company was in production. That didn't phase Cimino, or Zsigmond. They were out to tell the story – a true story of the Johnson County Wars. "So, we made it a little bigger than it was," he smiles. "It was still a true story and not one of the brightest spots in American history.

"I really loved working with Michael Cimino," says Zsigmond. "After *The Deer Hunter*, he decided he wanted to do a big Western epic. He wanted it to look a little like *McCabe and Mrs. Miller*, but not as grainy or fuzzy or soft. So, we decided to flash the film in the negative and positive, without soft effects filters. The idea was to keep it soft, using smoke, fireplaces, candles and, of course, the dusk on the exteriors.

"That is, of course, when we had dust," he laughs. "There is one big scene that I wanted to do in the morning light. It was a line-up type shot, after the battle. Kris Kristofferson is to walk through hundreds of dead people.

"We got to the location early and set up three cameras side by side. I was operating two — a wide-angle and a long-lens on a crane. I locked down one camera and got it ready to turn on, then got on the long lens that I had to operate. The shot looked beautiful — the sun was rising, but there was nothing interesting happening. There was no dust, no wind! It was too quiet.

"Suddenly, Michael Cimino walked in front of the camera and waved his arms. 'Wind. Wind.' He intoned. Everyone looked at him. We knew he was a little eccentric — but calling the wind?

"Damned if, ten seconds later, the wind didn't come up. 'Role the cameras,' someone screamed. God — or Michael Cimino — had gotten to Mother Nature! We had wind, and an incredible shot!"

Part of the adventure of making *Heaven's Gate* was the challenge in capturing the shots that Cimino wanted — with the equipment available. "A key sequence is set in 'Heaven's Gate' — the roller-skating rink where the immigrants went to entertain themselves," Zsigmond explains. "The rink was actually a tent. We had the ceiling painted like an 85 filter, so we could use the available light. It would simply have been too dangerous to put lights inside.

"Originally, we all learned to roller skate, so we could shoot the action with handheld cameras. However, that wasn't going to work. So, we used a golf cart, sometimes leading and sometimes following our actors around the rink.

"We had an assistant with a walkie-talkie outside the tent, giving us directions for our focus puller. 'Okay, get ready. The clouds are going over the sun. Ready, coming, okay. Now. On the assistant's mark, the focus puller would open up the lens.

"Then, 'okay, the sun is coming up, it's coming back, it's — okay. Now.' We would close the lens down. This way, we didn't have to cut the camera and do the shot again and again. We could get it in one long move."

From the Cimino epic, Vilmos Zsigmond went to a smaller thriller, pairing once again with the challenging Brian DePalma. "*Blow Out* was based on a story called *Blow Up*," he says. "Instead of a still photographer photographing a murder, it is John Travolta as a sound man, who captures a murder on tape while working on a sound recording. He tries to figure out who the murderer is, before someone else is killed."

DePalma wanted to create another new style with this picture. Working with production design, he and Zsigmond decided to pick primary colors for the palette, emphasizing the image as an "American picture," by using reds and blues — red for the murder and blue for the night scenes.

"Of course, Brian had to have at least one 360-degree shot in the film," Zsigmond smiles. "The one that stands out is near the end. This one was even trickier than *Obsession*. It is where Travolta is trying to save Nancy Allen from the murderer. He doesn't quite make it, and she is killed. He takes her into his arms, the camera circling them in a series of 360s.

"Brian wanted to see the sky with fireworks going on in the background. And, this being a difficult scene for the actors, we wanted to get it as easily and quickly as possible.

"Since it would be too expensive as well as difficult to build a city and set off all those fireworks, we shot the sequence against a plate — and rotated the actors and lights on a turntable, keeping the camera still and the shot simple."

In 1985, Zsigmond was nominated for another Oscar, this time for his work on the 1984 film *The River*. "The story was important to me," he says. "It was something I could relate to — this time it was farmers fighting the land developers who wanted to build a dam.

"We did a lot of shots in the wet and the mud, using our own dam to control the flooding and creating our own rain, because real rain doesn't photograph all that real.

"For me, one of the most memorable shots was done in a defunct steel mill," he recalls. "It is a shot where everyone stops working and they chase a deer that has wandered inside, for no reason. Because it would have been unsafe to shoot in a working mill, we didn't have the real effects (which Zsigmond had when he shot in a real mill for *The Deer Hunter*). To simulate reality as close as possible, we used orange light coming into the scene and pretend light effects for sparks. Sound effects would add the noise, later."

In 1987, Vilmos Zsigmond scored another first to his career — a comedy. A big comedy. *The Witches of Eastwick* was a challenge — lighting beautiful people in opulent surroundings. "At one point, we were shooting in the Boston Opera House as Jack Nicholson's (The Devil) living room," he smiles. "We used the old AFI, a big hall and huge palaces that we could get, that would be fancy enough for where The Devil might live.

"I think the most interesting shots were simple almost all 'in camera' special effects," he adds. "In the scene where Jack is being blown by the wind, he was being pulled by a cable — the feathers part of the scene, but also a device used to hide the cable.

"Then, there is the shots where they are supposed to be playing tennis." This time, Zsigmond starts to laugh. "All our actors were so sure they could play for real! When we got to the sequence, no one could hit the ball right. So, we had them pretending to hit the ball. We would put it in optically later.

"For an overhead shot, we had to shoot the tennis court with no shadows. We had someone sitting outside the location for days, watching the time and where the sun would be. When we figured out the time of day when it would be directly overhead, that is no shadows, we knew we could shoot.

"We had all of ten minutes for our window. We put the camera on a construction crane about 100 feet above looking down. That's how we shot the plate for the scene when the tennis ball freezes in space.

"Of course, today, people would laugh at this. CGI would do it so simply. But, in those days, we had to do it this way!"

Two years later, Zsigmond worked with director Roland Joffe on a rather expensive (for its time) picture, detailing the building of the atomic bomb. "We had to go to Mexico to build Los Alamos for *Fat Man and Little Boy*," he recalls. "For the first time, all I had with me from my crew was a gaffer (Bob Jason). I found the crews there tremendous — they worked really hard and, after the initial getting-to-know-what-we-wanted, things went great."

Vilmos Zsigmond was going from big picture to even bigger picture. The 1990 follow-up to *Chinatown*, called *Two Jakes*, was an interesting experience for this well-known cinematographer. Despite the controversy over the project, he had a great time working with Director/star Jack Nicholson in the "French hours" system — 8:00 A.M. to 6:00 P.M., with food available at all times.

"The system worked great," he says. "To go home every day at 6:00 P.M. was a dream! The long hours in Hollywood can kill a crew. You can't stay creative much longer than that – and this makes the quality of the film suffer."

Zsigmond made a conscious decision not to copy the lighting style of *Chinatown*. "Obviously, I loved *Chinatown*," he says. "But, to copy the style would have been too easy. Besides, *Two Jakes* happens much later in time. So, it needed a different approach. The idea was to make people feel like they were living within the period, when they watched the film. We wanted more reality. We wanted California bathed in the golden sunshine."

That reality included the way Nicholson was photographed. "The character is worn out," Zsigmond explains. "Jack gained weight and chose many angles that would enhance that attitude. However, I was still careful to light and angle the camera so that the attitude would be enhanced but the actor wouldn't look as tired or distressed as he was while making the project."

Part of the fun of *Two Jakes* was to get the character of the city of Los Angeles — including Mother Nature's little tricks — an earthquake. While people living in L.A. are used to her unexpected outbursts, Nicholson and Zsigmond knew they had to bring that reality to audiences around the world. They wanted to make the viewer feel the rolling in the pit of their stomachs.

"The whole set was built on hydraulics," Zsigmond explains. "It was a lot like the earthquake sequence at the Universal ride. The set could shake and move from side to side. We then put the camera on a crane, so it would not shake. This allowed the audience to feel a stillness, as the world around them shook. For the second quake sequence, we put the camera on a tripod and let it shake with the set."

To make the reality work, Zsigmond arranged the lights independent of the set. This way, they wouldn't shake while the set and cameras rolled. "We also chose what to emphasize in each sequence," he adds. "In the first quake shot, Jake Gittes calmly dives under his desk for safety. As he looks out at the camera, his eyes widen and his face tries to remain calm. We have a golf ball lazily roll off the top of the desk and onto the floor. It was the ordinary, in the middle of the insane."

There was only one major conflict between Director and cinematographer on this difficult shoot. "Jack wanted a sunset scene," Zsigmond recalls. "I calmly told him we had day backings and we had night backings. It wasn't possible to use either one for a 'sunset' sequence. He said we could. I said we couldn't. I finally convinced him to go shoot other scenes, while we would find or shoot another Translight with a sunset effect.

"A week later, we shot the scene with a beautiful Translight and after he had time to think about it, Jack realized I was right — and praised me for waiting for the right backing for the scene."

At times, Zsigmond's desire for reality put an extra pressure on everyone. "But, it was worth it," he says, smiling. "We had a scene at a golf course where Jake (Nicholson) is about to reveal he can tie Jake Berman (Harvey Keitel) to the complicated murder plot that is part of the story.

"There was no money for professional golfers, so we had to rely on Jack and Harvey," he laughs. "The crew stood there, holding their breaths. Jack did a great job smacking the ball down the middle of the fairway. Harvey's character, however, was to break the tee and smash the ball on a tree, smacking past Gittes."

To make this second shot, Zsigmond covered the sequence again, using a compressed-air gun firing balls off the tree. "That was easy," Zsigmond laughs. "Jack's character has to have the last laugh, hitting the rim of the hole, as he putts out."

The "normal" approach would be to shoot a close-up on the hole. "Not us," Zsigmond laughs. "We had a hole dug in the green and put the camera under the hole! This way, the audience sees the ball kiss the rim from underground.

"That gave it even more of an edge," he adds, somberly. "The audience sees the real trees, real sky, the silver of the hole's edge, and the real sun glancing off a shiny white ball."

Later that year, Zsigmond shot *The Bonfire of the Vanities*. "This picture had much more intricate camera moves," he says. "The movie starts with a five-minute 20-second long Panaglide shot."

The camera follows Bruce Willis (playing the writer of the story), as he drives up in a limousine, walks up the stairs, rides down a long hall in a golf cart, walks through a kitchen, along many corridors, to an elevator and is finally ushered into a hall with hundreds of people applauding. It is simply another way to tell a story."

The Steadicam (sometimes with the operator on a golf cart, stepping off at the right moment and leading or following Willis) and 360-degree shots were difficult to light. Zsigmond's problem — where to put the lights so that the camera wouldn't see them.

"Sometimes, we put them on dimmers which could be dialed up for ambient light and backlight, then down to avoid creating camera shadows," he explains. "In several places, we had three or four lighting technicians controlling those dimmers. They would watch the video monitors or look for the camera moves from hidden positions."

The crew took all day to rehearse the move. "We had to have it down exactly right," he explains. "If something went wrong and we delayed even a moment, we were in danger of not having enough film in the magazine. Actually," he adds with a smile, "we cheated a little. We made the rolls a little longer, creating 500-foot short ends from 1,000-foot rolls (film manufacturers still don't make 500-foot rolls for Panavision's 500-foot magazines)."

Still, the shot was a challenge. Zsigmond wanted to do it in the early morning, taking advantage of the blue coming into the sky, reflecting in the twin buildings near the Palm Court in New York. "Brian wanted the shot done, so we started at night," he recalls. "We finished about two in the morning. I was still fighting for early morning. 'What are we going to do until then?' he asked me. 'Everyone could go to their trailers and take a nap,' I answered. Then, we could use that morning light.

"Brian trusted my instincts," he adds. "So, we all took our naps, and came back just before sunrise. We managed to do three takes – when the sun was just coming up (too dark), a perfect time for reflections (the one we used) and another for protection (which was too light). The middle shot is in the film."

the stop changes, so we could work within the boundaries of the lenses, and still get all the shots we needed for the time lapse."

In 1995, Zsigmond got to do still another film tradition — shoot an action picture in *Assassins* (directed by Dick Donner). "The last time I did something like this was *Deliverance*," he says. "This one isn't a violent picture – we don't see blood or suffering — we see the effects of the life our two lead characters have led (Sylvester Stallone and Antonio Banderas), on themselves and the people around them."

The visual style Zsigmond set for this picture goes back to *Touch of Evil* and *The Third Man* — long shadows, hot flashes, deep focus shots. Both Zsigmond and Donner wanted the audience to see everything. "Film noir at its best," he says.

To do this, Zsigmond's lighting style featured either tungsten or HMI — but not a mix. "A lot of the time, we had to turn practicals off or remove them completely, so the color temperature wouldn't confuse the look," he says. "Isolating shots this way allowed us to enhance the mood and keep the film noir feeling — in color instead of black and white."

One of the biggest challenges of the picture was keeping the light even — and matching it from location to location. "A lot of the picture's action takes place in a burned-out hotel that is supposed to be in San Juan, Puerto Rico," he says. "Tom Sanders (Production Designer) did a great job creating the tri-level stage (at Lake Washington Naval Base outside of Portland).

"We had boarded-up windows, sun coming through holes in the walls, ceilings, shutters on the windows and doors. To keep the monochromatic look, we stayed with HMIs throughout the set.

"When we did the sunset and dusk looks, we used the same lighting, simply printing the shots differently at the lab. Night shots were done by pulling the LLD and keeping the painted backing dark, as well as pulling the fill light. When you looked at the dailies, it felt as if we changed the color of the gels on the lights – but it was really the lab's magic."

One of the pivotal shots in the exposition of Antonio Banderas's character has to do with him "assassinating" a piece of fruit. "He is preparing for his 'kill,'" Zsigmond explains. "He walks through the courtyard outside the bank where the assassins collect. He places an apricot on the top of the railing of a gate in front of the bank, then goes to his room and 'assassinates' the apricot.

"Dick wanted both the piece of fruit and Antonio's character (looking out the window of the hotel) in focus. To do this, we shot the scene with the 100mm lens on the Panastar, using a 120-frames-per-second rate. We put two baby spots for cross light, one 2k spot through a four-by-four frame of light grid for key light and a little bounce fill.

"In the background, we lit a big square of buildings — also the burned-out hotel. Here, we placed 12k and 6k HMIs (moonlight), with half CTO to take some blue out. The trees were lit with tungsten lights with quarter CTO gels.

"When Dick looked at the shot, there was a 'little' mark where the left side went out of focus. He wanted to use a second split diopter so that everything in this 100-plus-foot shot was in focus.

"That could have been a problem. So, what complicated maneuver did we do? We put a little Vaseline on the lens so that everything went out of focus on the left, as it was needed!" he laughs.

*Assassins* was a wonderful challenge for Vilmos Zsigmond, but not as challenging as shooting on location in South Africa (for Kenya), for *The Ghost and the Darkness*. "There was a mile-long set built in an open field near the river," he says. "Trees and grass were planted in red earth, which was trucked in from a neighboring state. A bridge and railroad station was built and a turn-of-the-century steam engine was trucked in from several hundred miles away. It was a marvelous production design.

"We also had real lions — four of them — and two animatronic lions. And, we brought in Samboro tribal dancers from Kenya. A challenge, since we were shooting a lot of scenes with lions attacking, day and night," he recalls. He still feels the adrenaline rush of working with these huge animals.

"These were huge sets. So, how to light them? The answer was to use firelight," he explains. "Most of the night scenes were illuminated with campfires. (Of course, Zsigmond's crew headed by gaffer Bob Jason hid photofloods on dimmers to create fluctuating light, simulating a real fire effect.)

"We added a blue moonlight fill, for warm effects," he continues. "Usually, the HMI lights are too blue, so we used a half CTO gel to create a realistic night look. Also, we added a quarter CTO to the fire effect light, to warm them up for that realistic fire effect.

"Instead of using gels on all the lights (HMI or tungsten), he decided not to correct them and let the laboratory do the correction. It saved us a lot of time. All we had to do to get good dailies was to give the lab a heated color chart and grayscale shot through a one-half blue CTB gel on the lens.

"If the lab printed the grayscale for normal white, the scene would turn into a realistic warm fire effect with acceptable blue moonlight. To correct the blue perfectly, we occasionally used a quarter CTO on the HMIs.

"The rain was another problem for us," he adds. "It was necessary to match shots filmed in sunshine with shots lit with HMIs using a one-quarter CTO gel, shot under cloudy skies. I did love the always clouded skies of

South Africa," he smiles. "We shot during the December through January rainy season.

"For the beautiful rainbows and cloud formations, we paid the price with flooded locations, washed-out bridges, and lightning storms. It was a joy to work with a good Director and wonderful actors (Val Kilmer and Michael Douglas). The film was awarded an A.S.C. Award nomination."

1998 found Zsigmond shooting an interesting slice-of-life story called *Playing by Heart*. For a man who began shooting commericals with available light, and vowed he preferred the idea of simple is better, Vilmos Zsigmond has changed his tune.

On this story of different ways of looking at love, he is using more than a few movie toys, "all of which are necessary to interpret the story — as they were when we were doing *Maverick* or any of the other more films," he says. "As stories get more sophisticated and technology improves, Directors are asking for more challenging shots and we're there to give them what they want."

In *Playing by Heart*, Zsigmond spent several days using the Technocrane to bring characters into and out of the story and to keep the audience involved. "One shot takes place in the exterior lobby of a Laemmle multiplex in Hollywood," says Zsigmond. "Director Willard Carroll wanted to see our two actors going down an escalator then walking off to the elevator. That means we had to use the Technocrane to put the camera in front of them as they go down the escalator. We then had to pan 90 degrees as they got off, travel ahead of them for about 60 feet, then pan another 180 degrees. The final move is to follow them as they walk the last 100 feet to the elevator.

"I know, it sounds simple. If we were going for a documentary style, we could have used the lights of the theater and the street. However, we are looking for a beauty shot — which means overpowering what is here with our lights.

"Since we were going anamorphic, we needed a little more than the mercury vapor lights there. So, we had to match the color temperature of the mercury vapor lights, light in many directions, and not have camera shadows. And, not compromise the look of the picture.

"That took HMI lights with half-plus green gels put as close to the frame lines as possible on all three levels of the structure," he explains. "It was all a matter of balance — of light, and of timing on the part of the camera crew."

The second Technocrane shot in *Playing by Heart* is even more complex. "In this shot, the crane was in the balcony of an old theater in Hollywood," he says. "People are dancing some 60 feet below. The shot started on the chandelier, moved down 30 feet to the crowd, making it even with the crane on the balcony, and then going an additional minus 30 feet, to come close in on one of our actors, dancing alone.

It sounds as though, after all these years, Vilmos Zsigmond has everything covered when he is shooting. "For the most part," he says, trying to keep a straight face. Then there is that little twinkle that usually comes to his eyes, when he's about to admit to being human. "When I don't, I just pray that luck will be there with me.

"On this picture, we wanted to do a time-lapse shot on a city street from night to morning. We started shooting at night, locked the camera down, and came back in the morning. Unfortunately, we forgot that we wanted a 'prop' in the shot, to make the shot more interesting — a city bus, for example. Only, we forgot to get our own bus!

"This is where we got lucky," he smiles. "Darned if a city bus didn't come through just at the right time — on the first shot. And, believe it or not, a bus came through — in the exact same place — when we went back for the morning shot!"

Luck has nothing to do with Zsigmond's ability to light a shot, however. He keeps crafting interesting visuals to add to his stories. When he is doing a "character" piece, as this one was, he finds special moments that will stick out in the audience's mind. "One of those is a wonderful scene that features the relationship between a boy and his mother," he explains. "As Jay Mohr's character lays in his hospital bed, dying, the rift between him and his mother (Ellen Burstyn) begins to mend.

"Since this is one of the more theatrical of the stories, we wanted to make the lighting more dramatic. We used a real (closed) hospital in Chicago. To give the room a day and night feeling, we used a Translight outside with a tent around the location to control the lighting. The biggest challenge was the wind, however, which kept flapping the tent.

"Because the boy is sick, we wanted to keep the room dark," he continues. "I used venetian blinds to break up the light, which came from practicals outside the windows.

"The room was small," he adds. "It had very little 'art direction,' so we took some 'theatrical license' and had a false wall built behind the bed. It stopped one foot from the ceiling, allowing us to light from the ceiling. We had a truss with baby 1ks above the frame line, to light through the blind.

"We then used the *Cool Hand Luke* look, adding a little rain on the windows. Unfortunately," he laughs, "the building was so old, we got water in the room."

At one point in the story, Burstyn's character goes into the bathroom. Willard wanted to see her in the mirror. "Okay, at first I said 'we can't do that,' and then I began to think. 'How do we do it without seeing the camera?' Simple, replace the real mirror with a one-way mirror between her and the camera. This way, we could get multiple images of Ellen, without seeing the crew.

"At the moment when the boy dies, we went a little theatrical," he admits. "We did a *One from the Heart* look, this time. The set was dressed in black and white and blue. We had a red chair on the left side of the room. When he dies, we pull away from the bed, with one light on the chair. We then, slowly, faded out into darkness. It was symbolic of his life fading away."

It is carefully planned and executed shots, like the startling images in *McCabe and Mrs. Miller* to the stark realities in *The River*, and the complex chases in *Assassins* or camp runaway coach shots in *Maverick* to the hospital scene in *Playing by Heart*, that have made Vilmos Zsigmond's mystical reputation in the movie industry.

His consistent ability to rise to and even supersede the challenges of top directors is legendary. That is why he was given the Lifetime Achievement Award by the A.S.C. in 1999, and why he is as much in demand today as he was 30 years ago.

Zsigmond isn't about to slow down. As he looks down on the city of fantasy from his hilltop house, he sees a lot of changes. There is smog in the air — tall buildings — and an overpopulation of architecture, where there once was a mystical beauty of a different and gentler Hollywood.

Yes, even the business has changed. However, he still finds ways to make movies the way he wants — simply and creatively. In a few days, he will take off for Israel, where his latest project will shoot. It will be another interesting challenge — sans Hollywood toys, he will be dealing with major locations, and probably not-so-easy-to-capture images. The shoot could go the way *Stalin* did — or it could be another *Ghost and the Darkness* — or a simple job, which no one expects.

Whatever it is, Vilmos Zsigmond always finds a way to get the story on film — his way — and satisfy the Director, the studio, all those other voices that need to be heard today — and, most of all, himself.